The State of Asian Pacific America

A Public Policy Report

THE STATE OF ASIAN PACIFIC AMERICA

A PUBLIC POLICY REPORT

POLICY ISSUES

TO THE YEAR

2020

Published by
LEAP ASIAN PACIFIC AMERICAN PUBLIC POLICY INSTITUTE AND
UCLA ASIAN AMERICAN STUDIES CENTER
1993

Leadership Education for Asian Pacifics (LEAP), 327 East Second Street, Suite 226, Los Angeles, CA 90012-4210

UCLA Asian American Studies Center, 3230 Campbell Hall, 405 Hilgard Avenue, Los Angeles, CA 90024-1546

Library of Congress Catalog Number: 92–061953

ISBN: 0–934052–22–0

Cover design: Mary Kao

Contents

Preface
The State of Asian Pacific America   **xiii**

Don T. Nakanishi
DIRECTOR
UCLA ASIAN AMERICAN STUDIES CENTER

J. D. Hokoyama
PRESIDENT AND EXECUTIVE DIRECTOR
LEADERSHIP EDUCATION FOR ASIAN PACIFICS (LEAP)

Acknowledgements   **xv**

Policy Recommendations   **xvii**

Asian Pacific American Public Policy Institute

An Overview of Asian Pacific American Futures:
Shifting Paradigms   **1**

Shirley Hune
ACTING ASSOCIATE DEAN
UCLA GRADUATE PROGRAMS, GRADUATE DIVISION
VISITING PROFESSOR
UCLA URBAN PLANNING PROGRAM

The Growth of the Asian Pacific American Population:
Twenty Million in 2020   11

Paul Ong

ASSOCIATE PROFESSOR
UCLA GRADUATE SCHOOL
OF ARCHITECTURE AND URBAN PLANNING

Suzanne J. Hee

UCLA ASIAN AMERICAN STUDIES CENTER

Exclusion or Contribution?
Education K-12 Policy   25

Peter N. Kiang

ASSISTANT PROFESSOR
GRADUATE COLLEGE OF EDUCATION
AND AMERICAN STUDIES PROGRAM,
UNIVERSITY OF MASSACHUSETTS/BOSTON

Vivian Wai-Fun Lee

DIRECTOR
NATIONAL CENTER FOR IMMIGRANT STUDENTS
OF THE NATIONAL COALITION OF ADVOCATES FOR STUDENTS
BOSTON, MASSACHUSETTS

Trends in Admissions for
Asian Americans in Colleges and Universities:
Higher Education Policy   49

L. Ling-chi Wang

CHAIR
ETHNIC STUDIES
UNIVERSITY OF CALIFORNIA, BERKELEY

Health Care Needs and Service Delivery for
Asian and Pacific Islander Americans:
Health Policy   61

Tessie Guillermo

EXECUTIVE DIRECTOR
ASIAN AMERICAN HEALTH FORUM
SAN FRANCISCO, CALIFORNIA

The Changing Asian American Population:
Mental Health Policy   79

Stanley Sue

PROFESSOR OF PSYCHOLOGY AND DIRECTOR
NATIONAL RESEARCH CENTER ON ASIAN AMERICAN MENTAL HEALTH
UNIVERSITY OF CALIFORNIA, LOS ANGELES

Asian American Arts in the Year 2020:
Arts Policy   95

Gerald D. Yoshitomi

EXECUTIVE DIRECTOR
JAPANESE AMERICAN CULTURAL AND COMMUNITY CENTER
LOS ANGELES, CALIFORNIA

Is There a Future for Our Past?
Cultural Preservation Policy 113

Franklin S. Odo

DIRECTOR
ETHNIC STUDIES PROGRAM
UNIVERSITY OF HAWAI'I, MANOA

Making and Remaking Asian Pacific America:
Immigration Policy 127

Bill Ong Hing

ASSOCIATE PROFESSOR OF LAW
STANFORD LAW SCHOOL

Work Issues Facing Asian Pacific Americans:
Labor Policy 141

Paul Ong

ASSOCIATE PROFESSOR
UCLA GRADUATE SCHOOL
OF ARCHITECTURE AND URBAN PLANNING

Suzanne J. Hee

UCLA ASIAN AMERICAN STUDIES CENTER

Legal and Civil Rights Issues in 2020:
Civil Rights Policy   **153**

William R. Tamayo

MANAGING ATTORNEY
ASIAN LAW CAUCUS
SAN FRANCISCO, CALIFORNIA

The Case of the Southeast Asian Refugees:
Policy for a Community "At-Risk"   **167**

Ngoan Le

DEPUTY ADMINISTRATOR
DIVISION OF PLANNING AND COMMUNITY SERVICES
ILLINOIS STATE DEPARTMENT OF PUBLIC AID

Empowering Our Communities:
Political Policy   **189**

Stewart Kwoh

PRESIDENT AND EXECUTIVE DIRECTOR
ASIAN PACIFIC AMERICAN LEGAL CENTER
LOS ANGELES, CALIFORNIA

Mindy Hui

ASIAN PACIFIC AMERICAN LEGAL CENTER
LOS ANGELES, CALIFORNIA

Out of the Melting Pot and Into the Fire:
Race Relations Policy   **199**

Michael Omi
ASSISTANT PROFESSOR
ASIAN AMERICAN STUDIES
UNIVERSITY OF CALIFORNIA, BERKELEY

Asian Pacific Islanders and the "Glass Ceiling"—
New Era of Civil Rights Activism?
Affirmative Action Policy   **215**

Henry Der
EXECUTIVE DIRECTOR
CHINESE FOR AFFIRMATIVE ACTION
SAN FRANCISCO, CALIFORNIA

Language Rights Issues
to the Year 2020 and Beyond:
Language Rights Policy   **233**

Kathryn K. Imahara
DIRECTOR
LANGUAGE RIGHTS PROJECT
ASIAN PACIFIC AMERICAN LEGAL CENTER
LOS ANGELES, CALIFORNIA

Meditations on the Year 2020:
Policy for Women   **253**

Elaine H. Kim
PROFESSOR
ASIAN AMERICAN STUDIES
UNIVERSITY OF CALIFORNIA, BERKELEY

Will the Real Asian Pacific
American Please Stand Up?
Media Policy   **263**

Diane Yen-Mei Wong
WRITER & EDITOR
FORMER EXECUTIVE DIRECTOR
ASIAN AMERICAN JOURNALISTS ASSOCIATION
SAN FRANCISCO, CALIFORNIA

South Asians in the United States
with a Focus on Asian Indians:
Policy on New Communities   **283**

Sucheta Mazumdar
ASSISTANT PROFESSOR
DEPARTMENT OF HISTORY
STATE UNIVERSITY OF NEW YORK, ALBANY

Appendix
Specific Policy Recommendations 303

Chapter Authors
Asian Pacific American Policy Experts 313

A Note to Our Readers

Each chapter provides an independent analysis of the major public policy implications for the demographic projections of the Asian Pacific American population to the year 2020 that are presented by Paul Ong and Suzanne J. Hee. To maximize this book's policy and curricular impact, each chapter is written to stand on its own, and to highlight the specialized knowledge and policy perspective that each writer brings to this project. As a result, each chapter can be read or used somewhat independently of all the others. However, by organizing this report in this fashion, we recognize that a few redundancies (e.g., the presentation of demographic data) as well as inconsistencies (e.g., the preference of each writer in using the terms "Asian Pacific American," "Asian and Pacific Islanders," etc.) will be apparent to anyone who reads this book in its entirety. We nonetheless hope our goal of allowing each expert to offer the fullest and most compelling presentation possible will be appreciated.

Preface

The State of Asian Pacific America

With this publication, our two institutions—Leadership
Education for Asian Pacifics (LEAP) and the UCLA Asian
American Studies Center—are proud to formally inaugurate
the nation's first Asian Pacific American public policy research
institute. We are hopeful that this report, like many others
which we plan to release in years to come, will serve to inform
public discussions and shape public policy deliberations on
major issues and concerns of the nation's rapidly growing and
diverse Asian Pacific American population.

We believe this policy report is particularly timely because
of the extraordinary political and social changes that are
occurring at all levels of our society and government. The
year 1993 marks not only the inauguration of President Bill
Clinton and a shift from a Republican to a Democratic
administration, but also a dramatic increase in the representation
of women and peoples of color from the United States Senate
to local city halls. The heightened presence of Asian Pacific
Americans in government and politics across the nation—from
their substantial increases of new registered voters to the large
numbers of leaders who have sought and have won elections—
has been equally impressive and significant. The year 1993
also represents a historical crossroads for our country's domestic
and international policy agendas. Every major policy issue
from education to employment will likely undergo vigorous
reexamination and perhaps major revamping, be it in response
to how the nation should compete effectively with the rest of
the world or how it should address the underlying causes of
its urban unrest.

This policy report on Asian Pacific America is intended to
have both an immediate and future impact and significance.
We have assembled a stellar group of policy experts and leaders
from across the nation who have rigorously and creatively
offered insights, perspectives, and recommendations on how
we should understand and respond to the extraordinary growth
and diversification that the Asian Pacific American population
is projected to undergo from now to the year 2020. In sharing

their specialized expertise in major policy areas like immigration and higher education, they have provided decision-makers, advocacy organizations, researchers, and the general public with practical and analytical guidance on how to address the most compelling policy challenges of Asian Pacific Americans during the decade of the 1990s and the early 21st century.

As the first of many reports and activities which will be undertaken by the LEAP Public Policy Institute and the UCLA Asian American Studies Center, this publication is reflective of the special strengths and goals of the two institutions that have come together to establish this joint policy research center. Founded in 1982, LEAP is a nonprofit, community organization which has sought to develop, strengthen, and expand the leadership roles played by Asian Pacific Americans through innovative professional seminars, public workshops, and other programs. The UCLA Asian American Studies Center, established in 1969, is one of four ethnic studies centers at UCLA, and one of the nation's oldest programs in Asian American Studies. Through its research, teaching, publishing, and public educational activities in fields ranging from literature to urban planning, the faculty, staff, and students of the Center have sought to advance scholarly and policy understanding of Asian Pacific Americans.

In closing, we would like to pay special tribute to Professor Paul Ong of the UCLA Graduate School of Architecture and Urban Planning for proposing this special policy project, and for generating the population projections of the demographic future of Asian Pacific Americans which serve as the unifying theme of this report. We also would like to express our gratitude to the Board of Directors of LEAP and the Faculty Advisory Committee of the UCLA Asian American Studies Center for supporting the establishment of our joint policy research center.

J.D. Hokoyama
President and Executive Director
Leadership Education for Asian Pacifics (LEAP)

Don T. Nakanishi
Director
UCLA Asian American Studies Center

Acknowledgements

We wish to thank the following individuals and institutions who have provided their generous support to the Asian Pacific American Public Policy Institute and have made this publication possible:

The James Irvine Foundation has been a major funder of the Public Policy Institute and a principal supporter of this policy report. We also wish to acknowledge the support of the following funders: The ARCO Foundation, Philip Morris Companies, Inc., Pacific Bell, Hughes Aircraft Company, Anheuser-Busch Companies, Inc., Federal National Mortgage Association (Fannie Mae) Foundation, and the Southern California Gas Company.

GTE Telephone Operations-West Area generously provided funds for the printing of this report.

Glenn Omatsu, publications editor and staff member of the UCLA Asian American Studies Center, provided invaluable guidance throughout the project, as did Russell Leong, editor of *Amerasia Journal*, who also edited and designed an accompanying brochure. Mary Kao at the Center was responsible for all the data entry and formatting of manuscripts. Jean Pang Yip proofread the final manuscript.

We also wish to acknowledge the assistance of Linda Akutagawa in the LEAP office who was, as always, most helpful in the project. Thanks also to Wendy Siu for assisting with proofreading the final manuscript. LEAP board members Tim T. L. Dong and Enrique B. de la Cruz also contributed to the effort. Graham Finney of the Conservation Company in Philadelphia provided guidance and objectivity. And finally, we wish to thank John Y. Tateishi who, as always, provided invaluable insights into the project.

Asian Pacific American Public Policy Institute

Policy Recommendations

The Asian Pacific American population has grown tremendously following the elimination of racially biased immigration quotas in 1965. From 1970 to 1990, this population doubled each decade from 1.5 million in 1970 to 3.7 million in 1980 to 7.9 million in 1990. Based on recent trends, we project the population to be about 20 million by the year 2020. A recent Census Bureau report confirmed and projected Asian Pacific Americans as the fastest growing group, increasing by 412.5 percent from 1992 to 2050 as compared to 50.2 percent for all groups (*New York Times*, December 4, 1992). This population has and will continue to enrich this country culturally, socially, and economically. However, there are also severe problems—growing racial conflicts, poverty, underemployment, and limited accessibility to the political process—that affect both the nation and Asian Pacific Americans.

We believe that it is time now to formulate public policies from an Asian Pacific American perspective and to address both current and future problems, many of which are discussed in the following chapters in this book.

The authors have developed an extensive and diverse set of recommendations, which are reproduced in the appendix. A common thread is not a call for new policies per se, but a call to re-articulate existing policies so they are relevant for an increasingly ethnically and racially diverse society.

Three Broad Recommendations

1. *Recognize and promote multiculturalism and inter-cultural sensitivity within existing legislation, programs, and agencies.*

The growth of the Asian Pacific American population, along with the growth of other minority groups, is transforming the United States into a pluralistic society. This change holds great promises in enriching this nation and in helping it prepare for a more integrated global economy. It is important that we adopt public policies that recognize this transformation and that provide a guideline for making this country a truly multicultural society.

In our public educational system, the cultures and histories of Asian Pacific Americans must be fully studied and researched, and the results be integrated into curricula and reflected in staffing.

In our social service agencies, programs and providers must be culturally and linguistically appropriate, so no one is excluded.

Similar changes are needed in development programs, including urban and labor policies, and in the arts and media.

2. *Modify the concept of civil rights so protection covers the types of discriminatory practices encountered by Asian Pacific Americans.*

Asian Pacific Americans should enjoy the civil rights protections afforded to all Americans, and especially the laws that protect minorities against discriminatory practices. However, some problems facing Asian Pacific Americans are not adequately covered by existing laws, which have been developed in a black/white context.

In the field of higher education, there must be protection against restrictive admission quotas based on race.

In the employment area, we call attention to the "glass ceiling," which prevents Asian Pacific Americans from moving into management positions; unfair personnel practices based on language and culture; restrictions limiting op-portunities and advancement in self-employment and other areas.

In the political sphere, Asian Pacific Americans must have access to the electoral process; their votes must be given full weight through the creation of influence districts; and if language is a barrier, appropriate bilingual material should be provided. In cases of anti-Asian bias and violence, the rights of Asian Pacific Americans need to be recognized and protected.

3. *Expand programs that help Asian newcomers adjust to U.S. society in order that they can contribute to America's economic, political and social development to their fullest potential.*

Given the large proportion of Asian Pacific Americans who are immigrants, many of whom came after the 1965 Immigration Act, and those who are refugees, there is a grave need for programs that help make these individuals full and productive members of our society.

For adults, there must be more English language instruction, skills development, and job retraining programs. Opportunities for the transfer of expertise, skills, and creative energies must be enhanced and obstacles eliminated.

For youth, attention must be given to those with limited English proficiency.

For Asian Pacific American women, most of whom work, affordable and culturally appropriate childcare and services in support of employment, health care, and related matters are needed.

Asian Pacific Americans are long-standing members of America's diverse population. Demographically, we are a larger proportion of the current and emerging diversity. We seek a more active role in policy-making that promotes national development. We also wish to address limitations in current policies that impede the contributions that Asian Pacific Americans can make to develop ourselves, our communities, and our nation at large. These broad recommendations and the more specific ones in the appendix are meant to advance the dialogue.

Paul Ong
Associate Professor
UCLA Graduate School of Architecture and Urban Planning

Shirley Hune
Acting Associate Dean
UCLA Graduate Programs, Graduate Division
Visiting Professor
UCLA Urban Planning Program

An Overview of
Asian Pacific American Futures:
Shifting Paradigms

Shirley Hune

ACTING ASSOCIATE DEAN
UCLA GRADUATE PROGRAMS, GRADUATE DIVISION
VISITING PROFESSOR
UCLA URBAN PLANNING PROGRAM

> The leadership of the United States depends in many ways on our making a commitment to solving issues of housing, health and the quality of life. That's what people have admired about this nation for decades, and now it is crumbling. I don't think it's possible for us to remain a world leader long into the future if we don't get our domestic house in order.[1]
>
> Adele Simmons
> President, John D. and Catherine T. MacArthur Foundation

In the 1990s, moving toward the 21st century, the nations of the world are undergoing a monumental transformation—a global political, economic, and social restructuring. The current responses are myriad. They include: a greater political and economic integration of the world community; the emergence of new centers of wealth, particularly in Germany and Japan, challenging the economic predominance of the U.S.; a widespread economic malaise; the rise of ethnic nationalism, religious fundamentalism, and racial hatred; the redrawing of national borders; more reliance on multilateral diplomacy to resolve international crises;

the globalization of a consumer culture; the growth in the transnational migration of workers; an increased awareness of the connection between development and the physical environment; and a recognition that violence and weapons of destruction cannot bring stability and peace.

This global transformation is the outcome of a *paradigm shift*—the end of the Cold War. A paradigm is an example, model, pattern, or proto-type. A paradigm shift is a change in the model. No other paradigm has so dominated foreign and domestic policies in the U.S. as the East-West conflict with its strategy of the containment of the U.S.S.R. Containment has shaped the nation's psyche, culture, institutions, and political priorities for half a century. Shifting the Cold War paradigm has yet to result in the formation of an alternative model of structuring American society and its politics and economics. Consequently, in this period of transition, many Americans view the current global restructuring and its domestic implications as a *crisis*, one fraught with dangers. The tendency, then, is to become pessimistic, even fearful, about social change. However, change is a dynamic process. It is also constant and inevitable. The Chinese ideogram for "crisis" is more complex. There is room for optimism and innovation. In combining two parts, one meaning "danger" and the other meaning "opportunity," into a single word to form "crisis," the Chinese remind us that events which appear to be a threat can have positive outcomes.

The development of the United States is a significant phenomenon in world history. It is an *experiment* in bringing together peoples of dif-ferent cultures, histories, languages, religions, social institutions, and other life experiences from all regions of the globe to live and work to-gether and to form a new nation, society, and common culture. It has offered hope and opportunities for individuals to change themselves and to tranform society. However, all communities are not valued equally. Racial minority groups have not and currently do not share in the nation's resources and its decision-making. Nor do they have much say in the direction of the affairs of their communities. Asian Pacific Americans are one such grouping. The gap between America's ideals and its reality remains, as was once entitled in a classic study by Gunnar Myrdal on the nation's relations with African Americans, *An American Dilemma*.

The United States faces many challenges as it prepares for the next century. It also has many opportunities, one of which can be closing the gap between its ideals and the social reality of inequities and racism. What will the nation look like in 2020? More important, what will the nation be like for its underrepresented populations and the poor? Given its present economic issues, how will it define its domestic agenda, especially the inner cities? How different will America's role in world affairs be in 2020? What will be the nation's goals? What is the United States committed to change or preserve? Who decides? Who will set public policy and determine priorities to be addressed? What is to serve as the data base and who will provide the expertise for defining needs and formulating policies? The demographic, economic, and political imperatives facing the nation, domestically and globally, can be viewed as impediments by those fearful of change. Or, these imperatives can be seen as opportunities for rethinking and planning its future.

Global restructuring involves both a nation's relations with other states and with its own people. International and national reorganization are inseparable. Over the last quarter century, Asian Pacific Americans have been the fastest growing minority group in the United States. Our earliest Asian American communities have deep roots in the building of this nation. We are an integral part of the country's historical development and of its future. As in the past, America's future in 2020 will rely heavily on the ingenuity of all its people and on what its leaders choose for the national agenda.

Asian Pacific Americans and the Necessity of Inclusion

The Asian Pacific American Public Policy Institute has initiated a project to forecast the Asian Pacific American population in 2020 and to consider the implications of these demographic changes for public policy. The major forecast is that the dramatic growth of our population over the past three decades will continue during the next three decades. It is estimated that the Asian Pacific American population will be approximately 20 million in 2020 or about 8 percent of the total American population, a substantial increase from that of being less than 1 percent in 1970. *In short, Asian Pacific Americans cannot be dismissed as an insignificant minority group.*

The Institute has also invited experts in a number of fields to identify issues around which policies can be formulated. Many of our interests and demands are shared by all Americans, such as adequate and affordable health care and housing and attention to our elderly and the education of our youth. Some concerns bring us into common identification with other minority groups. The issues we share include limited access to a wide range of employment opportunities, lack of representation in the political arena, misrepresentation and lack of representation in the media, arts, and general culture, and the increase in racial bias incidents and other violations of civil rights. Other issues are of particular concern to Asian Pacific Americans. These include accent discrimination, more support for the English-limited to acquire proficiency, and the critical need for culturally sensitive and competently trained service providers, especially for refugees and recent immigrants, in a range of areas from education, physical and mental health, to social services. Again, in short, Asian Pacific American issues are not marginal or peripheral to the core of American society.

Asian Pacific American concerns are central to the fulfillment of the mission of this nation. What has occurred in the past is the exclusion of our needs and interests from the public agenda rendering Asian Pacific Americans invisible. For example, at different times, Asian Pacific Americans have been defined as ineligible for a wide range of opportunities including small business loans, graduate fellowships, the right to purchase land and homes, and other entitlements. In a number of areas as wide-ranging as electoral politics, media and the performing arts, and research funds, Asian Pacific Americans are severely underrepresented. Containment from full participation in American society has been the predominant paradigm for Asian Pacific Americans. *In the present and the future, what Asian Pacific Americans seek is a paradigm shift in current public policy from exclusion to inclusion.* This volume speaks to the expectation and necessity of inclusion. By making Asian Pacific Americans visible in public policy, the United States will be taking a large step towards bringing current and future national policy closer to the reality of the population it is to serve.

The Need for New Frameworks

The major emphasis of this overview is to point out the need for shifting paradigms to take advantage of the opportunity for genuine restructuring. Many of the policies that currently exist have not solved "issues of housing, health and the quality of life" and others as stated by Adele Simmons, President of the John D. and Catherine T. MacArthur Foundation, and cited in the beginning of this overview. Given the ongoing global restructuring, it is timely as the nation approaches a new century to critically examine the limits of existing paradigms as they relate to domestic policies. The contributors to this volume recognize that we must go beyond simply asking for the inclusion of Asian Pacific Americans in the country's national agenda. *Inclusion is a first step.* Inclusion alone, within the framework of existing paradigms, will result in public policies with limited impact which will address the well-being of only a few Asian Pacific Americans and would likely generate resentment from other groups and sectors of American society. Throughout the volume, contributors challenge the premises around which policies are presently drawn as being outdated and misconceived. They also conclude that real change will require the *drafting of policies within new frameworks*, those that will more accurately reflect the social reality of the United States, or, what I have termed here as paradigm shifts.

What are some of the existing paradigms and what might some of these paradigm shifts be?

- Shifting the Paradigm of Race Relations in the U.S. as solely consisting of African Americans and European Americans (i.e., Blacks and Whites) to the reality of the nation's racial complexity. This is the paradigm shift that will *include* Asian Pacific Americans, Latinos/Latinas, American Indians and other groups in American public policy.

- Shifting the Paradigm of Racial Dynamics between the dominant white majority and each of the subordinate minority groups (i.e., White–African American, White–Asian Pacific American, White–Latino/a, White–American Indian) to include the dynamics between and amongst subordinate minority groups. U.S. Race Relations is beyond Majority–Minority Relations and includes Minority–Minority Relations. This will acknowledge the growing significance of interethnic and interracial relations (e.g., African Americans and Jews, African Americans and Koreans, Asians and Latinos, Latinos and African Americans) in public policy and the increased complexity of American Race Relations today.

- Shifting the Paradigm of Assimilation (defined as Anglo-Conformity) as the only and correct model of successful adaptation to a Paradigm of Cultural Pluralism.

- Shifting the Paradigm of America as a Monocultural Civilization based on the concept of the superiority of European values and institutions to a Paradigm of America as a Multicultural Civilization valuing and incorporating the diversity of all its cultures at all levels of society. Cultural pluralism is the social reality and it will be more so in 2020.

- Shifting the Paradigm of Cultural Diversity as Divisive to Cultural Diversity as Strength. The United States has been culturally diverse from its inception. It is the shared commitment to a common set of principles that has provided consensus and this does not require the suppression of cultural difference. It is the exclusion of racial, ethnic, and other forms of communities from full participation in American society that is disuniting and which promotes and fuels alienation.

- Shifting the Paradigm of American Immigration as consisting of only the poor, needy, and uneducated who, it is argued, take out more than they give to the nation, to an acknowledgment of the ideas, skills, expertise, capital, and other benefits provided to the country.

- Shifting the Paradigm of Ethnic and Language Maintenance as a threat and impediment to one of enrichment and asset to the country.

- Shifting the Paradigm of the United States as Land of Plenty with continuous rates of high growth and economic global supremacy to the current reality of a debtor nation with strong competition from other parts of the world. This recognition suggests that policies for 2020 need to be devised within the largest framework possible and not limited to sub-contexts, such as health and social welfare and military expenditures, or micro-areas, such as bilingual education.

The above paradigm shifts are merely suggestive. Many are not necessarily new concepts. What is new is that they are yet to be incorporated by decision makers in drafting policy.

Asian Pacific Americans, our contributing authors suggest, also need to consider new frameworks. The vast growth and diversification of our population and the ratio of new immigrants to long-established communities has had a significant impact, not only on the nation, but on older Asian Pacific American groupings. What kinds of paradigm shifts are required by Asian Pacific Americans for 2020?

■ Shifting the Paradigm of the Asian Pacific American Population as primarily focused on groups whose history in the United States dates from the 19th century, notably Chinese Americans and Japanese Americans, to encompass the wide range of Asian Pacific American groupings, especially those of the post-1965 period and those to come through 2020. The recognition of the diversification of our communities will require a sharing of power and representation with Filipino Americans, Korean Americans, Vietnamese Americans, Asian Indian Americans and others and a consideration of which policy issues are priorities for the different groupings.

■ Shifting the Paradigm of Defining the Asian Pacific American Experience solely by its pre-Civil Rights (i.e., institutionalized legal discrimination) period. An increased understanding of how the post-Civil Rights period has shaped the perspectives and struggles of our communities will help define public policy in the future.

■ Shifting the Paradigm of U.S. Race Relations beyond Majority-Minority Relations to include Minority-Minority Relations. We have set an example for coalition building in the creation of pan-Asian Pacific American structures and organizations while nurturing the autonomy of our national groupings. This needs to be expanded to create pan-minority institutions and organizations that can reduce tensions and conflict and promote cooperation toward shared goals. Critical attention needs to be given to minority-minority relations and to identifying policy issues that are common to other minority groups, especially as demographic changes point to minority populations increasing in greater percentage than the dominant majority through 2020.

Changing Ourselves and Transforming Society

This first publication of the Asian Pacific American Public Policy Institute has a number of objectives. Its *primary purpose* is to inform policy-makers and the general public of the significant presence and complexity of the Asian Pacific American population and of the potential effect its continued growth and diversification will have on American society and its institutions by 2020. A *secondary purpose* is to generate discussion within the Asian Pacific American population as to how we also will address the impact of the demographic changes on our communities. A *third purpose* is to demonstrate the importance of having community representatives and experts defining the issues and making policy recommendations.

Readers will be presented with an assessment and in-depth discussion of specific areas of Asian Pacific American life within a range of topics including the arts, cultural preservation, the economically-at-risk, education, immigration, labor, language rights, legal and civil rights, physical and mental health, the media, politics and empowerment, race and interethnic relations, social services, women, and the new communities. Our contributing experts also provide suggestions for addressing concerns toward 2020. This publication seeks to provide a foundation for the drafting of new public policies that will serve the needs of our population and, concomitantly, American society.

The United States is on the brink of a new century. Asian Pacific Americans have a stake in America's future. And, the United States has a commitment to all Americans.

Asian Pacific Americans seek a more direct role in defining the future of their communities and of the nation as a whole. We seek a greater response to our needs and concerns, in both the public and private sectors, and at all levels, national, regional, and local. We want opportunities for full and active participation in each segment of American society and for defining social policy. The empowerment of all Americans in community life is critical for restructuring. Asian Pacific Americans are prepared to do our share. It is with the hope of bringing the nation's reality with its inequities closer to its ideals that Asian Pacific Americans have prepared this volume.

Notes

1. *New York Times* (February 2, 1992), A11.

The Growth of the
Asian Pacific American Population:
Twenty Million in 2020

Paul Ong

ASSOCIATE PROFESSOR, UCLA GRADUATE SCHOOL OF
ARCHITECTURE AND URBAN PLANNING

Suzanne J. Hee

UCLA ASIAN AMERICAN STUDIES CENTER

The fastest growing minority group in the United States today is Asian and Pacific Americans. Although this group only comprised 2.9 percent of the total United States population in 1990, it increased in size by 95 percent from 1980 to 1990 (see table 1). Whites, on the other hand, make up 80.3 percent of the total U.S. population, yet their increase over the 1980s was merely 6 percent. African Americans were 12.1 percent of the total population in 1990 and saw only a 13.2 percent increase in the 1980s. And lastly, Hispanics, who constitute 9 percent of the total population, grew 53 percent from 1980 to 1990.[1] With an extraordinary growth rate, Asian Pacific Americans as a share of the total U.S. population grew from 0.7 percent in 1970 to 2.9 percent in 1990.

The rapid growth of the Asian Pacific American population over the last quarter of the century will likely continue well into the next century, and this increase poses an enormous policy challenge not only to the Asian Pacific American community, but also to the nation as a whole. To take a proactive stance requires us to go beyond reaction to today's pressing problems. We must create a vision for the next quarter century that will ensure that Asian Pacific Americans will find a just and equitable place in American society and the economy—a position that will also enable Asian Pacific Americans to contribute constructively to the building of a truly multicultural society.

TABLE 1. Asian Pacific Americans
Population by Ethnicity: 1980 and 1990

	1980	1990	Percent Growth
Total Asian Pacific	3,726,440*	7,273,662	95%
Chinese	806,040	1,645,472	104%
Filipino	774,652	1,406,770	82%
Japanese	700,974	847,562	21%
Asian Indian	361,531	815,447	125%
Korean	354,593	798,849	125%
Vietnamese	261,729	614,547	135%
Hawaiian	166,814	211,014	26%
Samoan	41,948	62,964	50%
Guamanian	32,158	49,345	53%
Other Asian Pacific	226,001	821,692	264%

*The 1980 number for Asian Pacific Americans in this table is slightly higher than that used in other published reports because it includes the count for "other" Asian Pacific American groups. Other published census reports include only nine specific Asian Pacific American groups for the 1980 count. Therefore, our calculation of percent growth is 95%, which is lower than the published 108% growth.[2]

Population projections are a key tool in helping frame a meaningful discussion of the policy issues facing Asian Pacific Americans.[3] Understanding current and future demographic patterns and trends provides insights to the struggles and conflicts in the educational, economic, and social service arenas, as well as the broad set of interracial and interethnic relationships that influence and shape public policy. Although the Bureau of the Census does project the white, black, and Hispanic populations, the Bureau unfortunately does not do so for the Asian Pacific American population. At best, we are in the residual "other" category.

This project fills the gap by projecting Asian Pacific Americans to the year 2020. Depending on the underlying assumptions regarding birth rates and net immigration, the Asian Pacific population in 2020 will be from 17.9 million to 20.2 million, a 145 percent to 177 percent increase from 1990.

Population Model

Our population model is an augmented cohort-survival model. Like any other projection model, our estimates are essentially educated guesses based upon reasonable assumptions. There is no guarantee that these will be accurate. Given the changing dynamics of the United States, it would not be surprising if these projections were inaccurate. Nonetheless, these Asian Pacific population projections provide us with valuable information of the changing demographics of the Asian Pacific population.

Following standard practice, the model estimates the population by gender and by age-cohorts in five-year increments. The projection for a given age group is calculated as the sum of the number of surviving persons of the younger age-cohort five years earlier plus net migrations for that group. For example, the 15-to-19-year-old population in 1995 is calculated to be the number of surviving 10-to-14-year-old children in 1990 plus the net migration of teenagers who would be 15 to 19 years old in 1995. This estimation is done for every age-cohort. The new 0-4 group is defined as the number of infants born during the five-year interval. This process is repeated five additional times to derive projections for the year 2020.

The 1980 and 1990 census data and California vital statistics were used to derive net migration, fertility rates, and mortality rates. The base population estimates were taken from the published 1980 Census' detailed population characteristics reports, the published 1980 Asian and Pacific Islanders census report, and the 1990 Census Summary Tape File 1 (STF1). The numbers are based on the racial self-identifier.

Along with the age and gender breakdowns, we project the Asian

Pacific American population by nativity and for two major regions in the United States. It is crucial to estimate the number of foreign-born Asian Pacifics because they face intense cultural and economic barriers that dramatically differ from those of American-born Asian Pacifics. Thus, these foreign-born individuals need special programs and social services to help them adjust to a new society. We also project the Asian Pacific American population for California and a region comprised of three Mid-Atlantic states (New York, New Jersey, and Pennsylvania).

California has been the primary area for Asian immigration. Initially, large numbers of Chinese immigrants came to California in pursuit of economic prosperity that was created by the Gold Rush. Subsequently, other Asian Pacific ethnic groups, such as the Japanese and Filipinos, settled in this area. As a result, ethnic communities and resources were established, which ultimately attracted more Asian immigrants such as Koreans and Southeast Asians. In 1970 the total number for the Asian Pacific population in California was 0.6 million. This population grew to 1.3 million in 1980, and to 2.8 million in 1990. In 1990, 2.8 million Asian Pacifics comprised 10 percent of the California population and 40 percent of the entire U.S. Asian Pacific American population.

The Mid-Atlantic area has a substantial number of Asian Pacifics. In 1970, there were .22 million, .51 million in 1980, and 1.1 million in 1990. New York has the largest population of Asian Pacifics among the three states. Of the Asian Pacific immigrants who entered the United States between 1982 and 1989, approximately 11 percent (210,000) indicated that New York was their proposed state of residence. Although it could have been extremely useful to have projections by ethnicity (e.g., Chinese, Japanese, etc.), the required data are not yet available, and using the existing data yields inconsistent results. We include as an appendix some information on several major Asian Pacific American ethnic groups.

Fertility and Survival Rates

The annual birth rates and corresponding fertility rates were calculated from California vital statistics.[4] We matched births in 1990 with the population reported in the Census. In order to minimize the influence of random fluctuations, we used data from three years to adjust 1990 births. The percentage distribution of live births to women (age 15 to 44) by five-year age groups was calculated for the period from 1988 to 1990, and this distribution was applied to the total number of births for 1990. Next, the estimated number of births per age group was divided by the number of females for the corresponding age group.

The completed fertility rate is defined as five times the sum of the annual birth rate for women in five-year age groups. This imputed fertility rate assumes that the current birth rates, or child-bearing behavior, remain stable over time. This is not a safe assumption. With economic mobility and acculturation, the fertility rates of Asian Pacifics decrease and approach the norm of non-Hispanic Whites.[5] Our estimated fertility rate is 2.01. This is lower than the 2.3 to 2.4 rate used by others.[6]

Survival rates are also estimated from vital statistics for California. We use the rates developed by California's Center for Health Statistics (1983), which are published as abridged life tables.[7] Rates are available by race, age-group, and gender.[8]

Immigration Rates

Immigration rates, which are the most important component of Asian Pacific American population growth, are calculated from Census reports, and cross checked with INS data and refugee information. The 1980 Census provides information on the native- and foreign-born populations and persons; however, the data on nativity of individual ethnic groups for 1990 are not yet available. This information will not become public until the year 1993. We estimate the 1990 foreign-born population by projecting the 1980 Asian Pacific population by nativity. The 1980-based projections for 1990 provide an estimate of the 1990 population with the assumption of no (zero) net immigration. Births during the 1980s are based on both the observed 1980 total Asian Pacific population and the 1990 total Asian Pacific population. We then define the net immigration for the 1980s as the difference between the 1990 estimates based on the 1980 population and observed 1990 population. By combining the new immigrants with the surviving immigrants from 1980, we derive a total foreign-born population for 1990. Our estimate (4.6 million) is very close to the number of persons born in Asia recorded in the 1990 Census (4.5 million).

Based on the above analysis, we then developed sets of immigration rates for the population model. In the baseline population projection, immigration is assumed to continue at the same level as in the 1980s at 210,000 Asian Pacific immigrants per year. The birth rates are also speculated to remain constant since the 1980s at 2.01 Asian Pacific births per female. This linear extrapolation simply assumes a continuance of past trends. The second projection posits a rise in the population of Asian Pacific immigrants, yet at the same time a decrease in the overall birth rates. The projected immigration begins with roughly 210,000 persons per year with an increase of approximately 40,000 over a ten-year period; and the birth starts at the higher 2.3 births per female with a decrease of about 0.1, or 4 percent to 5 percent, every ten years. The final projection surmises that the number of immigrants slowly increases at a rate of 10,000 per ten years. At the same time, the birth rate will also grow from 2.0 at a rate of 0.1, or 4 percent to 5 percent, every ten years. We believe that the second set of assumptions is the most realistic.

These three sets of assumptions are not meant to produce the traditional low, medium, and high projections. We believe that the second set of assumptions leads to the "best" or "most likely" projections. The other two sets of assumptions lead to low projections and provide us with a way of understanding how differences in birth rates and immigration can affect the outcome.

Overall Projections

This section discusses and analyzes our population projections for the year 2020. Table 2 shows the projections for the year 2020 for Asian Pacifics by age. Our second and preferred projection shows that the total population for all Asian Pacific ethnic groups will increase from 7.3 million in 1990 to 20.2 million in the year 2020. This shows a growth of approximately 145 percent. Interestingly, the first and third projections are similar, although when we developed the assumptions, arriving at similar projections was not the intent.

Our projections differ from the projections by U.S. Census Bureau.[9] Because the Census uses a residual category (i.e., not White and not Black) that is predominantly but not exclusively Asian Pacific American, we compare the absolute growth of the Bureau of the Census populations with ours. Our second projection shows that the Asian Pacific population will grow by 13 million, which is considerably higher than the 9.3 million in the Census' middle projection series. The major difference is that the Census assumes an annual net immigration of 176,000, which is significantly lower than the trend in recent years. The Census' high projections series, which is based on an immigration level of 220,000, produces an increase of 12.7 million, which is consistent with our second projection.

TABLE 2. Projections of the Asian Pacifics
in the United States by Age (x1000)

Asian Pacific Americans	1990	2020A	2020B*	2020C
<15	1,749	3,706	4,370	3,439
15-24	1,224	2,509	3,013	2,511
25-44	2,659	5,309	6,160	5,492
45-64	1,187	4,333	4,614	4,392
65+	454	2,057	2,089	2,065
Total	7,274	17,914	20,246	17,904

*preferred projection

Age Group Projections

The number of Asian Pacific children and young adults (age 0 to 24) will increase from approximately three million in 1990 to 6.2 million in 2020. This is an increase of 107 percent for the base projection. However, the number of foreign-born children and young adults shows a slight decrease of 1.2 million to one million, or roughly 16 percent. Our second assumption forecasts that the individuals age 0 to 24 will also increase by 150 percent, from three million in 1990 to 7.4 million in 2020. The foreign-born children and young adults show a growth as well: 1.2 million and 1.4 million, respectively, or 16 percent. And last, our third projection sees an increase of these individuals from 2.9 million in 1990 to seven million in 2020, or approximately 140 percent. The foreign-born children and young adult population shows a slight decrease from 1.2 million to 1.1 million, roughly 8 percent. In each of these projections, Asian Pacific children and young adults comprise approximately 34 to 38 percent of the total Asian Pacific population. Of this amount, roughly 15 to 18 percent are foreign born.

The growth of working-age Asian Pacifics will have a great impact on the labor force in the United States. Our baseline assumption projects that the working-age adults (age 25 to 64) will increase 151 percent, from 3.8 million in 1990 to 9.6 million in 2020. The second projection sees this age cohort increasing 180 percent, from 3.8 million to 11 million. And last, the third projection assumes that the Asian Pacific working-age group will increase 157 percent to 9.9 million by the year 2020. Of this age group approximately 67 percent were foreign born in 1990, and 71 percent are projected to be foreign born in 2020.

Table 3. Projections of Asian Pacifics in the United States by Nativity (x1000)

	US-Born	F-Born	Total	% F-Born	% US-Born	F-Born Growth	US-Born Growth
1990 Total	2,632	4,633	7,274	64%	36%		
2020A Total	8,211	9,703	17,914	54%	46%	110%	211%
2020B* Total	9,176	11,163	20,246	55%	45%	141%	244%
2020C Total	7,835	10,069	17,904	56%	44%	117%	197%

*preferred projection

The fastest growing age cohort among Asian Pacifics is the elderly (age 65 and older). Our three projections show that the total Asian Pacific elderly population will rise from approximately 450,000 in 1990 to 2.1 million in 2020, an increase of roughly 355 percent. The elderly comprised 6 percent of the total Asian Pacific population in 1990. However, in 2020, the elderly will make up approximately 12 percent of the total

Asian Pacific population. The foreign-born elderly will also see an increase of roughly 510 percent.

Foreign-Born and Regional Projections

The projections show that there will continue to be an increase of the Asian Pacific immigrant population (see table 3). For the baseline assumption (the birth rates and the immigration rates remain constant from 1990 to 2020), the immigrant population will rise from 4.6 million to 9.7 million, a growth of 110 percent over three decades. The second projection, with a decrease in the birth rate and an increase in the immigration flow, indicates the foreign-born population will show a growth of 4.6 million in 1990 to 11.2 million in 2020, or 141 percent. And last, the third assumption, a decreasing birth rate and a growing immigration rate, projects an expansion of the immigrant population of 4.6 million in 1990 to 10.1 million in 2020, an increase of 117 percent over 30 years. As a percent of the total population, the foreign-born population will show a decrease in all three projections. In 1990, the foreign-born population is 64 percent of the total Asian Pacific U.S. population; yet by 2020 this percentage will be between 54 and 56 percent. The majority of the foreign-born population will be the elderly.

Table 4. Asian Pacific Populations by Regions (x1000)				
	1990	2020A	2020B*	2020C
CALIFORNIA	2,850	7,410	8,530	7,520
Net Increase		160%	199%	164%
MID-ATLANTIC	1,100	2,920	3,400	2,300
(NY, NJ, PA)				
Net Increase		165%	209%	109%
*preferred projection				

The Asian Pacific population projections for California show a substantial increase. Table 4 shows the 1990 Asian Pacific American population was 2.85 million, and by 2020 it will grow to an estimated 7.4 million to 8.5 million. This is a net increase of approximately 160 percent to 199 percent. This growth is substantial to the growth of Asian Pacific populations in the United States.

Our projections for California are conservative compared to those by Bouvier.[10] His medium projection places the Asian population at 9.4 million, compared to our preferred projection of 8.5 million. A part of the difference can be attributed to Bouvier's inclusion of the residual "other" racial/ethnic group with Asians. Accounting for this factor, we believe that our projections are in line with those by Bouvier.

The Mid-Atlantic states, New York, New Jersey, and Pennsylvania, also show a large growth of Asian Pacifics. Although this population was merely 15 percent of the total U.S. Asian Pacific population, the increase of this group was equally dramatic. The Mid-Atlantic Asian Pacific population will increase from 1.1 million in 1990 to between 2.3 million and 3.4 million in 2020. This is a growth of 109 percent to 209 percent. Unfortunately, there is no other independent projection against which we can compare ours.

Our preceding projections provide the readers with a glimpse of future Asian Pacific populations in the United States. In a little more than a quarter century, there will be approximately 20 million Asian Pacific Americans. Although there are uncertainties in our projections, there are even greater uncertainties regarding the social and economic status of this population in the future. Because of this rapidly growing minority group, not only must the Asian Pacific American community be concerned with the challenges and conflicts in the education, employment and public service arenas, but the national community must be prepared to address these issues as well.

Appendix

The following table shows the data on the native- and foreign-born population and the number of persons by place of birth for 1980 and 1990. For place of birth for the Chinese, we used the number of persons born in the People's Republic of China, Hong Kong, and Taiwan. The numbers for the 1980 foreign born and country of birth and 1990 country of birth are taken from published reports from the Bureau of the Census. The total foreign-born population in 1990 is estimated by using a ratio of persons foreign born to persons by country of birth in 1980. This ratio is then applied to the 1990 population of persons by country of birth which gives the estimate of the 1990 foreign-born population. The estimated new immigration is determined by subtracting the 1980 Asian Pacific American foreign-born survivals from the 1990 foreign-born population. By doing so, the estimated new immigration accounts for the number of foreign-born deaths from 1980 to 1990. The published Immigration and Naturalization Service (INS) data report the number of persons that are from the specific country of origin.

Comparison of Immigration Data					
	Chinese	Japanese	Korean	Filipino	Vietnamese
1980 by foreign-born	514,000	203,000	293,000	506,000	222,000
1980 by country of birth	286,000	222,000	290,000	501,000	231,000
1990 by foreign-born	977,000	387,000	670,000	1,006,000	534,000
1990 by country of birth	543,000	422,000	673,000	998,000	556,000
Estimated new immigration	456,000	193,000	382,000	555,000	315,000
Publ. INS report (80-89)	419,000	41,000	337,000	467,000	396,000

The numbers for the Koreans and Filipinos are roughly of the same size and appear quite reasonable. However, some ethnic groups, such as the Chinese, Japanese and the Vietnamese, have some disparity in their numbers.

Due to the complex historical patterns of Chinese migration within the Asian countries, a good portion of the immigrants identified and categorized as racially and ethnically Chinese do not come from the traditional sending sources, such as the People's Republic of China, Hong

Kong, and Taiwan. Many are Southeast Asian refugees of Chinese descent, who had resided in Vietnam or Laos for many generations, and still consider themselves ethnically Chinese. Consequently, there is considerable variation in the numbers reported by the different sources in the above table.

The estimated Japanese foreign-born numbers also seem quite high. As in the previous table, the estimated new immigration is much greater than the INS reported population. This unusually high number of immigrants may be due to two factors: (1) the native-born Japanese who are born to Japanese-Caucasian couples may not define themselves as Japanese, and therefore may decrease the native-born population of the Japanese; and (2) the high estimation of the new immigration may be due to the number of Japanese nationals who were in the United States temporarily.

Vietnamese population numbers also present problems for the projections. The estimated new immigration for the Vietnamese is less than the reported INS data. This estimate may be underestimated because of the changing ethnic identity of the Southeast Asians of Chinese descent. Unfortunately, the census reports do not have data on Southeast Asians of Chinese descent, therefore making it difficult to determine who are of Chinese descent from the traditional sending sources and who are of Chinese descent from Southeast Asian countries.

Notes

Jane Takahashi provided assistance to this project during its early stage.

1. The Hispanic category includes all persons regardless of race, including a significant number of Latinos who are White. Consequently, the sum total of Whites, Blacks, Hispanics, and Asian Pacific Americans is greater than 100 percent.

2. U.S. Census Bureau, *United States Department of Commerce News*, Washington, D.C., June 1991.

3. Paul M. Ong, "California's Asian Population: Past Trends and Projections for the Year 2000," Graduate School of Architecture and Urban Planning, University of California, Los Angeles, May 1989.

4. We also reviewed national statistics but found the national data to be less detailed and complete than California's data.

5. The fertility rates differed considerably by ethnic groups. Among California's Asians, the Vietnamese have the highest birth rate at 2.68 with the Filipinos next at 2.40 births for women between 15 and 44 years of age. The Chinese and Korean population are almost identical

at 1.66 and 1.69 respectively. Similarly, the Asian Indians have a brith rate of 1.83. The lowest birth rate is for the Japanese at 1.57. Presently, the Japanese population consists of primarily U.S.-born second, third, and fourth generation Americans. The economic profile of this ethnic group approximates that of the Whites and they likewise have low fertility rates.

6. Leon F. Bouvier, *Fifty Million Californians?* (Washington, D.C.: Center for Immigration Studies, 1991), 11.

7. California Center for Health Statistics, "Data Matters," Sacramento, July 1983.

8. We used all the published rates except those for the oldest cohort (85+), which we adjusted upward slightly.

9. Gregory Spencer, "Projections of the Population of the United States, by Age, Sex, and Race: 1988 to 2080," U.S. Bureau of the Census, Washington, D.C., January 1989.

10. Bouvier, *Fifty Million Californians?*

Exclusion or Contribution?

Education K-12 Policy

Peter N. Kiang

ASSISTANT PROFESSOR, GRADUATE COLLEGE OF EDUCATION AND
AMERICAN STUDIES PROGRAM, UNIVERSITY OF MASSACHUSETTS/BOSTON

Vivian Wai-Fun Lee

DIRECTOR, NATIONAL CENTER FOR IMMIGRANT STUDENTS OF THE
NATIONAL COALITION OF ADVOCATES FOR STUDENTS, BOSTON

*Our children should not be placed in any position where their youthful
impressions may be affected by association with pupils of the Mongolian
race.*[1]

San Francisco School Board, 1905

In response to the challenge of changing demographics more than a
century ago, the San Francisco School Board established a segregated
Chinese Primary School for Chinese children to attend, including those
who were American born. By the turn of the century after Japanese
immigrants had settled in the wake of Chinese exclusion, the School
Board also applied the Chinese segregation policy to Japanese students.
School superintendent Aaron Altmann advised the city's principals:
"Any child that may apply for enrollment or at present attends your
school who can be designated under the head of 'Mongolian' must be
excluded, and in furtherance of this please direct them to apply at the
Chinese School for enrollment."[2]

Throughout their history, Asian Pacific Americans have confronted
a long legacy of exclusion and inequity in relation to school policies and

practices, particularly during periods of changing demographics, economic recession, or war. In spite of historic, linguistic, and cultural differences, distinct Asian and Pacific nationalities have been grouped together and treated similarly in schools. Furthermore, Asian Pacific Americans have had little administrative control or political influence over the shaping of educational policies and school practices.

Nevertheless, Asian Pacific Americans have individually and collectively worked to overcome and redefine exclusionary policies. Legal cases brought by Joseph Tape in 1885 and Wong Him in 1902, for example, challenged the Chinese Primary School segregation policies which denied their children the right to attend neighborhood public schools.[3] In the process, Asian Pacific Americans have, at times, improved conditions not only for their own communities, but expanded educational opportunities for many disenfranchised groups.

Most notably, the class action suit brought by Kinney Lau and eleven other Chinese American students against Alan Nichols and the San Francisco Board of Education in 1970 led to the historic *Lau* v. *Nichols* Supreme Court ruling which provided the foundation for the nation's bilingual education mandates. The court unanimously concluded in 1974:

> ... there is no equality of treatment merely by providing students with the same facilities, textbooks, teachers, and curriculum; for students who do not understand English are effectively foreclosed from any meaningful education.[4]

Like *Brown* v. *Board of Education*, the Supreme Court's decision in the *Lau* case fundamentally reformed U.S. educational policy. Thanks to the efforts of Chinese American students and parents, the educational rights of limited-English speaking students of all nationalities were formally recognized and protected.

In the two decades since the *Lau* decision, the profile of the Asian Pacific American population has changed dramatically. Demographic projections suggest that Asian Pacific American population growth and diversification will continue at least through the year 2020. What will this mean for schools and K-12 educational policy in light of Asian Pacific Americans' historic legacies of exclusion and contribution?

Demographic Changes into the 21st Century

During the 1980s, the school-age Asian and Pacific Islander population, defined as those between ages 5-19, grew by 90 percent from 929,295 to 1,761,901 in the U.S. In California and the Mid-Atlantic area of New York, New Jersey, and Pennsylvania, the Asian Pacific school-age population more than doubled, growing by 111 percent and 102 percent respectively.

In many local school districts, the magnitude of Asian Pacific population growth has been even more dramatic. In Lowell, Massachusetts—a city with fewer than a hundred Cambodian residents in 1980 that now represents the second largest Cambodian community in the country— the influx was so rapid that between 35 and 50 new Cambodian and Lao children were entering the Lowell public schools *each week* during 1987. In Lowell and across the country, the changing demographics of schools and society loom large as critical issues for educational practitioners and policy-makers.[5]

Their concerns, however, have tended to reflect immediate needs and crisis situations, as in the case of Lowell. Yet, educators must prepare to address these demographic trends for a sustained period of time into the next century.

According to projections developed by Paul Ong, the Asian Pacific American school-age population, which doubled between 1980 and 1990, will more than double once again from 1990 to 2020.

Ong's projections suggest that spectacular demographic growth will persist and that current K-12 educational policy issues involving Asian Pacific Americans will continue to be relevant well into the 21st century. According to population projections based on the assumption of increasing immigration, in 2020 there will be 10 percent more Asian Pacific immigrant children below the age of 15 in the U.S. and 25 percent more in California than in 1990. This is cause for serious concern, given that educational policies and practices have been unable to meet the needs of Asian Pacific immigrant students, even at current levels.[6]

Together with the large numbers of foreign-born, immigrant school-age cohorts in 2020, however, a major shift will occur in the demographic profile as the numbers of second-generation, American-born children with immigrant parents will dramatically increase. The implications of these demographic projections for educational policy are discussed below.

Although Ong's population totals are aggregated for all Asian and Pacific Islander groups and summarized for the U.S., California, and the Mid-Atlantic area, the significance of both ethnic diversity and locality should also be emphasized. Other demographic projections, for example, suggest that between 1980 and 2000, the rankings of the six largest Asian ethnicities will change from Chinese, Filipino, Japanese, Asian Indian, Korean, and Vietnamese to Filipino, Chinese, Vietnamese, Korean, Asian Indian, and Japanese.[7]

These changes, driven by immigration and refugee resettlement patterns as well as differential fertility rates, have important ramifications for educational policy because linguistic, cultural, and socioeconomic profiles vary widely by ethnicity. Hmong women, for example, maintain a fertility rate of nearly ten children per lifetime compared to Japanese American women whose rate is less than two.[8] When they become available, disaggregated Asian Pacific Islander data sets from the 1990 U.S. Census will be crucial for policy-makers and community advocates to analyze in detail.

In addition, background factors within each ethnicity, such as refugee wave, generation, and gender also matter. The contrast, for example, between a first-wave Vietnamese daughter of professionals who grew up in the U.S. for most of her life and a third-wave Vietnamese son of rice farmers who came to the U.S. unaccompanied five years ago is obvious and full of implications for educators.

Locality is also important in relation to ethnicity and school policy. Asians comprise 20 percent of the school enrollments in Long Beach and Fresno, California,[9] although Cambodians comprise the majority in Long Beach while Hmong represent the majority of Asian students in Fresno— each with distinct languages, world views, refugee experiences, and, by extension, educational needs.

Furthermore, the development and implementation of K-12 educational policy typically occurs at the local school district level, albeit within the parameters of state guidelines. The public school districts in Boston and San Francisco, for example, each serve about 62,000 students, of whom roughly eight out of ten are children of color. In Boston, however, African Americans make up 48 percent of the student body compared to

9 percent Asian Pacific Americans. In San Francisco, African Americans comprise 27 percent, while Asian Pacific Americans represent 31 percent of the total student body. The context for developing sound Asian Pacific American educational policies is obviously different in San Francisco compared to Boston, though the needs of Asian Pacific Americans in both cities are compelling.

Policy Implications

The remainder of this paper is organized thematically to focus on specific educational policy areas, including curriculum, school climate, teacher training and recruitment, language issues, assessment, support services, and parent empowerment.

CURRICULUM TRANSFORMATION

What I have learned has made a difference. Knowledge is responsibility. I have been able to share my knowledge and shed some light on my family members.

an Italian American student

I can relate a lot better to Asian students now.

an African American student

It helps me to revitalize all the memories and hardships I have gone through. . . . It is very helpful emotionally and academically.[10]

a Cambodian American student

Given projections that Asian Pacific Americans will continue to be the fastest growing subgroup in the nation well into the 21st century, the most important implication for educational policy is that the K-12 curriculum must provide systematic, in-depth opportunities for all students to learn about the historical experiences and contemporary realities of Asian Pacific Americans and their communities. This transformation of the curriculum differs from curricular emphases on the countries and cultures of Asia, and is imperative to implement, whether or not Asian Pacific students are present in individual classrooms.[11]

To meet this challenge, one curricular approach may focus on the particular histories and cultural backgrounds of specific nationalities, such as Koreans, Asian Indians, or Hmong in America. Alternative curricular strategies may focus on specific themes that cut across the experiences of various Asian Pacific nationalities in America, such as immigration, exclusion, settlement and community, labor and contribution, war and international relations, or identity and diversity.[12]

The thematic approach recognizes that various Asian groups share common experiences within the context of U.S. society. In spite of cultural and linguistic differences as well as historical conflicts between Asian and Pacific Islander nations, a distinct *Asian Pacific American* experience is well-documented by scholars.[13] This shared experience is also reflected, albeit crudely, in comments such as "they all look alike," or in incidents when Vietnamese are told to go back to China and Cambodians to go back to Vietnam.[14]

Using the thematic approach, students can also draw connections and parallels to the experiences of other groups in a multicultural curriculum. Themes such as migration, community, and the search for the American Dream are central, but not unique to Asian Pacific Americans, and can serve as the building blocks of a coherent, integrated curriculum that breaks down barriers between groups. Students learn to recognize the power of social forces such as race or class but also to appreciate various *human* qualities such as having dignity and determination to survive.

The thematic approach also facilitates the process of teaching and learning *across the curriculum* from social studies to language arts to mathematics. Research and practice in curricular reform throughout the country suggest that learning is enhanced when students explore themes in depth and make connections from the combined vantage points of several subject areas. A thematic focus on the Japanese American internment during World War II, for example, readily lends itself to lessons across the curriculum in history, writing, drama, civics, geography, health science, agricultural science, art, poetry, and math. With a common thematic focus, subject areas can reinforce rather than work in isolation from each other, and thereby create powerful learning opportunities for students.

We were coming from a meeting of the Asian Club and white students threw oranges at us. Before that we had been standing in the hall and the supervisor kicked us out. So we went outside and they threw oranges. So there is nowhere to go.[15]

a California-born Punjabi girl

People, can we all get along?

Rodney King

In the aftermath of the Los Angeles riots, teachers at the Wilton Place elementary school in Koreatown reported that many of their students had witnessed family businesses being looted or burned. On the first day after school reopened, the school's nurse observed that many Korean American students requested early dismissals due to stomach pains and headaches[16]—showing that dynamics in the local area and larger society affect the experiences of students in schools.

During the past decade, as rapid demographic changes have threatened established interests and sharpened historic contradictions in our society, bias-related crimes against African Americans, Asian Pacific Americans, Jews, and gays have proliferated throughout the country. Hate crimes reported in 1989 grew by 42 percent in Los Angeles, 29 percent in New York City, and 22 percent in Boston.[17]

Although often expected to overcome problems that the society as a whole has been unable to resolve, schools typically reflect and reinforce the structural barriers and social conflicts of the environment in which they are situated. For example, a 1990 national study of high school students conducted for Northeastern University and Reebok International revealed that 57 percent of the teenagers had witnessed a racial attack and 47 percent would either join in a racial attack in progress or feel that the group being attacked deserved it. Only 25 percent said they would report a racial incident to school officials.[18] Similarly, a 1991 survey of youth between the ages of 15 and 24 conducted by People for the American Way found that 50 percent of the respondents viewed race relations in the U.S. as generally bad.[19] Furthermore, if these studies had taken place after the acquittal of Los Angeles police officers charged with beating Rodney King, the percentages would have likely been even higher.

In their landmark 1992 study, the U.S. Commission on Civil Rights documented numerous cases of anti-Asian violence throughout the country's neighborhoods, workplaces, and schools that were fueled by stereotypes, "Japan-bashing" and a national climate of anti-Asian violence. The report states:

> The pervasive anti-Asian climate and the frequent acts of bigotry and violence in our schools not only inflict hidden injuries and lasting damage, but also create barriers to the educational attainment of the Asian American student victims, such as suspension from school and dropping out of school. . . . These consequences forebode a high price that not only the individuals involved but also our society as a whole are bound to pay in the future.[20]

Even elementary schools are not secure. In December 1988, for example, Patrick Purdy fired over one hundred rounds from an automatic assault rifle into the Cleveland Elementary School yard in Stockton, California—killing five Cambodian and Vietnamese children. Although news reports treated him as a generic mass murderer who fired at random, witnesses said Purdy aimed specifically at Southeast Asian children. The California Attorney General concluded in his investigation that "Purdy attacked Southeast Asian immigrants out of a festering sense of racial resentment and hatred," and that Purdy had often confronted people speaking a foreign language—telling them to speak English in America.[21]

The Stockton massacre, like the racist killings of Vandy Phorng, a 13-year-old Cambodian boy in Lowell, Massachusetts, and 17-year-old Vietnamese high school student Thong Hy Huynh in Davis, California, by schoolmates,[22] have been especially tragic, given that Southeast Asian refugees have already survived so much war, death and trauma in their home countries. Their children are not supposed to die here in the U.S.

As the Asian Pacific student population continues to grow rapidly, educational practitioners and policy-makers must not only develop timely, appropriate measures to respond to specific anti-Asian incidents, but more important, must address the underlying causes of violence and establish alternative environments characterized by respect and cooperation. Research has shown, for example, that the process of multicultural curriculum transformation described above not only strengthens students' knowledge and critical thinking skills, but also improves the climate and learning environment of the school or classroom.[23]

TEACHER TRAINING AND RECRUITMENT

Your voice is one I'd heard only distantly, tokenly, the "model minority"
a terrible reality, I realize in my head. . . . I somehow never saw the
*procession of American Indians to African Americans to **Asian** Americans.*
Now I see.[24]

a high school English teacher

To meet the challenge of changing demographics and enable these proposed curricular reforms, policies in the areas of teacher education and professional development must facilitate the training of current and future educators in relevant content areas and pedagogical strategies. For example, in recent years, a wide range of Asian American Studies primary source documents, oral histories, and works of historical fiction have been published. If teachers are not familiar with these resources, however, and do not have sufficient background knowledge or training to authorize Asian Pacific American voices in the curriculum, then students mistakenly believe that Asian Pacific Americans have been silent and played no role in U.S. history or society.[25]

With significantly more Asian Pacific students entering the nation's classrooms each year, teachers and school staff must also be able to enhance student self-esteem and encourage Asian American student voices that may otherwise be silent or silenced. Many Asian students, particularly those whose first language is not English, feel self-conscious about speaking in class because of the language barrier, cultural differences, and racism. A Vietnamese high school student from Boston notes, "when I came here, I don't feel free to speak and I always think that people don't want to hear me."

The urgency for teacher training and professional development to address these issues is also intensified by policies that seek to integrate or mainstream bilingual students as quickly as possible. The impact of these trends in bilingual education (and special education) policy is that all teachers and school personnel, not just the bilingual teachers, are increasingly responsible for establishing a supportive learning environment for immigrant students in school. To do so effectively, however, they need training.

Although the day-to-day context for addressing these issues of curriculum and pedagogy is the classroom within which individual teachers work, the larger policy issues are relevant to accreditation agencies, teacher education programs, and bodies responsible for teacher certification guidelines.

The Asian Pacific American communities must also take some responsibility, particularly in encouraging more Asian Pacific students to go into the field of education. Fifteen percent of all college students major in education compared to only 6 percent of Asian Pacific students in college.[26] While investing heavily in educational institutions, Asian Pacific Americans constitute only 1 percent of the teaching force nationally, and even less of the pool of school administrators, guidance counselors, educational researchers, *and policy-makers*.[27] The number of fully certified Asian Pacific bilingual teachers has actually declined between 1985-1990 in California, and the shortage of bilingual teachers, counselors, and aides in school districts throughout the country has reached crisis proportions.[28] While schools of education should do a better job of outreach and recruitment, parents and communities must take the lead in addressing this severe underrepresentation of Asian Pacific Americans in the education field.

SERVING ASIAN PACIFIC AMERICAN STUDENTS

The previous sections on curriculum, school climate, and teacher training focus on school-wide or system-wide policy concerns. The following sections examine policy areas related to meeting the specific needs of Asian Pacific American students.

Underlying these sections is a rejection of the distorted, albeit pervasive, model minority myth or "whiz kid" stereotype commonly associated with Asian American students. Many scholars have challenged the origins, validity, and consequences of the model minority image. Though not reported here, those critical analyses represent baselines for educators and policy-makers to understand and respond in meaningful ways to the realities experienced by Asian Pacific American students.[29]

DEVELOPING A PROFILE

Few national studies on Asian Pacific American students are available to drive educational policy.[30] The most recent is a 1992 report that examines language characteristics and academic achievement of 1,505 Asian Pacific eighth-graders based on the National Education Longitudinal Study (NELS:88 database) which sampled 25,000 eighth-graders in 1,000 public and private schools in 1988.[31]

Roughly 52 percent of the NELS:88 Asian sample were U.S.-born and 48 percent were foreign-born. Disaggregated by ethnicity, the sample included 20 percent Filipinos, 17 percent Chinese, 13 percent Southeast Asians, 11 percent Korean, 9 percent Pacific Islanders, 9 percent South Asians, 6 percent Japanese, and 15 percent others. Nearly three out of four students in the sample came from bilingual households, although only 12 percent indicated a high proficiency in their home language.

Among a variety of interesting findings, the study determined that socioeconomic status (SES) was associated with English proficiency and with reading and math performance levels. Of the Asian students from bilingual homes, for example, 78 percent of the high SES students had a high English proficiency compared to 50 percent of low SES students. Moreover, nearly 40 percent of the low SES students failed to achieve basic performance levels for both reading *and* math compared with fewer than 15 percent of the high SES students. In addition, when SES was controlled, students with low English proficiency were less confident about graduating from high school compared to those with greater proficiency (60 percent versus 83 percent). Confidence levels differed by ethnic group as well. For example, 86 percent of South Asians, 72 percent of Filipinos and 67 percent of Pacific Islanders were very sure about graduating from high school.

The NELS:88 study is important in empirically refuting the "whiz-kid" image that Asian Pacific students have no problems in school. It also clarifies the significance of background characteristics, including ethnicity, English language proficiency, and socioeconomic status. Furthermore, given that the NELS:88 study excluded students whose English-proficiency was judged by school personnel to be too low to complete the NELS instruments in English,[32] the findings, therefore, do not account for the profiles of many recent Asian Pacific immigrant and refugee students who, according to several studies, have the lowest levels of English proficiency and socioeconomic status while facing the greatest needs in school.[33]

Before I very silenced, afraid to talk to anybody. But now when I want to say something, I say it. . . . I want to have the right to talk, speak, or vote.[34]

a Vietnamese student

For limited English proficient (LEP) students, bilingual education has been mandated by law since the *Lau* v. *Nichols* ruling by the Supreme Court in 1974. In spite of local and national political controversies surrounding language policies,[35] there is growing consensus among educators and researchers that a wide variety of bilingual program strategies can be effective and appropriate in promoting cognitive development and academic achievement among LEP students.[36] The success of two-way bilingual programs throughout the country is especially encouraging and deserves further development with Asian languages, given the potential benefits not only for large numbers of both foreign-born and American-born Asian Pacific students, but also for non-Asian students in relation to the growing social, cultural, and economic influence of the Pacific Rim nations.

However, the U.S. Commission on Civil Rights, in its review of educational programs provided for Asian American LEP students, concluded:

Many Asian American immigrant children, particularly those who are limited English proficient (LEP), are deprived of equal access to educational opportunity. These children need to overcome both language and cultural barriers before they can participate meaningfully in the educational programs offered in public schools.

Providing equal educational opportunity to Asian American LEP students requires sound student assessment procedures and programs that can orient them and their parents to American society and American schools. Asian American LEP students need bilingual education and English as a Second Language (ESL) programs staffed by trained teachers to enable them to learn

English and at the same time to keep up in school. They need professional bilingual/bicultural counseling services to help them in their social adjustment and academic development. Our investigation has revealed that these needs of Asian American LEP students are being drastically underserved. In particular, there is a dire national shortage of trained bilingual/ESL teachers and counselors.[37]

The Commission's findings are especially troubling in light of Ong's demographic projections which indicate that the numbers of school-age Asian Pacific American immigrants in 2020 will be comparable to or only slightly less than current levels which are "drastically underserved."

Other studies show that some school districts have responded to the needs of Asian Pacific LEP students by incorrectly classifying them as learning disabled instead of providing them with appropriate bilingual instruction as required by law.[38] Local research reveals similar findings. For example, school ethnographers, Trueba, Jacobs, and Kirton, in their study on Hmong elementary school students, observe: "Illiteracy in English continues to be the most frequently recorded reason for classifying minority children as 'learning disabled.'"[39] At the same time, LEP students, particularly from low SES backgrounds, are also being denied federally mandated Chapter 1 compensatory education services, according to a June 1992 report from the U.S. Department of Education.[40]

ASSESSMENT POLICIES

These examples introduce larger issues of educational assessment that have local and national ramifications. Policies of placement, tracking, promotion, and graduation based on standardized testing, for example, are especially problematic because of linguistic barriers, cultural biases, and other disadvantages experienced by Asian Pacific students due to time pressure and the stress of the test-taking situation.

In principle, the purpose of student assessment and evaluation is to identify areas of weakness that can be strengthened through the targeting of appropriate services and strategies. Once targeted, resources should be mobilized to enable all students to overcome those weaknesses in order to achieve their full potential. In practice, assessment policies, particularly those based on standardized testing, have led to the inequitable distribution of educational resources, accompanied by the sorting of students, often according to race, socioeconomic status, gender, and English proficiency.[41]

The value and validity of national standards as well as assessment policies on the local level such as the controversial "Certificate of Mastery" proposals in Massachusetts will continue to be debated in the coming years, hopefully with consideration given to the needs of Asian Pacific students. Alternative assessment strategies, such as portfolios of student work collected over time and exhibitions that demonstrate students' learning and application of knowledge in a variety of domains, offer promise. Nevertheless, even those learner-centered approaches to assessment must attend to the importance of linguistic and cultural diversity in their implementation.

LANGUAGE AND CULTURE SHIFT

> *If you try to teach them you are not American, they will not believe it.*
> *I think if I try to tell about our generation, they will not want to learn.*[42]
>
> a Vietnamese refugee parent

> *I've been trying to put my life as a puzzle together but I don't know if*
> *I will be able to finish my puzzle. But I will do anything to try to finish*
> *my puzzled life.*[43]
>
> a Vietnamese American student

The most striking shift in the school-age Asian Pacific population according to Ong's projections is the marked increase in those born in the U.S.—with growth rates ranging from 125 percent to 225 percent, depending on projection assumptions, for the U.S., California, and the Mid-Atlantic area.

The NELS:88 Asian Pacific study may be instructive here. For example, even though three-fourths of the Asian student population came from bilingual families, nearly 60 percent indicated that they have low proficiency in their home language compared to 66 percent who have high proficiency in English. Interestingly, only 6 percent of those students from bilingual families reported attending a bilingual program of instruction during their first two years of school in the U.S. And, although the study noted that 73 percent of the Asian students came from bilingual homes, only 27 percent were identified as such by at least one of their teachers—suggesting that many linguistic and cultural issues faced by students in moving between their dual worlds of home/family and school are not recognized or addressed.

This profile is consistent with findings by Lily Wong-Fillmore and others in a landmark study providing evidence that as language minority children learn English in the U.S., they lose their native language—the younger the age, the greater the effect—due to the dominant status of English in early childhood education programs and in society.[44]

The researchers further suggest that as the home language is lost in the process of acquiring English, family relations also erode. The following example may well represent the future of parent-child relations in many Asian Pacific American families with immigrant parents and American-born children as projected in the coming decades:

> An interviewer told the story of a Korean immigrant family in which the children had all but lost the ability to speak their native language after just a few years in American schools. The parents could speak English only with difficulty, and the grandmother who lived with the family could neither speak or understand it. She felt isolated and unappreciated by her grandchildren. The adults spoke to the children exclusively in Korean. They refused to believe that the children could not understand them. They interpreted the children's unresponsiveness as disrespect and rejection. It was only when the interviewer, a bilingual Korean-English speaker, tried to question the children in both languages that the parents finally realized that the children were no longer able to speak or understand Korean. The father wept as he spoke of not being able to talk to his children. One of the children commented that she did not understand why her parents always seemed to be angry.[45]

It is ironic that the strengths and cultural values of family support which are so often praised as explanations for the academic achievement of Asian Pacific American students[46] are severely undercut by the lack of programmatic and policy support for broad-based bilingual instruction and native language development, particularly in early childhood education. The unfortunate cost of such policies is the sacrifice of substantive communication and meaningful relationships across generations within many Asian Pacific American families and the squandering of linguistic and cultural resources within the society.

SUPPORT SERVICES

> *As students are mainstreamed from a Cambodian bilingual class, or Laotian class. . .they are dropped—thud!—on the floor, because we have sort of an all or nothing thing, where they're in a full-time bilingual program, or they get no support at all.*[47]
>
> a state education official

> *My parents don't like my clothes, my hair, the way I talk. They don't like my future plans. They don't like anything about me.*[48]
>
> an Asian American student

As noted in previous sections, large numbers of Asian Pacific immigrant and refugee students have critical needs that are unaddressed because of the lack of bilingual/bicultural school personnel to provide appropriate counseling and guidance services.

While the need for bilingual counselors, advisors, tutors, and other support service personnel is expected to remain at current crisis levels given the population projections for school-age immigrants through 2020, there will also be a dramatic increase in the need for bicultural/multicultural school counselors and for teacher training in culturally appropriate counseling methods to attend to the complex issues of identity and cultural dissonance that will follow from the huge increase in second-generation school-age Asian Pacific Americans with immigrant parents.

The need for targeted support services to deal with post-traumatic stress disorder (PTSD) and other consequences of the Southeast Asian refugee experience should decline, assuming that no new waves of refugees flee from Asia to the U.S. Given the continuing war within Cambodia as well as the instability of other countries such as Thailand, Vietnam, the Philippines, and Myanmar (Burma), however, the future of refugee resettlement policy is difficult to predict. Initial research on the children of U.S.–Vietnam combat veterans with PTSD also suggests that there are second-generation effects, such as a higher than average incidence of attention-deficit disorder and other learning disabilities. If so, then the continuing social consequences of the Vietnam War may persist for another generation of American-born children of refugees, and will demand recognition from policy-makers and service-providers.

At the same time, urban youth and schools in the 1990s have faced wars of a different kind here at home. Many Asian Pacific American youth, in spite of the model minority myth, have been profoundly affected by guns and gang violence, drugs, and the AIDS epidemic. Whether these public health crises will gain relief by 2020 is unclear, but the signs so far are pessimistic. In response, urban schools are evolving into multi-service centers, in addition to being institutions of teaching and learning. Local health centers, social service agencies, and other community-based organizations are essential partners for the future development of effective school policy and practice. In areas with significant Asian Pacific populations, the experience and involvement of Asian Pacific community organizations will be invaluable to schools in the coming years.

Furthermore, although the issues of identity, language and culture shift, and intergenerational conflict, as highlighted above, will present major challenges to schools, families, and communities in the coming years, these issues are not new to some Asian Pacific American groups such as Japanese, Chinese and Filipino Americans. Research and counseling methods, outreach strategies, and organizational models from those communities may be transferrable. Therefore, it will be increasingly important to share lessons, expertise, and resources across communities in a coordinated manner in order to provide maximum support for the education and healthy development of new generations.

PARENT EMPOWERMENT

> *The refugee parents are frustrated. On the one hand, they want to push their children academically, they want them to become someone in this society, to work hard, to study well. On the other hand, they cannot effectively intervene in the education process, they cannot even attend school functions... even school conferences, because of the language, but most often they are not familiar with the process, with... how things get done here.*[49]

> a Vietnamese community leader
> and candidate for elected office

For a variety of reasons, ranging from cultural expectations to long work hours and lack of transportation to the language barrier, Asian Pacific parents play limited roles in direct relation to the schools their children attend. Meanwhile, many schools exclude Asian Pacific American parents from meaningful participation as a result of the language barrier, lack of training and cultural sensitivity, poor outreach and follow-up, and lack of respect.

Yet, parents are the initial, and often most influential "teachers" in their children's lives. In turn, teachers and administrators who remain unaware of their students' home environments are neither able to make connections between the curriculum and students' own experiences nor prepared to provide appropriate support when students confront difficulties.

As policies for reforming school governance increasingly focus on decentralized structures of school-site management that grant greater decision-making authority to stakeholders within schools, such as principals and teachers, parents must also claim their rightful place at the table. Culturally appropriate outreach, training, and follow-up are critical to enable Asian Pacific parents to play significant roles in school reform and governance. Models for Asian Pacific American parent organizing, parent training, and parent/school partnerships need to be identified, refined, and disseminated.

Inevitably, parent organizing and advocacy efforts lead to issues of political representation and empowerment on school boards. Speaking for a coalition of Latino and Southeast Asian parents who sued the Lowell School Committee and the City of Lowell, Massachusetts, for Title VI discrimination, Alex Huertas asserted in 1987: "The lack of Latino and Asian representation has made our struggle harder. In next year's elections, we need to promote our own candidates."[50]

Data from the National Association of School Boards shows that only 0.1 percent of the nation's school board members are Asian Pacific American. In a handful of cases, primarily in California, individuals such as Warren Furutani in Los Angeles, Wilma Chan and Jeanne Quan in Oakland, Leland Yee in San Francisco, and Michael Chang in Cupertino, California, as well as Alan Cheung in Montgomery County, Maryland, have run successfully for election to local school boards and have had significant impact on district policies. Through her election to the St. Paul, Minnesota, school board in 1991, Choua Lee became the first

Hmong American elected public official in the country. In 1992, Won So was appointed as the student representative and became the first Asian Pacific American to serve on the New York City school board.

New York's schools—the largest system in the country—are governed through a decentralized structure of community boards representing each district of the city. Any parent is eligible to vote in community school board elections, regardless of their status as a registered voter. The New York City policy of parent empowerment is especially significant for immigrant Asian Pacific and Latino parents who may not be citizens, but who desire and deserve a voice in school board decision-making.

Given the large numbers of immigrant Asian Pacific parents through 2020, such a structure could have far-reaching impact if adapted in other cities with large Asian Pacific population centers. At the same time, the numbers of American-born Asian Pacifics will also increase dramatically— magnifying the importance of voter registration, leadership development, and other foundations of political empowerment in order to gain greater influence over school board policies.

IMPLICATIONS FOR FURTHER RESEARCH

In addition to recommendations presented in the sections above, more comprehensive research on Asian Pacific Americans—research that is not skewed either by model minority assumptions or by excluding LEP Asian Pacific students from sample populations—is needed to drive national and local educational policy. Quantitative and qualitative educational research studies, disaggregated by ethnicity and conducted in native languages, are especially important to initiate. Given the increases in Asian American poverty during the 1980s,[51] relationships between education and socioeconomic status are also critical to explore.

In light of Ong's population projections, foundations and government agencies along with universities and schools must take greater responsibility for Asian Pacific American research and policy development. However, consistent with conclusions from a recent report on Asian American poverty in Boston,[52] the capacity must also be developed *within* Asian Pacific American communities to conduct systematic research and policy analysis on educational issues and related concerns.

Conclusion:
Recognizing Strengths for the Future

As the nation prepares to move into the 21st century toward the year 2020, it is clear that the economic, cultural, and political influence of Asia will become increasingly decisive in international affairs, and that the Asian Pacific American population will continue to grow at a fantastic pace.

Asian Pacific Americans, particularly the first generation, invest heavily in education. Maintaining deep respect for teachers and holding high expectations for student achievement based on hard work, Asian Pacific Americans have much to contribute to the debate over educational policy and the process of educational reform.

Yet, the strengths offered by Asian Pacific Americans to society are typically not recognized.[53] For example, even though educational reports written by everyone from the President and the Secretary of Education to local school boards and chambers of commerce are unanimous in lamenting the low level of U.S. students' foreign-language skills, none of those reports calls for strengthening the educational support for immigrant students who already speak many languages other than English. Why do we fail to embrace our students who are native speakers of languages like Korean, Vietnamese, or Chinese? Why do we not enable them to stay in school and develop their multilingual/multicultural skills in English? Rather than seeing them, at best, as special needs populations outside of the mainstream of our schools or, at worst, as foreigners whose accents are aggravating and who should go back where they came from, we have to learn to see what great contributions they can make to our schools and society because of their multilingual and multicultural backgrounds.

Similarly, a recent trend in management training at leadership academies promotes physical workouts and survival tests designed to develop character, discipline, and stamina. Yet, do we consider the experiences of refugees and immigrants or even those of urban Latinos and African Americans who have come through real-life survival tests, walking hundreds of miles without food or crossing the sea in sinking boats or dealing with gang warfare in the streets? They are real survivors who have already developed and proven their strength of character, discipline, and stamina. They have all the qualities we look for in leaders, but they are never recognized. At best, they are seen as helpless or needy clients; at worst they are resented as a burden to society.

Will K-12 educational policy in the 21st century promote Asian Pacific American exclusion or contribution? If informed by demographic analyses, then the imperative is clear. For if the strengths of Asian Pacific Americans continue to go untapped, especially in the field of education, then we as a society have not progressed very far in the hundred years since the San Francisco school board mandated that the city's children should not associate with or be influenced by their peers "of the Mongolian race."

Notes

1. *San Francisco Chronicle* (May 7, 1905); cited in Victor Low, *The Unimpressable Race* (San Francisco: East/West, 1982), 88.

2. Superintendent's Letter to Principals, Circular No. 8, January 12, 1906; cited in Low, *The Unimpressable Race*, 89.

3. Low, *The Unimpressable Race*.

4. Ling-chi Wang, "*Lau v. Nichols*: History of Struggle for Equal and Quality Education," in *Asian-Americans: Social and Psychological Perspectives*, vol. 2, edited by Russell Endo, Stanley Sue, and Nathaniel N. Wagner (Palo Alto, California: Science and Behavior, 1980), 181–216.

5. Peter Nien-chu Kiang, *Southeast Asian Parent Empowerment: The Challenge of Changing Demographics in Lowell, Massachusetts*, Monograph No. 1, Massachusetts Association for Bilingual Education, 1990.

6. Joan McCarthy First and John Willshire Carrera, *New Voices: Immigrant Students in U.S. Public Schools* (Boston: National Coalition of Advocates for Students, 1988), 6; U.S. Commission on Civil Rights, *Civil Rights Issues Facing Asian Americans in the 1990s*, Washington, D.C., February 1992, 76.

7. Robert W. Gardner, Bryant Robey, and Peter C. Smith, "Asian Americans: Growth, Change, and Diversity," *Population Bulletin* 40:4 (October 1985).

8. First and Carrera, *New Voices*; U.S. Commission on Civil Rights, *Civic Rights Issues Facing Asian Americans in the 1990s*.

9. Council of the Great City Schools; cited in "25 Largest Public School Districts," *Black Issues in Higher Education* (May 7, 1992), 62.

10. Unpublished student essay, 1989.

11. School District of Philadelphia, *Asian/Pacific Americans: Getting to Know Us—A Resource Guide for Teachers*, 1988; and John Nobuya Tsuchida, *A Guide on Asian & Pacific Islander American Students* (Washington, D.C.: National Education Association, 1991).

12. For further development of these ideas and for examples of specific learning activities based on a thematic approach, see Peter N. Kiang,

Asian American Studies Curriculum Resource Guide (Massachusetts K–12), University of Massachusetts and Massachusetts Asian American Educators Association, May 1992.

13. Sucheng Chan, *Asian Americans: An Interpretive History* (Boston: Twayne, 1991); and Ronald Takaki, *Strangers from a Distant Shore* (Boston: Little Brown, 1989).

14. This occurred when the movie *Rambo* opened in Boston in May 1985.

15. Margaret A. Gibson, *Accommodation without Assimilation: Sikh Immigrants in an American High School* (Ithaca, New York: Cornell University Press, 1988), 143.

16. Peter Schmidt, "L.A. Events Seen Touching Schools 'for Years,' " *Education Week* (May 13, 1992), 1, 12.

17. Larry Tye, "Hate Crimes on Rise in U.S.," *Boston Globe* (July 29, 1990).

18. Anti-Defamation League of B'nai B'rith, "Young and Violent: The Growing Menace of America's Neo-Nazi Skinheads," New York, 1988; and Diego Ribadeneira, "Study Says Teen-agers' Racism Rampart," *Boston Globe* (October 18, 1990).

19. Peter Schmidt, "New Survey Discerns Deep Divisions among U.S. Youths on Race Relations," *Education Week* (March 25, 1992), 5.

20. U.S. Commission on Civil Rights, *Civil Rights Issues Facing Asian Americans in the 1990s*, 97–99.

21. *Asian Week* (October 13, 1989).

22. Kiang, Southeast Asian Empowerment; and George Kagiwada, "The Killing of Thong Hy Huynh: Implications of a Rashomon Perspective," in *Frontiers of Asian American Studies*, edited by Gail M. Nomura et al. (Pullman, Washington: Washington State University Press, 1989), 253–265.

23. Sonia Nieto, *Affirming Diversity* (New York: Longman, 1992).

24. Unpublished essay, 1991.

25. For further discussion about the importance of voice in multicultural education, see Antonia Darder, *Culture and Power in the Classroom* (New York: Bergin & Garvey, 1991); Nieto, *Affirming Diversity*; and Catherine E. Walsh, *Pedagogy and the Struggle for Voice: Issues in Language, Power, and Schooling for Puerto Ricans* (New York: Bergin & Garvey, 1991).

26. American Council on Education, 1989.

27. Glass ceiling studies suggest that the disproportionately small number of Asian Pacific Americans in leadership positions in both public and private sectors face particular difficulties due to stereotypes, cultural barriers, and contradictory expectations. This deserves further study in the education field.

28. U.S. Commission on Civil Rights, *Civil Rights Issues Facing Asian Americans in the 1990s*, 77–79.

29. Bob H. Suzuki, "Education and the Socialization of Asian Americans: A Revisionist Analysis of the 'Model Minority' Thesis," *Amerasia Journal*

4:2 (1977), 23–51; Ki-Taek Chun, "The Myth of Asian American Success and Its Educational Ramifications," *IRCD Bulletin* 15:1&2 (Winter 1980), 1-12; Won Moo Hurh and Kwang Chung Kim, "The Success Image of Asian Americans: Its Validity, and Its Practical and Theoretical Implications," *Ethnic and Racial Studies* 12:4 (October 1989), 512–538.

30. National Education Association, *Report of the Asian and Pacific Islander Concerns Study Committee*, June 1987; Joan C. Baratz-Snowden and Richard Duran, *The Educational Progress of Language Minority Students: Findings from the 1983–1984 NAEP Reading Survey*, Princeton, Educational Testing Service, January 1987.

31. National Center for Education Statistics, *Language Characteristics and Academic Achievement: A Look at Asian and Hispanic Eighth Graders in NELS:88*, Washington, D.C., U.S. Department of Education, February 1992.

32. *Ibid.*, 3.

33. First and Carrera, *New Voices*, 15–70; and U.S. Commission on Civil Rights, *Civil Rights Issues Facing Asian Americans in the 1990s*, 68–103.

34. Unpublished essay, 1988.

35. James Crawford, ed., *Language Loyalties: A Source Book on the Official English Controversy* (Chicago: University of Chicago Press, 1992); Kenji Hakuta, *Mirror of Language: The Debate on Bilingualism* (New York: Basic Books, 1986).

36. Kenji Hakuta and Lucinda Pease-Alvarez, eds., "Special Issue on Bilingual Education, American Educational Research Association," *Educational Researcher* 21:2 (March 1992); and Sandra Lee McKay and Sau-ling Cynthia Wong, *Language Diversity: Problem or Resource?* (New York: Newbury House, 1988).

37. U.S. Commission on Civil Rights, *Civil Rights Issues Facing Asian Americans in the 1990s*.

38. National Education Association, *Report of the Asian and Pacific Islander Concerns Study Committee*, Washington, D.C., June 1987.

39. Henry T. Trueba, Lila Jacobs, and Elizabeth Kirton, *Cultural Conflict and Adaptation: The Case of Hmong Children in American Society* (Basingstroke, United Kingdom: Falmer Press, 1990), 91.

40. Peter Schmidt, "L.E.P. Students Denied Remedial Help, Study Finds," *Education Week* (June 17, 1992), 11.

41. First and Carrera, *New Voices*, 42–55; and Joan First, John B. Kellogg, Cheryl A. Almeida, and Richard Gray, Jr., *The Good Common School: Making the Vision Work for All Children* (Boston: National Coalition of Advocates for Students, 1991), 51–86, 135–165.

42. Unpublished essay, 1989.

43. Unpublished essay, 1991.

44. Lily Wong-Fillmore et al., "When Learning a Second Language Means Losing the First," *Early Child Research Quarterly*, in press.

45. Lily Wong-Fillmore, "Preschoolers and Native Language Loss," *MABE Newsletter*, Massachusetts Association for Bilingual Education (Spring 1991), 2.

46. Nathan Caplan, John K. Whitmore, and Marcella H. Choy, *The Boat People and Achievement in America* (Ann Arbor: University of Michigan Press, 1989).

47. First and Carrera, *New Voices*, 50.

48. Gibson, *Accommodation without Assimilation*, 135.

49. Vu-Duc Vuong, quoted in First and Carrera, *New Voices*, 77.

50. Kiang, *Southeast Asian Parent Empowerment*, 13.

51. In Boston, for example, Asian Americans were the only group whose poverty rate increased during the 1980s. See Irene Sege, "Recent Arrivals," *Boston Globe* (June 17, 1992), 1, 32; and Dean S. Toji and James H. Johnson, "Asian and Pacific Islander American Poverty: The Working Poor and the Jobless Poor," *Amerasia Journal* 18:1 (1992), 83–91.

52. Carlton Sagara and Peter Kiang, *Recognizing Poverty in Boston's Asian American Community* (Boston: Boston Foundation, 1992), 66.

53. This section is adapted from Peter N. Kiang, "Social Studies for the Pacific Century," *Social Education* 55:7 (November/December 1991), 458–462.

Trends in Admissions for
Asian Americans in Colleges and Universities:

Higher Education Policy

L. Ling-chi Wang

CHAIR, ETHNIC STUDIES
UNIVERSITY OF CALIFORNIA, BERKELEY

Gaining access to prestigious institutions of higher education will continue to be a top priority for most Asian American families, even if admissions into such institutions become increasingly competitive and the cost of attending them becomes prohibitive. Less noticeable, but just as important, is the quality of education or the lack of it given to even larger numbers of Asian Americans from immigrant and working class backgrounds in community colleges and state universities and colleges.

This article explores the future trends and emerging issues in these two sectors of higher education for Asian Americans as they look to the 21st century. I shall begin with a historical background and analysis of patterns on Asian enrollments in higher education, setting the stage for a proper understanding of several current controversies over the so-called "over-representation of Asian American students," "model minority," and "reverse discrimination." This will be followed by a discussion on what we can expect in the early decades of the 21st century and what Asian Americans must do to protect their rights and the rights of others.

Historical Patterns of
Asian American Enrollments

Historically, two distinctive patterns of Asian enrollment in higher education can be identified. On the one hand, most of the elite, church-affiliated universities and colleges made a point of recruiting some exceptional students directly from Asian countries partly to enhance the work of American missionaries in Asia and partly to help train leaders knowledgeable and friendly to the U.S. For example, all Ivy League universities and most of the elite liberal arts colleges maintained the presence of a small group of foreign students from Asian countries. Upon graduation these foreign students returned to their countries to become government officials, educators, professors, and church leaders. This explains the high visibility and prestige these institutions enjoy throughout East Asia to this date.

Foreign graduate students from Asian countries increased sharply during the Cold War as higher education expanded rapidly with federal assistance and as U.S. industries, especially the hi-tech industries and research universities, eagerly absorbed them into their work forces. Instead of returning to their home countries after the completion of their training, most of "the best and brightest" settled permanently in the U.S. For example, about 100,000 Chinese graduate students came to the U.S. for advanced degrees between 1950 and 1983 and most of them, about 85 percent, stayed and raised their children in the U.S. In the process, they disproportionately increased the percentage of high achievers among the Asian American population and contributed inadvertently to the stereotype of Asian Americans as a "model" or "super" minority. This explains also the eagerness and determination, including willingness to incur financial sacrifices, with which they send their children to these same institutions.

On the other hand, the American-born Asians were ironically kept out of these same institutions because of overt discriminatory policies against racial minorities and women. In spite of their low socioeconomic status, the children of working class immigrants from Asia in the pre-World War II period were encouraged and motivated to pursue the highest possible education accessible and affordable to them. The hope and sole strategy within the Asian American communities was to use education to overcome poverty and prejudice for the next generation. Unfortunately most institutions of higher education and graduate professional schools maintained policies of either excluding outright Asian American students or limiting their access to a tiny annual quota. The high cost of entering the elite private colleges and universities also effectively prevented the highly motivated, but working class Asian American children from entering these institutions. Historically, about the only institution readily accessible to them before World War II was the tuition-free University of California at Berkeley and Los Angeles. It was this opening that set the precedence and established the patterns for future generations for Asian Americans seeking affordable quality higher education. To most Asian Americans to this date, the University of California still represents their best hope of getting admitted without prejudice and receiving a high quality education their parents can afford to pay.

The most significant increase in Asian American enrollment in higher education began in the mid-1970s. According to the National Center for Education Statistics, there were 406,000 Asian Americans in all types of institutions of higher education in 1988. As a percentage of total enrollment in higher education, Asian Americans represented only 3.8 percent in 1988, a very substantial increase from 1.8 percent in 1976. In the same period, the percentage of Whites dropped from 82.6 percent to 78.8 percent and black students declined from 9.4 percent to 8.7 percent while the Hispanic share rose from 3.5 percent to 5.2 percent. (There were 881,000 Blacks and 587,000 Hispanics in colleges and universities in 1988).

It is important to note that the increase occurred across the spectrum of higher education, from the most elite private universities to the small liberal arts colleges, from the top public research universities to the two-year community colleges. Needless to say, the University of California at Berkeley and Los Angeles continue to be among the most popular choices, again, because of their quality, accessibility, and low cost. Other public Ivies, such as Michigan, Illinois, Wisconsin, for the same reasons, have also seen their Asian American enrollments go up.

Several factors account for the sharp increase which continues to this date. First and foremost, the removal of the restrictive racial quotas allocated to immigrants from Asian countries in 1965 caused a sudden surge in Asian immigrants, many of whom were either child-bearing women or women with young children who reached college-age by the mid-1970s. Second, the African American civil rights movement forced the elite universities and colleges to open their doors for the first time to domestic racial minorities and women through affirmative action programs. Most of these universities and colleges soon discovered a huge reservoir of Asian American applicants, many of whom possessed both academic qualifications and financial resources. This development allowed Asian American high school graduates for the first time to have more choices of universities and colleges beyond the University of California and a few public universities in metropolitan areas with high concentrations of Asian Americans and caused a steady decline in the matriculation rates at UC Berkeley and UCLA. Third, the U.S.-China detente in 1972 and the U.S. withdrawal from Vietnam in 1975 precipitated a major geopolitical realignment in East and Southeast Asia and ushered in a new era of political instability for Asian dictatorial regimes sponsored and protected, up until then, by the U.S. As a result, many upper- and middle-class families from South Korea, Taiwan, Hong Kong, the Philippines, Thailand, Indonesia, Malaysia, and Singapore decided to move to the U.S. for a more secure and brighter future for their children through education. Most in this group knew the reputation of the elite private universities and pushed their children to gain admissions into them. Lastly, the evacuation of refugees from Vietnam in 1975 and the "Boat People" crisis in 1978 eventually brought over one million refugees from Indochina, many of whom came also with the hope of giving their children a chance to start anew in the U.S. through education.

The above factors led to a rapid increase of Asian American enrollments in several major sectors of higher education in the early 1980s, especially among the most select private universities and colleges in the East Coast and at UC Berkeley and UCLA, the two historically favored institutions for Asian Americans. By about 1983, most of the Ivy League universities, MIT, Cal Tech, Johns Hopkins, Julliard School of Music, and the University of Chicago had at least 10 percent Asian American undergraduates, and by 1990 even the top elite liberal arts colleges were enrolling anywhere from 7 percent to 17 percent (e.g., 8 percent at Amherst, Swarthmore, and Williams; 7 percent at Oberlin; 9 percent at Reed; 14 percent at Pomona and Bryn Mawr; 17 percent at Wellesley and Barnard; and 9 percent at Smith). At UC Berkeley and UCLA, Asian American freshman enrollments increased at such alarming rates that they threatened to outnumber the dominant white student population.

In fact, the rapid rise of Asian American enrollments among these universities led some—for example, Brown, Harvard, Princeton, Stanford, MIT, UC Berkeley, and UCLA—to review and revise their respective admission policies in such a way as to cause either an unexpected slowdown or a decline in the admission of Asian American applicants. Allegations of discrimination and use of illegal means, including alleged quotas for Asian Americans, led to several self-studies by some institutions (Brown, Princeton, MIT, and Stanford) and external investigations by government agencies at the federal and state levels in the late 1980s (audit on UC Berkeley by the California Auditor General and investigation of Harvard and UCLA by the U.S. Office for Civil Rights). Even though these self-studies and investigations have yielded mixed findings, they brought about several far-reaching changes in admission policies, most notably at Stanford, UC Berkeley, and UCLA, and resulted in significant increases in Asian American admissions in most institutions. For example, the freshman class of Harvard, Yale, and Stanford in 1990 had respectively 20 percent, 15 percent, and 24 percent Asian Americans and for the first time in history, Asian American freshmen outnumbered Whites in both UC Berkeley and UCLA in 1990.

Enrollment by Class and National Origin

The national attention given to the Asian American struggle against discriminatory admission policies and their phenomenal success in gaining access to the most prestigious institutions and in fighting against racial discrimination among the top universities and colleges in the United States should not in any way obscure the less publicized struggles by the majority of Asian Americans seeking access to basic and general education necessary to survive and compete in the job market.

As mentioned above, a total of 406,000 Asian Americans were in higher education in 1988. In spite of their smaller population (7.3 million, or 2.9 percent of the total U.S. population in 1990), the enrollment of Asian Americans was equal to Hispanics in private institutions (3.2 percent) and four-year institutions (4.6 percent), but the enrollment of Asian Americans was substantially less than Hispanics in public institutions (4 percent to 5.8 percent) and two-year institutions (4.1 percent to 7.9 percent). In other words, between 1976 and 1988, the representation of Asian American students in higher education more than doubled (1.8 percent to 3.8 percent), and more Asian Americans were enrolled in public institutions (4 percent) and in two-year institutions (4.1 percent), as opposed to private institutions (3.2 percent) and four-year institutions (3.6 percent).

Without doubt, the highly visible presence of Asian Americans in the top private and public universities in the U.S. has overshadowed the vast majority of Asian Americans from working class background, most of whom belong to the immigrant generation. Their numerical presence in the public institutions and in the two-year community colleges represent the values they attach to degrees in higher education, even if they are severely limited by their language background, cultural difference, academic preparation, and financial capability.

Typical of this kind of enrollment are students at California State University at San Francisco and the City College of San Francisco located in a region known for not just its Asian American concentration but also proximity to two of the top universities in the U.S.: UC Berkeley and Stanford University, both of which have high Asian American enrollments. In 1991, CSU San Francisco reported 33 percent Asian Americans out of a total undergraduate student body of 14,672, and the City College of San Francisco had over 40 percent out of 70,000 part-time and full-time students. Students enrolled in these two institutions receive either general education or job-related training programs. In City College, the largest single bloc of Asian American students are enrolled in survival English classes. Through basic English classes and job training programs, they learn to survive in their new, adopted country. Their perennial problems are having to wait for a long time to get into the English classes and getting trained for jobs that hopefully will still exist when they leave school.

In short, the patterns of Asian American enrollment in higher education reflect the bifurcated Asian American population. In general, the children from the middle class are motivated to attend the very top public and private universities and colleges across the nation while the children of the working class pursue higher education on the basis of their needs and academic and financial ability.

However, it would be a mistake to assume all Asian American college-age children attend colleges of different types. According to the U.S. Bureau of the Census, 34.3 percent of all Asian Americans were college graduates in 1980. However, only 2.9 percent among Hmong, 5.6 percent among Laotians, 7.7 percent among Cambodians, and 12.9 percent among Vietnamese were college graduates. In fact, a very significant percentage of college-age Asian Americans is not attending college. They tend to be the poor, non-English-speaking immigrants who invariably are compelled to do menial jobs with Asian American employers who frequently do not even pay the minimal wage. In spite of their high propensity toward college attendance, not all Asian Americans are high achievers in education and not all Asian Americans are enrolled in the high-prestige universities and colleges, as the popular stereotype of "model minority" implies. In fact, the stereotype has had an adverse impact on Asian American youth.

Even though there are no data collected on the national origins of Asian Americans in higher education, an informal survey of Asian American students in the Ivy League universities and in the University of California show very clearly that Chinese Americans, South Asian Americans, Japanese Americans and Korean Americans are well represented at the undergraduate level, and Chinese Americans and South Asian Americans are best represented at the graduate level. Among the least represented are the Indochinese Americans, and within this group, Vietnamese Americans far outnumber the Hmong, Laotians, and Cambodians.

Therefore, the two major factors that determine college attendance rates and the types of institutions Asian American students attend are socio-economic status and national origin. To achieve a better understanding of Asian Americans in higher education, we need more refined and reliable data collection. Just as important is the need not to make generalizations on Asian American success in higher education. This brief analysis demonstrates the diversity and disparity among Asian Americans in higher education.

Future Trends in Asian American Enrollments

Will the patterns of Asian American enrollment in higher education outlined above persist in the next two decades or so? If these patterns persist, how will different types of institutions of higher education respond to the steady rise of Asian American enrollment? How well will they meet the diverse educational needs of Asian American students? Will the foreign students from Asian countries continue to come to the U.S. for advanced degrees and settle as permanent residents?

Even though the Cold War has ended and many of the immigrant-sending countries in East Asia have become developed countries in recent years, there is no reason to doubt that the well-established patterns of immigration in the past three decades and thus the patterns of Asian

American enrollment in higher education will not persist.

This conclusion is based on the following reasons. First, the Asian immigrants from China, Taiwan, Hong Kong, the Philippines, and Indochina in the last two decades will be eligible to sponsor their relatives to come to the U.S. Unless there is a change in the U.S. immigration law, the influx of Asian immigrants will continue, even though the reasons for emigration may be different from the previous period. Second, the lure of better economic opportunity and a better chance to provide a college education for their children will continue to stimulate additional emigration from Asian countries. Third, the U.S. will remain a main attraction for ambitious students from Asian countries where research universities are either non-existent or too few to meet their demands. In spite of the high cultural value and social prestige assigned to education in most East Asian and Southeast Asian societies, education in most of these countries remains largely inaccessible to most people. Access to education is highly restrictive because of exorbitant tuition and keen competition for access to a small handful of institutions. Several Asian countries are trying to build world-class research universities, but it will be a long time before they can become competitive. Many of these foreign students will eventually establish families in the U.S. and send their children to college.

In other words, the growth rates and enrollment patterns of Asian Americans in higher education established since the mid-1970s will continue in the foreseeable future, indeed, well into the next century. This means that the pool of highly motivated and competitive Asian American applicants to all types of institutions of higher education will continue to swell.

Emerging Issues

This being the case, Asian Americans can expect steeper competition for access into top universities and colleges as university resources shrink and tuition and admission standards are raised. Similarly, the children of working class immigrants will continue to seek access to higher education even though they will find access increasingly difficult as public universities raise their admissions standards and community colleges cut their services for survival English and job training programs.

Four major issues are likely to incite public debates:

First, the debate over the so-called "overrepresentation" of Asian Americans at the top national universities and colleges is likely to continue because the percentage of Asian Americans admitted each year will continue to rise. Among the top public universities, the percentage of Asian American freshmen exceeded Whites at UC Berkeley and UCLA last year. In fact, the gap will continue to widen as the Asian American applicant pools in these two public institutions expand and the white pools shrink. For the first time this year, the pool of Asian American applicants to UCLA surpassed Whites while the number of Asian American applicants at Berkeley closed in on the white applicants. Likewise, although at a slower rate, both in numbers and percentages, the admissions of Asian Americans among the nation's top private universities and colleges are rising steadily. The percentages of Asian Americans in the 1991 freshman class at Harvard, Yale, and Stanford reached 19 percent, 15 percent and 24 percent respectively.

Second, the perceived overrepresentation of Asian American students in these institutions will intensify the ongoing national debate over the usefulness of some of the traditional universal meritocratic criteria that began in the early 1980s when several universities noted the alarming growth rates of Asian American students on their campuses. The debate is likely to center on the proper weight to be assigned to traditional academic criteria (test scores and GPA) and non-academic criteria of infinite variety (extracurricular activities, leadership quality, race, socioeconomic status, geographic location, age, disability, music or athletic talent, veteran status, career choice, children of VIP, "legacy" status, i.e., children of alumni, etc.) Behind this debate is the issue of overrepresentation and how best to achieve a balanced, diverse student body without abandoning these institutions' commitment to the principle of academic excellence. Since the leaders of the U.S. have historically come out of these world-class universities and colleges, the hidden agenda and ultimate issue behind the overrepresentation debate may very well be the future leadership in the U.S. and how we conceive our national identity. This, in fact, was the real issue behind the three-century-old "Jewish Question" until it was finally overcome in the late 1950s.

Third, just as important on the other side of this debate on overrepresentation is whether affirmative action programs designed to correct past injustices against racial minorities are being eroded by rising

Asian American enrollment on the one hand *or* are rapidly becoming an obstacle for more Asian Americans seeking to gain access to these same institutions. At the heart of the debate over the merit, legitimacy, and legality of affirmative action programs is whether the *Bakke* decision (1978) should be left alone or challenged. Under *Bakke*, the U.S. Supreme Court permitted universities to establish temporary affirmative action programs not only to correct past injustices against racial minorities but also to create a diverse student body for reasons, presumably, of pedagogy, as long as race, color, or national origin is not the sole basis for framing such programs. At issue therefore are the fairness and longevity of such programs under *Bakke*. Led by Assistant Attorney General William Bradford Reynolds, Gary Curran of the Office for Civil Rights (OCR), and Congressman Dana Rohrabacher, conservative Whites and some Asian Americans have been using the legitimate complaints of Asian Americans to advance their objective to dismantle affirmative action programs through the Office for Civil Rights since the late 1980s. They consider such programs unfair and no longer necessary. The recent decision by OCR to conduct compliance review at UC Berkeley, UC Davis, UCLA, and UC San Diego is further indication of this line of thinking and attack.

Fourth, the shrinking public and private resources for higher education, the virtually mandatory college degrees for success in the job market, and the anticipated rise in demand for access to higher education in the next decade are forcing institutions of higher education to raise tuition and admission standards as convenient devices to reject applicants. Unfortunately, the net result of this strategy is to force, in mass, middle- and lower-middle-class applicants to seek admission into the less selective and cheaper public universities, compelling these institutions also to raise their fees and admission requirements. The end result is the displacement of large numbers of working class children from these traditionally affordable institutions. For example, the University of California system has nearly doubled its fees in the past two years alone. Many Asian American students from the working class will find it increasingly difficult to gain access to these institutions. They will be compelled to look to community colleges where fees, likewise, have been moving up steadily. Under this bumping process, Asian Americans will probably continue to do well because of their commitment to higher education and their willingness to sacrifice for the sake of education. This means that they will become more visible and "overrepresented" at all levels of the educational hierarchy, a condition most conducive to multiracial conflict.

Asian American Response to Emerging Issues

Given the scenario outlined above, Asian Americans must chart their course of actions along the following lines:

- Asian Americans must actively monitor and participate in the ongoing debate over the criteria for admissions and be prepared to take action against any unfair targeting of Asian Americans for exclusion;

- As a racial minority who have benefitted and will continue to benefit from affirmative action programs in other sectors of the society, Asian Americans must continue to support legitimate affirmative action programs on the one hand and forcefully oppose efforts by Whites and some Asian Americans to challenge and dismantle such program under *Bakke*;

- Because affirmative action programs are defined legally as transitional programs whose usefulness will eventually expire, Asian Americans must support efforts to gradually shift the predominantly race-based affirmative action programs to class-based affirmative action programs. Such programs in the long run will benefit all races in a society in which the poor are getting poorer and the rich richer; and

- Asian Americans must work with institutions of higher education to develop English language and job training programs that will adequately serve the needs of working class Asian immigrants.

Health Care Needs and
Service Delivery for
Asian and Pacific Islander Americans:

Health Policy

Tessie Guillermo

EXECUTIVE DIRECTOR
ASIAN AMERICAN HEALTH FORUM
SAN FRANCISCO, CALIFORNIA

As the Asian and Pacific Islander American population increases and its demographics change, the need for health care is a subject of much concern. Central to any discussion about health care services for Asian and Pacific Islander Americans is the issue of access. Although access to health care has been a widely researched topic in the United States, and in fact much time and effort has been spent in outlining the barriers to care that face Asian and Pacific Islander individuals, existing health care policies do little to eliminate these barriers. In fact, among the most widely debated policy issues of the day is the reform of the existing U.S. health care system to ensure accessibility for all; but an examination of current proposals reveals that they do not address language and cultural factors in the delivery of care, two factors that affect the use of health services.[1] Because Asian and Pacific Islander communities are relatively new and relatively small, little is known about our health care needs. In the absence of a better empirical basis for policy formation, the requirements for health services for Asians and Pacific Islanders remain difficult to assess.

While the issue of access is critical to any discussion of health care services, it is beyond the scope of this article to provide a complete analysis of this problem. However, indicators relating to access can be measured by examining Asian and Pacific Islander population characteristics. This article will describe the need for health care services by highlighting certain population characteristics and analyzing the existing health care delivery system in terms of the availability of services for Asian and Pacific Islanders. Finally, this article will conclude with policy recommendations.

Sociodemographic Profile:
Key Predictors for Access to Health Services

The context for evaluating current health care services for Asians and Pacific Islanders is the sociodemographic profile of "at-risk" populations (see table 1).

Table 1 lists sociodemographic characteristics which are key indicators and predictors to the use of health services. Factors such as age, sex, race/

Table 1. Characteristics of Population At-Risk
(Indicators of Potential Use of Health Services)*

PREDISPOSING	ENABLING	NEED
Age	Residence (Location)	Morbidity
Sex	Income	Mortality
Race/Ethnicity	Employment Status	Limited Activity Days
Language	Occupation	Family Health History
Nativity	Level of Insurance	
Education		

* Adapted from behavioral model of health access developed by Aday et al., *Health Care in the United States: Equitable for Whom?* (New York: Sage Publications, New York, 1980).

ethnicity, language, nativity, and education are identified as "predisposing" characteristics. These factors are assumed to exist prior to any recognition of the need for health care. "Enabling" characteristics include such factors as residence, income, employment status/occupation, and level of insurance. They describe the resources available to a population to gain access to services.

Table 2 describes the Asian and Pacific Islander population by age/sex breakdown using 1990 Census data. As the table shows, 53.2 percent of females in 1990 are of childbearing age, suggesting the need for reproductive, maternal and child health and other primary health care services.

Table 2: U.S. Asian and Pacific Islander Population by Age & Sex, 1990

	Percent of Population	
Age	Male	Female
75 and over	1.9	2.3
65 to 74	3.7	4.5
55to 64	5.8	7.0
45 to 54	9.8	10.0
35 to 44	16.4	17.7
25 to 34	19.4	19.5
15 to 24	18.0	16.0
5 to 14	16.4	15.2
4 and below	8.4	7.7

Source: U.S. Bureau of the Census, 1990 Census
© 1992 Asian/Pacific Islander Data Consortium—ACCIS; San Francisco, CA

Projections for the year 2020 indicate a two to threefold increase in the elderly population, suggesting the need for additional attention to elderly needs in the future and more chronic disease prevention services in the present.

Table 3 lists ethnicity and nativity characteristics from the 1990 Census. The 1990 Census currently categorizes up to 17 different Asian ethnicities and eight Pacific Islander ethnicities, in addition to two "other" categories. Although 1990 data is not yet available on language characteristics of ethnic groups, the 1980 Census indicated that 85 percent of Asians and Pacific Islanders spoke a language other than English at home. According to 1990

TESSIE GUILLERMO, "Health Care Needs and Service Delivery"   63

Table 3. Ethnicity and Nativity Characteristics of
Asian and Pacific Islander Americans in 1990

Race/ Ethnicity	Population	Race/ Ethnicity	Population
Chinese	1,645,472	Hawaiian	211,014
Filipino	1,406,770	Samoan	62,964
Japanese	847,562	Guamanian	49,345
Asian Indian	815,447	Tongan	17,606
Korean	798,849	Fijian	7,036
Vietnamese	614,547	Palauan	1,439
Laotian	149,014	No. Mariana Islander	960
Cambodian	147,411	Tahitian	944
Thai	91,275	Other Pacific Islander	13,716
Hmong	90,082	Total Pacific Islander	365,024
Pakistani	81,371		
Indonesian	29,252	**Total Asian Pacific Islander**	**7,273,662**
Malaysian	12,243		
Bangladeshi	11,838	White	199,686,070
Sri Lankan	10,970	Black	29,986,060
Burmese	6,177	Amer. Ind., Eskimo & Aleut	1,959,234
Okinawan	2,247	Other Race	9,804,847
Other Asian	148,111	Hispanic Origin	22,354,059
Total Asian	6,908,638	**Total U.S. Population**	**248,709,873**

Table 4: U.S. PMSA/MSA with the Largest 1990 Asian and Pacific Islander Population

Rank	State	PMSA/MSA	1990 A/PI Population	% of Total PMSA/MSA Population	% of 1990 State A/PI Population
1	CA	Los Angeles-Long Beach	954,485	10.8%	33.5%
2	NY	New York	556,399	6.5%	81.2%
3	HI	Honolulu	526,459	63.0%	76.8%
4	CA	San Francisco	329,599	20.6%	11.6%
5	CA	Oakland	269,566	12.9%	9.5%
6	CA	San Jose	261,466	17.5%	9.2%
7	CA	Anaheim-Santa Ana	249,192	10.3%	8.8%
8	IL	Chicago	229,492	3.8%	80.4%
9		Washington, DC-MD-VA	202,437	5.2%	71.0%
10	CA	*San Diego	198,311	7.9%	7.0%
11	WA	Seattle	135,251	6.9%	64.1%
12	TX	Houston	126,601	3.8%	39.6%
13	CA	*Sacramento	114,520	7.7%	4.0%
14	PA	Philadelphia	104,595	2.2%	76.1%
15	CA	Riverside-San Bernadino	100,792	3.9%	3.5%
		Total of U.S. Asian Pacific Islander Population	4,359,165		59.9%

*Signifies an MSA.

Source: U.S. Bureau of the Census, 1980 & 1990 Censuses.
Asian/Pacific Islander Data Consortium-ACCIS; San Francisco, CA

Census data, Asians and Pacific Islanders had the highest percentage of all persons five years and over who were characterized as "linguistically isolated." In California in 1990, 32.8 percent of all Asian and Pacific Islander households that spoke an Asian Pacific language were "linguistically isolated," as compared to 27.8 percent of Spanish-speaking households and 14.9 percent of households speaking "other" languages, according to data collected and analyzed by the Asian/Pacific Islander Data Consortium.

The existence of many different Asian and Pacific Islander communities means that distinctions in language, practices and beliefs must be taken into consideration in the organization and structure of health services, particularly when coupled with data indicating that the overwhelming majority of Asian and Pacific Islanders will continue to be foreign born up to the year 2020. The need to provide health care services to culturally and linguistically diverse populations presents special challenges now and in the future.[2]

ENABLING CHARACTERISTICS

Asian and Pacific Islander Americans in 1990, as in 1980, resided primarily in urban areas, and in the western United States, as indicated by table 4.

Of the top 15 PMSA/MSAs in the U.S. for Asian and Pacific Islander Americans, 11 are in the western region (Los Angeles-Long Beach, Honolulu, San Francisco, Oakland, San Jose, Anaheim-Santa Ana, San Diego, Seattle, Houston, Sacramento and Riverside-San Bernadino), one in the midwest (Chicago), and three are in the eastern region (New York, Washington, D.C., Philadelphia). Among other things, this concentration has significance for physician provider match-ups (see chart 1 showing the distribution of Asian and Pacific Islander physicians).

Paul Ong's population projections for 2020 indicate a 160 percent growth in California's Asian and Pacific Islander population to 7,411,136 in 2020, and a growth in the northeast Mid-Atlantic region (New York, New Jersey, Pennsylvania) population to 2,925,671. Given the current distribution of the physician population, it would appear that unless a major redistribution of physician resources occurs in the next 30 years, Asian and Pacific Islander Americans will continue to experience a physician service deficit in the future.

Educational attainment for Asians and Pacific Islanders represents a bimodal pattern consistent with other socioeconomic indicators. Approxi-

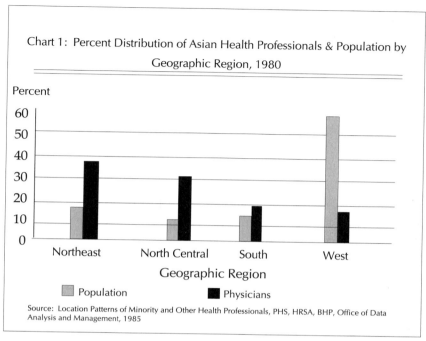

Chart 1: Percent Distribution of Asian Health Professionals & Population by Geographic Region, 1980

Percent

Geographic Region

▢ Population   ■ Physicians

Source: Location Patterns of Minority and Other Health Professionals, PHS, HRSA, BHP, Office of Data Analysis and Management, 1985

mately 18.5 percent of Asians and Pacific Islanders 25 years or older in 1990 were high school graduates, 22.7 percent had a bachelor's degree and 13.9 percent had a graduate or professional degree. While this information indicates a high level of educational achievement, 13.7 percent of Asians and Pacific Islanders 25 years or older had less than a ninth grade education as compared to Whites at 8.9 percent. In California, the percentage was 8.7 percent for Asians and Pacific Islanders, second only to "Other Race" (20.3 percent) in this cohort. Level of education, of course, has important consequences for income earning potential, as well as for knowledge of healthy behaviors, service availability and options for acquiring health care.

In 1990, 94.5 percent of civilian Asian and Pacific Islander females and 94.9 percent of males over 16 years of age were employed in the United States. However, this apparently high level of employment does not guarantee health insurance coverage, as 28 percent of Asians and Pacific Islanders in the U.S. were uninsured, compared to Whites at 20 percent.[3] Over 14 percent of Asians and Pacific Islanders lived below the poverty level as compared to Whites at 9.8 percent. In California, per capita income for Asians and Pacific Islanders averaged $13,733, $5,295 lower than per capita income for Whites. The ability to pay for health care services through direct purchase of insurance is limited for low-income individuals, and for Asian and Pacific Islander Americans, the high proportion of immigrants among the low-income stratum often precludes obtaining care through public subsidy because of limits on eligibility for the newly-arrived.

HEALTH STATUS

The final category of characteristics which make up the determinants of health care use includes need indicators such as mortality, morbidity, limits of physical activity, and medical emergencies. Although as noted above, little documentation exists to characterize the health status of Asian and Pacific Islander ethnic groups, it is important to summarize some of what is known about the different groups in order to substantiate distinct health needs and service requirements.

Among Asian and Pacific Islander Americans, the distribution of health problems varies among ethnic groups. While heart diseases are more prevalent among the white population, cancer and cerebrovascular diseases are more highly prevalent among Chinese, Japanese and Filipino Americans.[4] Filipinos have a high incidence of hypertension, and Southeast Asian refugees have a high prevalence of tuberculosis infection, hepatitis B, intestinal parasites and anemia. While Filipino females have a lower incidence of breast cancer (41 per 100,000) as compared to Japanese and Chinese (56 per 100,000), they have the lowest survival rates (74 percent) as compared to Japanese and Chinese (85 percent) and to Whites (78 percent). Hawaiians are five times more likely to die of stomach cancer than their white counterparts, and have a higher prevalence of diabetes (48.8 percent) as compared to Whites (7.3 percent). Recent studies reveal smoking rates of 24 percent for Filipinos, 35.8 percent for Koreans in California and up to 72 percent for Lao among Asian males.[6]

Assessing health status by measuring the leading cause of death (LCD) for Asians and Pacific Islanders has recently been the subject of a monograph developed by the Asian American Health Forum in California.[7] This LCD ranking is the only population-based analysis of mortality *by specific ethnic group* to be accomplished to date (see tables 5 and 6).

As table 6 shows, the ten leading causes of death for Asians and Pacific Islanders roughly resembles the same profile as for Whites, and except for AIDS (13th) and suicide (8th), are also similar to other population groups.

Table 5: Leading Causes of Death in California
Number of Deaths and Rank, by Race, 1989

Cause of Death§	Total		Asian & Pacific Islander		Other		Hispanic		Black		White	
	No. of Deaths	Rank	No. of Deaths	Rank	No. of Deaths	Rank	No. of Deaths	Rank	No. of Deaths	Rank	No. of Deaths	Rank
Diseases of the Heart	69,457	1	2,335	1	215	1	4,875	1	5,267	1	56,765	1
Malignant Neoplasms	48,110	2	2,198	2	125	2	3,493	2	3,498	2	38,796	2
Cerebrovascular Disease	15,725	3	833	3	43	4	1,151	4	1,169	3	12,529	3
Unintentional Injuries	10,791	4	496	4	93	3	2,559	3	919	5	6,724	6
Pneumonia and Influenza	10,479	5	394	5	24	7	772	7	620	6	8,669	4
C.O.P.D.*	9,759	6	253	6	25	6	445	12	488	8	8,548	5
AIDS	4,367	7	70	13	12	13	647	9	543	7	3,095	7
Liver Disease***	4,000	8	119	12	41	5	840	6	313	11	2,687	9
Suicide	3,832	9	158	8	20	10	433	13	179	13	3,042	8
Diabetes Mellitus	3,364	10	172	7	22	9	591	10	430	10	2,149	10
Homicide	3,270	11	139	9	28	11	1,091	5	1,068	4	944	11
Perinatal Period**	2,137	12	126	10	19	12	745	8	466	9	781	13
Congenital Anomalies	1,615	13	121	11	13	8	502	11	187	12	792	12
Other Causes	29,024		1,214		155		3,020		2,442		22,193	
Total Number of Deaths	215,930		8,628		835		21,164		17,589		167,714	

* Chronic Obstructive Pulmonary Disease and Allied Conditions
** Certain Conditions Originating in the Perinatal Period
*** Chronic Liver Disease, Cirrhosis

Source: California Department of Health Services
Prepared by: Survey and Research Program of the Asian American Health Forum
©1992 Asian American Health Forum, Inc.

Table 6: Rate of Death from All Causes by Race or Ethnicity: California, 1989

Race or Ethnicity	Number of Deaths from All Causes	1990 Population in California*	Rate of Death from All Causes per 100,000 of the Population C/D x 100,000
Japanese	1,558	312,989	498
Other Pacific Islander	85	19,176	443
Samoan	123	31,917	385
Asian Specified**	223	58,058	384
Chinese	2,545	704,850	361
Filipino	2,412	731,685	330
Korean	626	259,941	241
Hawaiian	75	34,447	218
Guamanian	54	25,059	215
Cambodian	130	68,190	191
Vietnamese	450	280,223	161
Thai	47	32,064	147
Asian Indian	221	159,973	138
Asian Unspecified	156	127,087	123
Total Asian & Pacific Islander	8,628	2,845,659	303
Other	835	4,181,234	20
Hispanic	21,164	7,687,938	275
African American	17,589	2,208,801	796
White	167,714	20,524,327	817
Total	215,930	29,760,021	

* 1990 Census population data were used as a denominator since no 1989 population estimates were available.

** Asian Specified includes Lao and others presumed to be Lao.

Source: California Department of Health Services, U.S. Bureau of the Census
Prepared by: Survey and Research Program of the Asian American Health Forum
© 1992 Asian American Health Forum, Inc.

Table 7: Diseases of the Heart
Primary Leading Cause of Death among
Asian and Pacific Islander Americans in California, 1989

Race or Ethnicity	Number of Deaths from Diseases of the Heart	1990 Population in California*	Rate of Death from Diseases of the Heart per 100,000 of the Population C/D x 100,000
Japanese	447	312,989	143
Other Pacific Islander	22	19,176	115
Filipino	758	731,685	104
Samoan	32	31,917	100
Chinese	694	704,850	98
Hawaiian	27	34,447	78
Guamanian	14	25,059	56
Asian Specified**	30	58,058	52
Korean	133	259,941	51
Asian Indian	76	159,973	48
Asian Unspecified	37	127,087	29
Cambodian	19	68,190	28
Vietnamese	60	280,223	21
Thai	5	32,064	16
Total Asian & Pacific Islander	2,335	2,845,659	82
Other	215	4,181,234	5
Hispanic	4,875	7,687,938	63
African American	5,267	2,208,801	238
White	56,765	20,524,327	277
Total	69,457	29,760,021	

*   1990 Census population data were used as a denominator since no 1989 population estimates were available.
**   Asian Specified includes Lao and others presumed to be Lao.

Source: California Department of Health Services, U.S. Bureau of the Census
Prepared by: Survey and Research Program of the Asian American Health Forum
© 1992 Asian American Health Forum, Inc.

Table 8: Certain Conditions Originating in the Perinatal Period—Tenth Leading Cause of Death among Asian and Pacific Islander Americans in California, 1989

Race or Ethnicity	Number of Deaths from Certain Conditions*	Number of Live Births**	Rate of Death from Certain Conditions Originating in the Perinatal Period per 100,000 Live Births C/D x 100,000
Asian Unspecified	14	1,960	714
Thai	3	637	471
Asian Indian	7	2,333	300
Japanese	10	3,363	297
Cambodian	7	2,525	277
Asian Specified***	13	4,743	274
Other Pacific Islander	3	1,169	257
Chinese	24	9,698	247
Filipino	30	13,679	219
Korean	9	4,261	211
Samoan	2	1,007	199
Vietnamese	12	6,107	196
Hawaiian	0	488	0
Guamanian	0	405	0
Asian & Pacific Islander	126	52,375	241
Other	19	5,037	377
Hispanic	745	211,696	352
African American	466	47,555	980
White	781	252,645	309
Total	2,137	569,308	

*   Deaths include infant deaths as well as deaths of the mother; therefore, these rates should not be confused with infant mortality rates.
**   No. of Live Births was used as a denominator to determine rate of death.
*** Asian Specified includes Lao and others presumed to be Lao.

Source: California Department of Health Services, U.S. Bureau of the Census
Prepared by: Survey and Research Program of the Asian American Health Forum
© 1992 Asian American Health Forum, Inc.

The overall crude death rate for Asians and Pacific Islanders (303 per 100,000) is lower than for African Americans and Whites, but higher than Hispanics and "Others." Table 6 presents the death rates for Asians and Pacific Islanders, broken down by ethnicity.

A look at the first and tenth leading cause of death for Asians and Pacific Islanders in California illustrates the importance of disaggregation of data and the implications for health services and intervention (see tables 7 and 8). The overall death rate for Asians and Pacific Islanders due to Diseases of the Heart, the first leading cause of death, is 82 per 100,000, which ranks third highest among all population groups. When broken down by ethnicity, the death rate ranges from a high of 143 per 100,000 for Japanese to a low of 16 per 100,000 for Thai. For the tenth leading cause of death, Perinatal Related Conditions, the overall death rate is 241 per 100,000 for Asians and Pacific Islanders, the lowest of all population groups. When disaggregated by ethnicity, however, a tremendous range is represented, from 714 per 100,000 for "Asian Unspecified" to 196 per 100,000 for Hawaiians. This range graphically illustrates the implications of using aggregated data to develop policy and establish services.

In the past, policies geared towards preventing deaths from these causes have made use of aggregated Asian and Pacific Islander health data, or more likely no data, resulting in programs and services that have had little impact.

The differences in health condition that the above statistics describe indicate distinct at-risk profiles for Asian and Pacific Islander ethnic groups. This information needs to be taken into account in order to formulate policy that will assure the delivery of primary care services and health promotion/ disease prevention programs for these populations.

Health Delivery System

The United States health delivery system is quite fragmented, with limited coordination of services. Except for a few models of health delivery programs—for example, community-based primary care and some health maintenance organizations—"mainstream" medicine does not emphasize comprehensive health care programs. Under a comprehensive care program, a person with multiple health concerns can receive the necessary care in a coordinated fashion, including services such as mental health, family planning, nutrition counseling, health promotion and education programs for smoking cessation or weight control. Findings from a recent survey of health providers involved in bilingual primary care services cited a lack of coordination between various health care facilities in a given geographical area as an impediment for providing access to comprehensive health care.

The availability of appropriate and quality health services is a major factor influencing access to care. This includes providing a range of culturally and linguistically appropriate care: adequately trained translators, bilingual providers and support personnel, culturally sensitive methods of care, and the ability of a patient to obtain care within a reasonable time frame in a supportive environment. According to data from the Association of Asian/Pacific Community Health Organizations (AAPCHO), only eight community health centers among over 400 federally funded centers provide comprehensive, primary care to low-income, limited English speaking Asian and Pacific Islander communities in the United States. These eight centers provide care to over 60 percent of the estimated Asian and Pacific Islander population eligible to receive subsidized care in their service areas, while the remaining 40 percent receive care from one of 86 centers nationwide.[8]

The results from a recent needs assessment conducted by the Association of State and Territorial Health Officers (ASTHO) in the U.S. on state-sponsored bilingual health services reported that only 26 percent of the states responding indicated that linguistically appropriate service delivery is a high priority; 54 percent rated it an average priority, and 20 percent rated it below average or as a low priority.[9] The same report indicated that bilingual/bicultural services were not uniformly offered across all service programs. Overall, the number of bilingual services offered across all state health programs ranged between three and 49, with STD/HIV/AIDS programs having the highest number of bilingual/bicultural services available.[10] Immunization and TB and Maternal and Child Health programs ranked second and third for bilingual/bicultural services. For distribution of educational/information services, 70 percent of respondent states had material in Vietnamese, 52 percent in Cambodian, and 21 percent in Chinese languages. For the various programs, the most utilized method for written or oral translation was to contract individuals as needed.

In a national survey conducted by the Asian American Health Forum of health promotion/disease prevention programs implemented by Asian and Pacific Islander community-based organizations or public entities, 62 percent of respondents indicated some health program in place targeting

Asian and Pacific Islander populations. As with the ASTHO survey, the largest number of programs were HIV/AIDS programs, followed by infectious disease, mental health, nutrition and substance abuse programs. Health Education ranked highest as the type of service delivered, followed by screening, counseling, research and, lastly, primary care.

Very little other data exists to assess the ability of the health care delivery system to respond to the needs of Asian and Pacific Islander Americans. In light of the above attempts to collect national data, however, it is apparent that current community-based and publicly financed attempts to provide health care services to Asians and Pacific Islanders are not sufficient. If, as projected, our population continues to experience exponential growth, then policies and programs will have to see our needs of as a priority.

Equity in Access to Health Care: Policy Recommendations

A more complete analysis of access requires an in-depth study of Asian and Pacific Islander behaviors with regard to health practices, satisfaction with and utilization of services and patient outcomes. Further, the health delivery systems must be examined thoroughly concerning commitment of resources, both public and private, to Asian and Pacific Islander health needs. Much more research and better data collection are needed to adequately formulate policy in this area.

However, even with these stated limitations, the above analysis provides some direction for policy recommendations, assuming that equity in access to health care is a desired objective of policy formation.

The population characteristics presented earlier in this article as indicators of risk, or predictors for service utilization, serve as the basis for our policy recommendations. Immutable, or unalterable characteristics, such as age, sex, race/ethnicity, language, nativity and residence (location), are grouped primarily within the predisposing category and generally cannot be changed through policy intervention. Characteristics that are considered alterable through policy intervention are grouped primarily within the enabling category and include income, employment, occupation and insurance. They also include factors such as education, health practices and attitudes.

Service delivery systems have characteristics which affect access to services but which can be altered and improved. These include organization (e.g., definition of target populations, patient's waiting time, health plan/ program participation) and resources (e.g., types of providers and practices, and supply and distribution of providers and facilities).

It is clear from the sociodemographic profile presented earlier that Asians and Pacific Islanders are at health risk. In order to respond to these needs, health policy development should focus on alterable characteristics in individuals and the delivery system. The following recommendations are grouped by general, individual and system specific categories.

GENERAL RECOMMENDATIONS

1. Prioritize the institution of culturally competent health care service delivery in all proposals for health care reform.

2. Modify current national and state data collection methods and reporting systems to codify Asian and Pacific Islander populations by ethnicity and, where appropriate, break down morbidity, mortality, health care use and expenditures by specific ethnic group.

3. Create financial and other incentives for research institutions to conduct community sensitive health services and outcomes research on Asian and Pacific Islander Americans.

POPULATION AT-RISK RECOMMENDATIONS

1. Prioritize educational attainment for Asians and Pacific Islanders as a means to ensure gainful employment and access to health insurance coverage; provide employer incentives to improve the health of their workforce through employer-based wellness programs as well as adequate health insurance coverage.

2. Establish universal health care as a means to assure health services access to all Americans, regardless of employment, income or educational status.

3. Expand and fund health promotion/disease prevention

programs targeted towards limited English proficiency populations and newcomer communities that are community based and population specific.

1. Increase the number and capacity of community-based primary care facilities to target Asian and Pacific Islander American communities.

2. Modify minority education and training program eligibility to include Asian and Pacific Islander health professionals from ethnic communities that are at-risk and underrepresented.

3. Create financial and other incentives to encourage the development of more primary care providers available to serve the Asian and Pacific Islander community, and motivate a redistribution of providers to better serve population concentrations.

4. Develop standards for health service translation or interpretation through a certification procedure, with reimbursement mechanisms tied to the usage of certified translation services.

5. Coordinate services used by limited English proficient and culturally distinct populations, such as WIC, maternal and child health, immunization services, primary care, as well as social services and mental health services.

Notes

Portions of this paper were adapted from "Health Policy Framework for Asian and Pacific Islander Americans" by Ninez Ponce and Tessie Guillermo, a chapter written for a pending publication of the Asian American Health Forum. The AAHF has granted permission for adapted portions of the chapter to be included in this paper.

1. Asian American Health Forum, *Partners in Human Services: Shaping Health Care and Civil Rights Policy for Asian and Pacific Islander American* (Washington, D.C.: AAHF, 1992).

2. Asian American Health Forum, Third Biennial Forum, "Dispelling the Myth of a Healthy Minority," Washington, D.C., 1990.

3. National Center for Health Statistics, *Health, United States, 1990* (Hyattsville, Maryland: Public Health Service, 1991).

4. Asian American Health Forum, *Leading Causes of Death Among Asians and Pacific Islanders in California, 1989,* Monograph Series No. 3 (San Francisco: AAHF, 1992).

5. National Center for Health Statistics, *Health, United States, 1990.*

6. Barbara L. Levin, "Cigarette Smoking Habits and Characteristics in the Laotian Refugee: A Perspective Pre and Post Resettlement," unpublished manuscript, Cook County Department of Public Health, Maywood, Illinois, 1990. See also, D. Burns and J. P. Peirce, *Tobacco Use in California 1990-91* (Sacramento: California Department of Health Services, 1992).

7. Asian American Health Forum, *Leading Causes of Death Among Asians and Pacific Islanders in California, 1989.*

8. L. Mayeno, personal communication, 1992.

9. Association of State and Territorial Health Officials, *State Health Agency Strategies to Develop Linguistically Relevant Public Health Systems: Report and Recommendations* (Washington, D.C.: ASTHO Bilingual Health Initiative, July 1992).

10. *Ibid.*

The Changing Asian American Population:

Mental Health Policy

Stanley Sue

PROFESSOR OF PSYCHOLOGY AND
DIRECTOR, NATIONAL RESEARCH CENTER
ON ASIAN AMERICAN MENTAL HEALTH, UCLA

This report examines the population projections of Asians and Pacific Americans in the United States and raises policy implications for mental health issues. Obviously, the validity of the implications drawn are highly dependent on the adequacy of the projections, the quality of the available research, and the assumptions made. At this time, the projections concern Asian and Pacific Americans as an aggregate. While place of birth and age distributions are included, we do not know the projections for individual Asian and Pacific American groups, and other characteristics such as gender, socioeconomic class, and precise geographic distribution. Furthermore, mental health research on this population is scarce and relatively recent. Given these limitations, this report represents a preliminary attempt to identify mental health implications for the year 2020. While the focus is on mental health, many of the implications are pertinent to health, social, and human service issues in general.

The most striking aspect of the projections is the estimate that the Asian and Pacific American population will show substantial increases. According to Ong, the population of Asian and Pacific Americans will have a percentage growth of over 150 percent between the years of 1990 and 2020. The percentage increase of foreign born will probably be about 109 percent to 141 percent compared to the estimated figure of 197 percent to 244 percent for the American born. Thus, growth will be higher for American-born than foreign-born Asian and Pacific Americans. The population in 2020 is likely to be somewhat older, with a slightly higher proportion of persons 65 years of age and older and a slightly lower proportion of those under age five. The most important projection is that the population will be over two-and-one-half times larger during this 30 year span. Given these possible changes, what are the implications for the mental health field? What kinds of policy recommendations should be made?

From the very outset, let me address myths and misunderstandings that have guided current mental health policies and practices and offer some recommendations in planning for the year 2020 in the areas of psychopathology, use of mental health services, adequacy of services, manpower, and community interventions. Action on these recommendations should have already been initiated years ago; it is particularly urgent now because of the anticipated heavy growth of the Asian and Pacific American population and because fruits of such actions take time to bear.

> *Myth #1: Asian Americans are relatively well adjusted.*
> *Recommendation:* Immediate attention should be placed on the initiation and funding of research dealing with Asian American mental health issues.

> *Myth #2: Asian and Pacific Americans tend to avoid using social and mental health services and have less need for such services.*
> *Recommendation:* We must increase the awareness that demand is not equivalent to need for services. Means must be found to increase the utilization, funding, and adequacy of services.

> *Myth #3: Since Asian and Pacific Americans as a group do well educationally and are relatively well adjusted, there is no need to recruit and train more bilingual and/or bicultural personnel in order to work with, and to conduct basic and applied research on, Asian and Pacific Americans.*
> *Recommendation:* Systematic efforts be made to increase the pool of mental health researchers and practitioners who can contribute to Asian and Pacific Americans.

Myth #4: Mainstream forms of services and community inter-
ventions can be applied to Asian and Pacific Americans.
Recommendation: Culturally relevant services and interventions
need to be developed and established. While some Asian and
Pacific Americans may be well served by mainstream services,
many simply find such services unhelpful, strange, or foreign.

Myth #5: The general public as well as the Asian and Pacific
American community is well aware of mental health issues.
Recommendation: Immediate efforts be made to educate Asian
and Pacific American communities as well as the society at large
about mental health issues.

Myth #6: By improving mental health services and by promoting
the acculturation of Asian and Pacific Americans, we can
adequately address their mental health needs.
Recommendation: Facilitating acculturation and improvement of
services are insufficient courses of action. More generally, conditions
that foster stress—stereotypes, racial intolerance, discrimination,
poverty, culture conflicts, etc.—need to be addressed in improving
mental health.

Initiation and Funding of Mental Health Research
on Asian and Pacific Americans

A paucity of research exists on Asian and Pacific Americans. Consequently, little is actually known about the mental health needs of Asian
Americans, planning and systematic development of service programs
have been hindered, and the general public has been free to incorrectly
perceive Asian and Pacific Americans as being an exceptionally well-
adjusted group. The fact is that the available research findings show that
Asian and Pacific Americans do face significant mental health problems
and stressors.

MENTAL HEALTH PROBLEMS

The public stereotype that Asian and Pacific Americans are relatively
free of adjustment difficulties has hindered serious attempts to understand the mental health of this population. The critical issue is not
whether mental health problems exist, since all groups encounter these

problems. The meaningful issues involve the extent of mental disorders, the nature of psychopathology, and the particular Asian and Pacific American groups at risk for disorders. Without understanding these issues, it is likely that the mental health needs of Asian and Pacific Americans cannot be adequately addressed, now and in the future when the population is expected to continue to rapidly grow.

What is the actual extent of mental disorders among Asian and Pacific Americans? The unfortunate fact is that no large-scale prevalence studies, which are used to specify rates of mental disorders, have been conducted on this population. The consequence is that we have no direct knowledge of the rates of mental disorders and cannot compare the various Asian and Pacific American groups with each other and with non-Asian-and-Pacific American groups. Since the current population is relatively small (about 3 percent of the U.S. population is Asian and Pacific American) and is composed of many different groups, researchers have had difficulty finding adequate and representative samples on which to conduct studies. Furthermore, lack of funding for research on Asian and Pacific Americans, problems in finding cross-culturally valid measures of psychopathology, etc., have also hindered attempts to study prevalence. The few available investigations of Asian and Pacific Americans are small-scale studies, often based on selected groups or on selected disorders; some are not true prevalence studies. They do, however, provide evidence that rates of psychopathology among Asian and Pacific Americans have been underestimated. Examples of selected groups included the work of Westermeyer and his colleagues who studied a small group of Laotian Hmong refugees in Minnesota.[1] Using various measures of psychopathology, they found that the refugees had very high rates of psychiatric disorders. Other studies have also revealed that Southeast Asian refugees are at risk for mental disorders.[2] Investigations by Kuo examined community samples of four different Asian American groups: Chinese, Japanese, Pilipino, and Korean.[3] Kuo found that Asian Americans had higher average scores on the measure than did Whites. About 19 percent of the Asian Americans were identified as being potential cases of depression on the measures. Other studies also suggest that the rates of emotional disturbance among Asian and Pacific Americans are not low.[4]

Personality studies also point to adjustment problems of Asian and Pacific Americans. D. Sue and his colleagues found evidence that Japanese and Chinese American college students compared with non-Asian students tended to experience greater feelings of anxiety, loneliness, and discomfort.[5] Problems encountered by students were also found more recently by Sue and Zane who obtained similar results.[6] Chinese American students were found to experience anxiety, especially among recent immigrants. While the academic achievement levels (i.e., academic grades) of the Chinese students exceeded those of the general student body, these students still had high levels of anxiety. Obviously, personality studies as well as epidemiological investigations are subject to bias, since the measures used to assess psychopathology and adjustment may not be valid for different cultural groups. This possibility points to the unfortunate state of research on Asian and Pacific Americans in which the validity of assessment tools can be questioned. Nevertheless, *the outcomes from such research do not support the popular stereotype that Asian and Pacific Americans are well adjusted. The consistency of research findings from different investigators and from different research strategies strongly suggest that significant mental health problems exist.* Because the population is expected to increase rather rapidly in the next three decades, much more research is urgently needed.

HIGH RISK GROUPS

High risk groups are those that are particularly exposed to stressors and/or lack mental health resources (such as social supports, responsive mental health services, etc.) or encounter other conditions that increase the chances of mental disorders. At various times and by various constituencies, a whole host of groups such as the elderly, women, Southeast Asian refugees, and immigrants has been identified as high risk. I would like to focus on immigrants. With respect to Southeast Asian refugees, who have been traumatized by events in their native countries of Cambodia, Laos, and Vietnam, it is unclear what conditions will exist in these Southeast Asian countries in the future and whether refugees from these countries will continue to come to the U.S. What we do know is that the population projection shows a continuing high rate of immigration to the U.S.—easily doubling the current population of immigrants.

Recent immigrants certainly encounter numerous problems involving English language skills, minority group status, cultural conflicts, employment, etc., which are basic to survival and well being. The study by Sue and Zane demonstrated that new Chinese immigrants are more likely to report anxiety than immigrants with longer periods of U.S. residency or American-born Chinese.[7] Other studies have revealed that Southeast Asian refugees are at particular risk for depression and post-traumatic stress disorder.[8] Although refugee status is not equivalent to immigrant status, many similar problems of living in a new culture exist. *The fact is that the continuing high rate of immigration and the implications for mental health demand immediate attention and the acquisition of more knowledge. This requires increased funding opportunities for research from local, state, and federal agencies.*

Mental Health Services

In the past, utilization of mental health services was used as an indicator of psychopathology in particular populations. The assumption was that if one group had a high prevalence of mental disorders, that group would tend to utilize services more often than a group with a lower prevalence rate: Demand for services was a reflection of *need* for services. It is now widely recognized that demand does not indicate need, especially for some groups. Nevertheless, utilization of services must be examined since it reveals possible cultural differences in defining and approaching mental health problems, provides knowledge about the kinds of problems clients have, indicates the responsiveness of the mental health care system, and yields some insight into how to better treat or prevent problems. Discussed are studies of utilization and the adequacy of mental health services.

UTILIZATION

Almost all of the past studies of utilization rates of mental health services have demonstrated low rates of utilization among Asian and Pacific Americans. Kitano presented findings on the admission of patients to California state mental hospitals.[9] Admission rates for mental disturbance were many times lower for Japanese and Chinese Americans than for Caucasian Americans during each of the years from 1960 to 1965. Data from the state of Hawaii also revealed low Asian and Pacific American rates of admission to state hospitals for mental disorders. Chinese, Hawaiian, Japanese and Pilipino Americans all exhibited lower rates of admissions than expected from their proportions in the population.[10]

These and more recent studies consistently demonstrate that Asian Americans tend to be underrepresented in psychiatric clinics and hospitals compared to their populations.[11] The underrepresentation occurs whether students or non-student populations, inpatients or outpatients, and different Asian and Pacific American groups are considered. In one of the most comprehensive analyses, Matsuoka examined Asian and Pacific Americans' use of services at state and county mental hospitals, private psychiatric hospitals, Veteran Administration psychiatric services, residential treatment centers for emotionally disturbed children, non-federal psychiatric services in general hospitals, outpatient psychiatric clinics, multi-service mental health programs, psychiatric day/night services, and other residential programs in the U.S.[12] In general, Matsuoka found that utilization of services by Asian/Pacific Islander populations was low, regardless of their population density in various states of the U.S. The only exception to findings of underutilization is the results of a study by O'Sullivan, Peterson, Cox, and Kirkeby.[13] Analyzing the utilization rate for ethnic groups in the Seattle area, the investigators found that Asian Americans were not underrepresented as users of community mental health services. It is unclear why the results of this study are at variance with all of the others. One potential explanation is that the utilization figures for 1983 were compared with Seattle population data from the 1980 Census. If the Asian and Pacific American population showed a marked growth from 1980-1983 (Asian and Pacific Americans have been the fastest growing ethnic minority group in the U.S.), then they may indeed be actually underrepresented as clients. Perhaps the findings are unique to Seattle. In any event, underutilization appears to be the rule rather than the exception.

SEVERITY OF DISTURBANCE

The term "underutilization" implies that Asian and Pacific Americans are not using services when they need to. Is it possible that this population is relatively better adjusted than other populations, so that greater utilization of services is unnecessary? Every population underutilizes in the sense that not all individuals with psychological disturbance seek help from the mental health system. For example, in the Epidemiologic Catchment Area study which compared the prevalence rate of mental disorders with the rate of utilization of mental health care services, the vast majority of afflicted individuals did not seek services.[14] The real issue is whether Asian and Pacific Americans with psychiatric disorders have a greater propensity to avoid using services than other populations. While this issue cannot be fully addressed in the absence of information on prevalence rates, considerable indirect evidence exists that Asian and Pacific Americans are more likely than the general population to underutilize services. As mentioned earlier, the available small-scale prevalence, personality, and needs assessment studies of Asian Americans suggest that considerable mental health problems exist; and yet, utilization is dramatically low. Other lines of evidence, such as severity of disturbance, also point to underutilization.

Sue and Sue analyzed the Asian American (primarily Chinese, Japanese, and Korean) students who utilized the student psychiatric clinic at the University of California, Los Angeles.[15] The findings revealed that Asian Americans underutilized mental health services and exhibit greater disturbance among the client population. Sue and Sue's inference was that moderately disturbed Asian Americans, unlike Caucasian Americans, are more likely to avoid using services (unless one takes the unusual and unsupported position that Asian Americans have low rates of overall disturbance but high rates of severe mental disorders).

Other studies demonstrate that the phenomena of low utilization and greater severity among Asian and Pacific American clients are not confined to students.[16] The National Research Center on Asian American Mental Health at UCLA acquired a large dataset on thousands of clients seen in the Los Angeles County Mental Health System from 1983-1988. Preliminary analysis of the dataset revealed that Asian and Pacific Americans are underrepresented in the outpatient mental health system. While they represented 8.7 percent of the County population, they comprised only 3.1 percent of the clients. Latinos were also underrepresented. On the other hand, Blacks used services proportionately greater than expected by their relative population. When the proportions of clients having a psychotic diagnosis were tabulated by ethnic group, Asian and Pacific Americans were more likely than Whites, Blacks, and Latinos to have individuals with a psychotic diagnosis in inpatient and outpatient services.

The evidence is quite convergent that few Asian and Pacific Americans use the mental health service system. This underutilization is found among all Asian and Pacific American groups studied, among inpatient or outpatient facilities, and among students or adults. Furthermore, the studies consistently show that on a variety of measures Asian and Pacific Americans have greater disturbance levels than non-Asian clients. The alternative explanation that low utilization of services is caused by the low rate of mental disturbance is weakened by findings that Asian and Pacific Americans who do seek treatment are more severely disturbed than are Caucasian Americans. *These findings suggest low utilization of services does not mean that there is low need for services.* Lin, Inui, Kleinman, and Womack found that Asian Americans were more likely than Whites to have a delay in the recognition of mental health symptoms and then to actually participate in a treatment program.[17]

A number of factors affect utilization and effectiveness of mental health services. Some of the factors involve accessibility (e.g., including ease of using services, financial cost of services, and location of services), availability (e.g., existence of services), cultural and linguistic appropriateness of services, knowledge of available services, and willingness to use services. Obviously, the nature of one's problems influences utilization. Culturally-based factors are also important to consider, such as shame and stigma, conceptions of mental health, and alternative services as factors that affect utilization and appropriateness of mainstream services (i.e., services that are available to the general population of Americans). These have all been implicated as factors that account for low utilization among Asian and Pacific Americans.[18]

If Asian and Pacific Americans do not want services or do not use services, why should we be concerned? First, since Asian and Pacific Americans pay taxes for services, they are not receiving their fair share of services. Second, we cannot always demand that different clients adjust to a mental health system that responds only to a particular segment of the population. Services in a multicultural society must be multicultural and flexible to accommodate diverse ethnic groups. Third, the increasing size of the Asian and Pacific American population will mean increased pressures to address their mental health needs and increased demands for having services that are effective.

RECOMMENDATIONS FOR SERVICES

What kinds of services should be established? Under the concept of culturally responsive services, Uba and Sue have offered three suggestions to more effectively meet the mental health needs of Asian and Pacific Americans.[19] First, in mainstream mental health facilities where there are few Asian and Pacific American personnel, service providers can receive training to work with Asian and Pacific American clients. Such training would cover assessment, psychotherapy, and case management and include issues such as cultural values and behaviors, pre- and post-migration experiences, etc. The intent of the training would be to enhance skills and knowledge about Asian and Pacific Americans. Special Asian and Pacific American consultants should be available to the service providers. Second, mainstream mental health programs should employ more Asian and Pacific American personnel, who are bilingual and bicultural. Such personnel can be of immense benefit in providing effective services. Sue et al. have found that when Asian and Pacific American clients are matched with therapists who are of the same ethnicity and who speak the clients' language, they stay in treatment longer, tend not to prematurely terminate services, and have better treatment outcomes.[20] Third, parallel or non-mainstream services should be created. Parallel services are those that may be similar to mainstream ones (e.g., a clinic or hospital) but specifically designed to service an ethnic population. For example, specific wards at San Francisco General Hospital and the Asian Pacific Counseling and Treatment Center in Los Angeles were created to serve Asian and Pacific Americans. They typically employ bilingual and bicultural personnel, post notices in English and Asian languages, serve "Asian" foods or drinks, etc.—all in an attempt to respond to the cultural needs of Asian and Pacific Americans. *These culturally-relevant services should be strengthened, and new parallel programs should be established. Local, state, and federal agencies should place these services and programs as a high priority in terms of funding and development.*

Manpower and Personnel

Asian and Pacific Americans are underrepresented in the mental health field. For example, Howard et al. found that few doctorates in psychology were awarded to members of this population.[21] They noted that ". . .psychology has performed poorly in attracting Asian Americans to the discipline." Furthermore, the underrepresentation was particularly evident in the human service rather than academic areas of psychology. The same may be true of other disciplines pertinent to mental health (e.g., social work, sociology, psychiatric nursing, public health, anthropology, etc.).

Earlier, it was noted that when Asian American clients have therapists of the same ethnicity, they tend to stay in treatment longer and to have better treatment outcomes. The effect was particularly strong for clients who did not speak English as the primary language. This suggests that it is important for Asian and Pacific Americans to have mental health professionals who are of the same ethnicity. *That Asian and Pacific Americans are probably underrepresented as mental health care providers and that having them as therapists is beneficial strongly imply that the mental health field should make special efforts to recruit and train more Asian and Pacific Americans. The beneficial effects also extend to research and theory development where the insights and experiences of Asian and Pacific Americans are needed.*

Community Education

One of the most common stereotypes that Asian and Pacific Americans have had to combat is the popular belief that the group is a "model" minority. Such a belief undermines efforts to truly understand the group and to address mental health and other needs. For example, during the Los Angeles riots after the Rodney King verdict, the primary perception of the nation was that this was a Black-White issue. Efforts to rebuild Los Angeles were primarily directed to inner-city black areas. While such efforts should be undertaken, the nation as a whole was largely unaware that Korean Americans suffered about half of the total property damage from the rioting. The lack of knowledge of Asian and Pacific Americans, their needs, and problems must be rectified. *The media, educational system, community institutions, and leaders must acquire and transmit more accurate information about Asian and Pacific Americans.*

Mental health education is important for Asian and Pacific American communities. Many Asian and Pacific Americans are unfamiliar with Western mental health concepts and services available. They may consider mental health problems as shameful or private matters and lack understanding of how services can help. In such situations, education is needed to modify attitudes and to indicate methods by which problems can be addressed. The educational efforts can be made through schools, media (radio, television, ethnic newspapers, etc.), community forums, and other institutions, coordinated with mental health agencies.

Several points are important to make in educational messages:

1. Personal and interpersonal problems are common. These problems can involve generational conflicts in the family, difficulties

in adjusting to American society, anxieties, and depression. Unless the problems are addressed, individuals will continue to feel upset, have interpersonal problems, and fail to achieve more. There is no need to be ashamed of them. Shame simply hinders one's willingness to find means of overcoming problems.

2. Much can be done to prevent or overcome problems. Learning how to anticipate or manage problems by oneself and talking with others are often very helpful approaches. (The early identification of potential emotional problems, stress management techniques, and communications skills should be emphasized.)

3. Individuals should seek services for mental health problems when they confront problems that they cannot handle. While traditional, ethnic folk healing may be helpful, mental health services can be effective. One's problems are kept confidential (in accordance with laws) and therapists are available who can speak the ethnic language of clients. (A description of where services are available and the kinds of services available would be very helpful.)

These educational programs are intended to more accurately describe mental health problems and services, to offer a means of handling problems, and to make services more accessible and acceptable.

Broader Social Issues and Mental Health

Understandably, many researchers and practitioners have advocated for changes in the mental health field in order to respond to the needs of Asian Americans. Others believe that cultural conflicts and adjustment problems will diminish, once Asian and Pacific Americans become more acculturated. The fact is, however, that mental health status is a function of many factors such as social class, access to resources, social environment, etc. For Asian and Pacific Americans, as well as other ethnic minority groups, cultural conflicts as well as minority group status are important considerations in mental health. The use of the term "minority" within the phrase "ethnic minority group" has been criticized. "Minority" has historically been associated with notions of inferiority and deficits. Furthermore, the concept of minority implies that there is a majority, and one could argue that there is no real ethnic majority group in the United States (Whites can be conceived as including many different ethnic groups) or in the world. My use of the term is intentional. Rather than to imply that ethnic minority groups should be viewed as inferior or deficient, I want to convey the fact that minority status has an impact on the groups. Thus the situation of Asian and Pacific Americans, as well as African Americans, American Indians, and Latino Americans, is not solely a function of their own cultures. Rather, historical and contemporary forms of prejudice and discrimination have also been experienced. *To fully understand as well as to promote the well being of these groups, culture and minority group status must be analyzed and used as the basis for intervention.* Minority group status is used as a general concept to convey ethnic relationships in which some groups have experienced prejudice and discrimination. It is this status that distinguishes cross-cultural research, in which different cultural groups are examined, from ethnic minority research, in which cultural differences *and* ethnic relations are critical to consider.

Obviously, the effects of culture and minority status can be easily confounded. Over time, cultural values of a group may change as a result of ethnic relations. The main point is that the two effects are pertinent to the understanding of ethnic minority groups in general and Asian and Pacific Americans in particular. The particular cultural features of Asian and Pacific Americans and experiences with stereotypes, racial intolerance, and discrimination—all of which have a bearing on mental health—are important to address.

Notes

Portions of this paper were adapted from "Mental Health Issues for Asian and Pacific Islanders" by Stanley Sue, a paper written for the Asian American Health Forum, San Francisco. We gratefully acknowledge the Forum's permission to include the adaptations.

1. J. Westermeyer, T. F. Vang, and J. Neider, "Symptom Change Over Time among Hmong Refugees: Psychiatric Patients versus Nonpatients," *Psychopathology* 17 (1984), 168–177.

2. J. W. Berry and T. Blondel, "Psychological Adaptation of Vietnamese Refugees in Canada," *Canadian Journal of Community Mental Health* 1 (1982), 81–88; see also, K. M. Lin, "Psychopathology and Social Disruption in Refugees," in *Refugees and Mental Health*, edited by C. L. Williams and J. Westermeyer (Washington, D.C.: Hemisphere Publishing Corporation, 1986), 61–73.

3. W. H. Kuo, "Prevalence of Depression among Asian-Americans," *Journal of Nervous and Mental Disease* 172:8 (1984), 449–457; see also, W. Kuo and Y. Tsai, "Social Networking Hardiness and Immigrant's Mental Health," *Journal of Health and Social Behavior* 27 (1986), 133–149.

4. W. M. Hurh and K. C. Kim, "Correlates of Korean Immigrants' Mental Health," *Journal of Nervous and Mental Disease* 178 (1990), 703–711; see also, C. Loo, B. Tong, and R. True, "A Bitter Bean: Mental Health Status and Attitudes in Chinatown," *Journal of Community Psychology* 17 (1989), 183–296; Y. Ying, "Depressive Symptomatology among Chinese-Americans as Measured by the CES-D," *Journal of Clinical Psychology* 44:5 (1988), 739–746.

5. D. W. Sue, "Ethnic Identity: The Impact of Two Cultures on the Psychological Development of Asians in America," in *Asian Americans: Psychological Perspectives*, edited by S. Sue and N. N. Wagner (Palo Alto, California: Science & Behavior, 1973), 140–149; see also, D. W. Sue and A. C. Frank, "A Typological Approach to the Psychological Study of Chinese and Japanese American College Males," *Journal of Social Issues* 19:2 (1973), 129–148; D. W. Sue and B. A. Kirk, "Differential Characteristics of Japanese-American and Chinese-American College Students," *Journal of Counseling Psychology* 20 (1973), 142–148.

6. S. Sue and N. Zane, "Academic Achievement and Socioemotional Adjustment among Chinese University Students," *Journal of Counseling Psychology* 32 (1985), 570–579.

7. *Ibid.*

8. E. Gong-Guy, *The California Southeast Asian Mental Health Needs Assessment* (Oakland, California: Asian Community Mental Health Services, 1987); see also, Westermeyer et al., "Symptom Change Over Time among Hmong Refugees."

9. H. H. Kitano, "Japanese-American Mental Illness," in *Changing Perspectives in Mental Illness*, edited by S. C. Plog and R. B. Edgerton (New York: Holt, Rinehart & Winston, 1969), 256–284.

10. Hawaii State Department of Health, *Statistical Report of the Department of Health* (Honolulu: Department of Health, 1970).

11. T. R. Brown, K. Huang, D. E. Harris, and K. M. Stein, "Mental Illness and the Role of Mental Health Facilities in Chinatown," in *Asian-American: Psychological Perspectives*, 212–231; see also, F. K. Cheung, "Culture and Mental Health Care for Asian Americans in the United States," paper presented at the Annual Meeting of the American Psychiatric Association, San Francisco, 1989; L. R. Snowden and F. K. Cheung, "Use of Inpatient Mental Health Services by Members of Ethnic Minority Groups," *American Psychologist* 45:3 (1990), 347–355; S. Sue, "Community Mental Health Services to Minority Groups: Some Optimism, Some Pessimism," *American Psychologist* 32 (1977), 616–624; Los Angeles County Department of Mental Health, "Report on Ethnic Uitlization of Mental Health Services," unpublished manuscript, Los Angeles, 1984; S. Sue, D. Fujino, L. Hu, D. Takeuchi and N. Zane, "Community Mental Health Services for Ethnic Minority Groups: A Test of the Cultural Responsiveness Hypothesis," unpublished manuscript, 1991.

12. J. Matsuoka, "The Utilization of Mental Health Programs and Services by Asian/Pacific Islanders: A National Study," unpublished manuscript, 1990.

13. M. J. O'Sullivan, P. D. Peterson, G. B. Cox, and J. Kirkeby, "Ethnic Populations: Community Mental Health Services Ten Years Later," *American Journal of Community Psychology* 17:1 (1989), 17–30.

14. S. Shapiro, E. Skinner, L. Kessler, M. Von Korff, P. German, G. Tischler, P. Leaf, L. Benham, L. Cottler, and D. Regier, "Utilization of Health and Mental Health Services," *Archives of General Psychiatry* 41 (1984), 971–978.

15. S. Sue and D. W. Sue, "MMPI Comparisons between Asian- and Non-Asian-American Students Utilizing a University Psychiatric Clinic," *Journal of Counseling Psychology* 21 (1974), 423–427.

16. T. R. Brown et al., "Mental Illness and the Role of Mental Health Facilities in Chinatown"; see also, S. Sue, "Community Mental Health Services to Minority Groups."

17. K. M. Lin, T. S. Inui, A. Kelinman, and W. Womack, "Sociocultural Determinants of the Help-Seeking Behavior of Patients with Mental Illness," *Journal of Nervous and Mental Disease* 170 (1982), 78–85.

18. B. L. C. Kim, *The Asian-Americans: Changing Patterns, Changing Needs* (Montclair, New Jersey: Association of Korean American Christian Scholars in North America, 1978); see also, S. Sue and J. Morishima, *The Mental Health of Asian Americans* (San Francisco: Jossey-Bass Publishers, 1982); T. J. Tracey, F. T. L. Leong, and C. Glidden, "Help Seeking and Problem Perception among Asian Americans," *Journal of Counseling Psychology* 33:3 (1986), 331–336.

19. L. Uba and S. Sue, "Nature and Scope of Multicultural Mental Health Services for Asian/Pacific Islanders," in *Handbook of Social Services for Asian and Pacific Islanders*, edited by N. Mokuau (Westport, Connecticut: Greenwood Press, 1991).

20. S. Sue et al., "Community Mental Health Services for Ethnic Minority Groups," 1991.

21. A. Howard, G. M. Pion, G. D. Gottfredson, P. E. Flattau, S. Oskamp, S. M. Pfafflin, D. W. Bray, and A. G. Burstein, "The Changing Face of American Psychology: A Report from the Committee on Employment and Human Services," *American Psychologist* 41 (1986), 1311–1327.

Asian American Art in the Year 2020:

Arts Policy

Gerald D. Yoshitomi

EXECUTIVE DIRECTOR
JAPANESE AMERICAN CULTURAL AND COMMUNITY CENTER
LOS ANGELES, CALIFORNIA

Today: Nine million Americans of Asian ancestry. Over 65 percent are foreign born. Limited numbers are in the audiences of our arts institutions and in our groupings of professional artists. Only a small percentage is American born and over 30 years of age, the principal range from which audiences and artistic product are drawn.

The Future: More Americans of Asian ancestry in the year 2020 than in 1992. In 2020 there will be 20 million Americans of Asian ancestry. Yet, more than 50 percent will be foreign born, and only a small number will be American born and over the age of 30. How many will be recipients of multiple cultures and how many will be third, fourth and fifth generation Americans? How many artists will there be? From what traditions and experiences and training will their art be based? In what context will their art be presented? What will be the role of museums and performing arts institutions, not to mention media centers, public arts agencies and university training programs in responding to these populations and the individuals who comprise its diversity? How will these populations respond as audiences? How many will attend performances and exhibitions which reflect traditions outside of their native culture? How many from outside of these cultures will want to share in their richness and bring them into their own communities, often for the first time? What will be the role of the importation of "home country" culture to both the preservation of "home country" culture in the United States as well as its impact on "American culture" as it is defined, supported and developed in the third decade of the 21st century? What will be the impact of this "invasion" of people and cultures and investment from off-shore sources on the preservation of the American arts facilities and institutions so painstakingly developed during the latter half 20th century with public and private support? How can public policy institutions in the arts respond to cultures they do not understand, and become sensitive to new disciplines and values that they have not experienced?

These are just a few of the questions public policy specialists in the arts must address now, as we develop policies which address the needs of all of our communities as they evolve into the next century. We engage in this debate at a time when historians and cultural specialists are examining the bases of what is American culture and how it should be taught and studied. We're not certain whether we're in the "melting pot" or "stir-frying" our food or eating it as *sashimi*. It is in this context that publications as this volume are vitally important.

However, it is generally acknowledged that the support and interest for publications and studies about Asian Americans have only come about as the "critical mass" of Asian Americans has exceeded 10 percent of the American population in certain regions. The majority of Japanese Americans and Chinese Americans (as well as many Pilipino and Korean Americans) have been in the United States for at least four generations. The development of the West over the past one hundred years would have been markedly different were it not for the work of the Chinese American laborer or the Japanese American farmer. I was asked once to speak about the "Changing Face of Los Angeles." I had to remind the audience that my face had been in Los Angeles for over forty years, and that other Japanese American faces had been here for over one hundred years. Possibly we were invisible before.

Yet only now with the large influx of Asian immigrants are there sufficient numbers of Americans of Asian ancestry to be considered a political or consumer force. This newly found power by coalition building is well represented by groups as the Asian Pacific American Legal Center, Leadership Education for Asian Pacifics, and the Coalition of Asian Pacific Americans for Fair Reapportionment, all in Los Angeles, which have demonstrated strength in confronting issues of discrimination and representation. However, the same factors which lend to coalition building for political purposes provide a limited basis for the development of comprehensive public policies in the arts. While issues of reapportionment and the American concept of affirmative action are based on race, the peoples of Asian ancestry who now are part of the American citizenry, while being of the same race, are of different cultures and national origin. Furthermore, these differences are even more amplified by generational differences in each ethnic group. In other words, in fact, we are all "Asian" for the census, but there is no "Asian culture," only Vietnamese culture, Malaysian culture, Chinese culture, etc. There is no Asian dance or Asian music, and no one is an Asian artist. On the other hand, we can be grouped as "Asian" artists from various cultures, and there can be an "Asian music" concert representing the traditions of various cultures. It is important that this distinction be made, lest we label without the proper knowledge. Acknowledgement of political geography is different from the acceptance of each group's cultural diversity. We, in fact, are divided by our cultural traditions, yet it is those traditions which give us the strength and resiliency to be a part of this American culture, and to fight to retain our cultural values within this broader context.

"Best of Both Worlds"

The one important exception to this concept of cultural separation is the active development of "Asian American art" by younger artists, often of third and fourth generations, whose contemporary work represents an amalgam of cultural traditions, both from "home country," as well as from other American and Asian bases. They are developing and sharing a new sensibility within their genre which represents the "Best of Both Worlds," to quote songwriter and choreographer Nobuko Miyamoto. This Asian American work is being created by the young musicians and songwriters in the Jazz fusion band "Hiroshima," by the drummers in San Jose Taiko, and by composer Jon Jang writing about Tiananmen Square, as well as by comedienne Amy Hill and filmmaker Robert Nakamura. This work represents tentative first steps by third and fourth generation artists who draw from experience and training in several cultural traditions and represents the future of Asian American work in this country as it is drawn into the mainstream, yet also pulls the stream toward itself through its strength and integrity.

And there are even younger artists now receiving their creative training in the rap music of the 1990s, the *Nihon Buyo* of *Kabuki*, the *Kulintang*,

Yamaha music schools, and the skateboard parks of our California communities. These younger artists in training are having to reach back further to gain the strength of the Asian cultural heritage, but also reach further forward to address the complexity and advanced technology of the next century. They have the advantage of pursuing art which comes from many cultures in a world in which our technology allows us to see, hear, and cross many cultural borders. The future work that comes from their talent and experiences will be revolutionary in its world view, but will also address the conservation of traditions which have spanned the past millennium.

But to address the artists and audiences who are here today, as well as to address the needs of the arts and audiences which will be developed in the future, is a daunting task. No other area of public policy is more acutely in need of a policy of diversity and pluralism in response to these demographic shifts than public arts policy. By definition, public arts policy responds to the cultural needs of its communities and artists and develops public support mechanisms, often through the creation of facilities, grants programs, and regulations and tax incentives which encourage the creation, presentation, and participation in the arts of our citizens and the cultures from which they come.

These issues are being made even more complex by the diversity of Asian Pacific American groups, and the generational and demographic differences within each national group. In the political process, there are stages of empowerment which are related to a group's power to reapportion boundaries in legislatures reflective of the racial groupings in a community. As citizenship and voter registration increase, our political power can go beyond reapportionment to the next stage, where we can use our greater numbers to elect Asian Pacific officials.

In the arts, the nine million (now) or 20 million (in 2020) Asian Pacific Americans represent both an audience pool as well as a resource for potential artists. However, the demographic, cultural, economic, social, and age differences within the entire population will prevent homogeneous attempts to respond to Asian Pacific artist or audience needs. The older, newly-arrived people will more likely cling to their traditional cultures, much as they clung to their children to keep them on the boats when they escaped their country. Younger, newly-arrived people may hold tightly on to their CD players listening to a new breed of Asian Pop Music in their native languages, while the youngest will easily toss away the traditional costumes to dance to the sounds of Rap Music on their Boom Box. Second and third generation Asian Americans may wait in line to get those last tickets to the Frank Sinatra or Beach Boys concert, and possibly some of the fourth generation will study flower arrangement and *tai-chi*, but only to get their "heads straight." Others will fight diligently, across time zones and continents, to keep their cultural traditions and values to pass on those vital symbols, sounds, and musical instruments to the next generation. And still others will take these instruments to play a unique sound to the entire world.

Audiences will reflect this diversity and will be much broader than the scene described above. Their needs as consumers and their interests as ticket buyers will encourage them to "cross over" to become part of a larger American fabric of arts attendees. Some will not necessarily support the younger artists of their cultures, particularly those who will be seen as having "left" their cultural traditions. Others will encourage their children to leave those traditions behind and to jump fully into the searing "melting pot" of American cultural activity. In either case, there will be a tremendous time lag, much as there is from Asian Pacific efforts to elect members of our community to Congress. I was once asked how many years it would take, and the learned response given back to me was "generations." There are still only a few Asian Pacific members of Congress from the mainland of the United States.

This time lag will have a tremendous impact on arts policy-makers, as they attempt to support the audiences of the current day, while also supporting the training and development of the artists of the future. Some have even said that there will be a two-generation time lag between the arrival of the immigrant and the creation of newly developed creative work. If that is true, during this time lag, what is our responsibility to the artists, to potential audiences, and to the entire citizenry? Besides patience, what do we do while we are waiting for the work to be developed? What policies do we develop which will retain cultural traditions, as well as encourage the hastening of this process?

A Culture Rooted in Pain, Pride and Hope

Throughout American history, we have demonstrated a resiliency to accept new cultures and adopt them into our American way of life. Yet the resiliency of our broader American culture to accept and adapt has not necessarily benefited the cultures which we have included within our sphere, often through means of force and oppression. At times Americans have attempted to change cultural forms and values and at times destroyed those cultures and art forms in the process. We have commercialized cultural symbols and utilized them as hood ornaments on our mode of transportation and mascots for our athletic teams. In the name of art, we have denigrated the color of peoples' skin and made fun of the sounds made by their voices and musical instruments.

> Many of these cultures and people have been scarred by centuries of violence against them. Their traditions are lost or in jeopardy, and their communities have been subjected to exile and economic deprivation. . . . Many cultural experiences are rooted in pain as well as pride and hope. These histories, and the images and expressions that have grown from them, must be recognized and supported.[1]

Yet at other times, we have formed sponsor groups to support emigre musicians as well as indigenous American art forms, such as jazz. In our finest moments, we have understood that all citizens of this country are Americans, no matter what their country of origin, or the country of origin of their parents or even great grandparents. In the early part of this century, we welcomed European immigrant artists, and this population brought with them a hunger and demand for European-style performing arts events. Our cities and counties, as well as publicly supported universities, built symphony halls and opera theatres to present this work. In the early part of the century, we encouraged the charitable income tax deduction to support cultural activities, and in the sixties, established public arts agencies to provide support for these works. We have accepted the culture that these artists shared with us, yet we wonder if the same will be true of the art which has come from the many cultures of Asia. Immigrant audiences are supporting Chinese opera, Japanese *Shigin* and Pilipino dance, yet we wonder whether the stages of those same halls and theatres will be open to the work of our traditions. Will public facilities be built to accommodate *Kabuki*, *Kulintang* and Shadow Puppets? Will university music schools add *Gagaku* and *Gamelan* to their curriculum, and will the *sitar* and *koto* be taught in music programs like the violin and trumpet? Even more complex is the question about whether we will be able to accommodate the Asian American compositions of Jon Jang or Dan Kuramoto, let alone that future amalgam of work which is indeed Cuban-African-Chinese-Irish-Mexican-American, and which we can just call American work.

James Baldwin wrote in *Notes of a Native Son* that America is "White no longer and it will never be White again." That pointed statement written only 40 years ago couldn't predict the complexity of the America of this current decade or even this year of 1992. We are not merely shifting from one paradigm to another. Rather, we are shifting from one to many. If that is the case, what can we say about the public arts support system and its capacity to support this broader society? At one time one could say that the Baldwin quotation referred to a white versus black society, but now we have over one hundred ethnic groups who make up the mix of what it is to be American, and many of them reflect the diversity of Americans of Asian ancestry.

Our great experiment of democracy in America has survived by incorporating each of our cultures into its great fabric. We have not always been able to do it with grace or compassion, and we have made tragic mistakes about which we must be constantly reminded and diligently redress. Yet we have the resilience to accept the next dilemma and welcome the next immigrant. We omitted slaves from our Declaration of Independence, but fewer than one hundred years later endured a Civil War to guarantee (we thought) freedom. And we joined freedom rides one hundred years after that to fight for freedom once again.

We know as Americans that we will always have to give of ourselves to guarantee our own rights and the rights of others. When a woman's right to choose is taken away and a person's sexual preference results in discrimination, we know as Americans that we must speak out. We know that we must accommodate to views which are different from ours, or else the right to express our own views may be taken away. As a society, beginning with the first killing of Native Americans by the immigrant explorers, we haven't always been able to address the issues with timeliness to prevent the tragedies of violence, death, and great human suffering. Yet possibly we've had the benefit of learning from our hundreds of years of history to understand our cultural differences and the need to incorporate those differences into our communities, our broader American culture, and our laws. We've always believed in the potential of this country to address its issues and to solve them by incorporating the broadest spectrum of the American public into that process.

But now our confidence has been shaken. We have more cultures in this country than each of us can possibly understand, and although the process of incorporation can occur quickly, we do not know if we have the resources, both public and individual, to incorporate all of these cultures into what we hope will be the America of the 21st century. We don't know if so many cultures can be amalgamated so quickly into the fabric of America. We are faced with this great American dilemma of the 21st century: Will the country depicted in the Emma Lazarus poem at the base of the Statue of Liberty, "Give me your tired...," succumb to the quick and easy answer of requiring everyone to accept American mass culture and to leave behind the culture which serves as the basis of their humanity, or are we willing to deal with the complexity of each of our cultures, and to work to incorporate those cultural perspectives into the broad fabric of what it is to be an American? And furthermore, are we willing to assist in the search for cultural background of those whose rush to jump into the melting pot has seared away their cultural roots?

We've been told that the arts can provide a perspective to redefine what it is to be an American. Yet this process of redefinition, or at least refinement, creates a dilemma for each of us. In this time of demographic and social change, how do we encourage the new without losing the old? How do we promote diversity without becoming unfocused? How do we fully accept each other without losing some of ourselves?

Some have suggested that we must adopt an open and color-blind approach which throws out the old standards and only accepts the standards of "artistic quality." However, these standards of "artistic quality" often ignore the standards of "cultural quality" which have existed for centuries throughout Asia and have existed for over a century within communities of Americans of Asian ancestry. To get to the level of acceptance necessary to accommodate the multitude of cultures now comprising the United States, one cannot develop an immediate color-blind approach. We must first recognize the integrity of each person's cultural heritage and the art which comes from that heritage.

Overcoming the Generational Time Lag

History informs us that it has taken several generations for the arts of newly-arrived groups or immigrants to be accepted by the "mainstream" of America, or for the newly arrived to receive sufficient training and experience in the United States to develop a form which combines their two traditions and is accepted by the broader American public. In the Japanese American community, this can be said about the achievements and success of Minoru Yamasaki, architect, George Tsutakawa, sculptor, and George Nakashima, furniture designer, architect and craftsman. Each was able to blend their Japanese sensibilities and perspective with their American and European training to reach a level of accomplishment as artists in the United States. Others have been able to gain national and international recognition when their training and subsequent work have reflected a western or European sensibility, again combined with Japanese traditions, such as in the case of Isamu Noguchi, who worked with Brancusi at a young age. Native-born Asians have gained success in the United States when they have brought with them the training from their own cultural traditions and combined it with western training. On occasion, a classically trained Asian artist such as Ravi Shankar is able to combine his work with other western musicians to gain success, but generally speaking, it is the second and third generation Asian American who will gain artistic success in the United States, and it is the second and third generation members who will be the audience for the broader productions. These artists of talent have overcome the generational time lag described above and succeeded against all odds. It was due to their individual vision, based in their own cultural traditions, often assisted by training from outside their culture, and then nurtured and supported by the entirety of American cultural, ethnic and religious groups. This, then, is the context in which artistic work must be assisted:

■ Acknowledgement and support of native cultural traditions, often brought to this country at great sacrifice, and often involving spiritual and religious references and elements. This must be carried on for generations.

■ The economic resources and systems to sustain those traditions given the dire circumstances of many new immigrant groups. We cannot let cultural traditions slip away, yet we must also allow the popular to play its role in encouraging traditional cultural activity.

■ Encouragement of training, both from within and traditional cultural systems and the broader society.

■ Encouragement of audience development to broaden the thinking of Americans about arts and culture to include traditional cultures.

■ Support for the development of the new and risk-taking projects which push the boundaries of accepted cultural norms (both traditional and contemporary culture).

Los Angeles is today seen as one of the most culturally diverse American cities and a potential prototype of the American diversity of the 21st century. In a report to Mayor Tom Bradley in 1987, the Los Angeles 2000 Committee stated, "More different races, religions, cultures, languages and people mingle here than in any other city in the world."[2] The Committee went on to note that to ignore diversity risks an increasingly divided community with intensifying political conflicts, escalating crime, shrinking economic opportunity, racial isolation, and ultimately, marked deterioration in the quality of life. Instead, the Committee urged a view of diversity as a positive force and recommended that we embrace it, nurture it, and draw strength from it:

. . .think of the diversity. . .as a broad and complex system of cultures—each with its own beliefs, social structures, language and thought patterns, and art forms. These cultures, and particularly their art forms. . .offer ways to know and respect each other, thereby enriching our diversity. Therefore, we must recognize the essential role that the arts and culture play in building a sense of community. Through art and culture a community identifies itself and sees itself reflected in the greater whole.[3]

A public policy, then, must be designed to strengthen our arts and cultural institutions. Such a policy would embrace a dual challenge: first, to encourage contributions to the arts from the city's many ethnic and culturally specific groups, and second, to broaden existing centralized arts organizations.[4]

Yet, today's American public "arts policy" often has a narrow view of what is art. Music is often defined as that which is played by symphonic orchestras and quality media what is broadcast by public broadcasting. In contrast, most cultures generally define art as the work which reflects the spirit and enhances the soul. The oldest forms of arts support, particularly in Asia, reflected the perceptions of a people about their culture and the importance of the sounds and symbolisms which reinforced and enhanced that culture. Each individual had a strong appreciation of culture, and only the work which reflected that quality received support. *Our Many Voices, A New Composition*, an interim report of the "2000 Partnership," the successor organization to the "Los Angeles 2000," stated:

> Current American arts policy, however, is based on an idea of 'a superior culture.' This rests on a European definition of art, embracing that which hangs in the museum or is performed in the concert hall or the theatre; or is secular or derived from court tradition; or is contemporary and professional. And even though this policy is intended to serve our pluralistic society, we actually place little value on art that is based in another cultural tradition or is derived from a social, communal, occupational, religious, or family context. In practice, the policy is limited by design. The funding systems, cultural facilities, and the managers are simply inappropriate to serving these diverse forms of cultural expression. As a result, the support for different cultural voices—the real challenge of pluralism—has been sporadic and inadequate. Only as a result of constant political pressure has arts policy been grudgingly augmented and re-tooled to encourage the variation in regional and cultural customs and practice found throughout the country.[5]

A Melting Pot—Or Something Else?

At issue is the question of whether the United States is indeed the proverbial melting pot, or whether another analogy is appropriate. As a young child, when I learned about music and art from school textbooks, I learned that the Japanese prints which my grandmother carefully displayed on the walls at home were not "real" art. I learned that *ikebana* and *bonsai* were hobbies, not art. I learned that the *barrio* mural painted by my classmate's uncle wasn't art either, and that the jazz played by our neighbor down the street wasn't music. As a child, I mourned the loss of my culture and parts of myself, as my cultural symbols and those of my friends were systematically eliminated from our experience. Instead, my school taught me about the great European composers and musicians. Of the Americans I did learn about, I heard Copeland and not Ellington, and of course all the authors I read were men. Those days are not so long ago. I wonder if 25 years from now if my children will remember only learning about Shakespeare, Bradbury and Herman Melville, and not about Willa Cather and Chikamatsu.

Rather than the melting pot, some have suggested that the pertinent analogy for the future would be that of a stew, bouillabaisse, or mixed salad, in which each culture stays intact, but mixes with the influences of others to develop a culture which is greater than the sum of its parts. However, this American culture is much more complex than can be described or captured within a single paradigm.

Many now suggest an America which functions within multiple paradigms, envisioning not just one bowl or pot cooking on the stove, but a number of diverse pots, both large and small, each reflecting the diverse cultures of America. There might be big containers to accommodate the stews, bouillabaisse and salads, but also smaller containers, in which specific cultures and tastes would choose to be nurtured, preserved, and modified, prior to (and possibly instead of) joining the larger kettles. There would be pots which would represent the Mulligan Stew of several cultures, and there would be some plates with dividers upon which someone would make their selections from the Smorgasbord of tastes and flavors. This model would reflect both an integration of cultures, as well as a process of selective separation, nourishment and sustenance. There would, of course, be many cooks, and each culture would be integral to several of the pots. It is important to note that none of these models is absolute. Rather, no one actually lives only in one culture, and as Guillermo Gomez-Peña says, all of us live on the borders. Each of us would actually live in several "pots." Most people travel back and forth from culturally specific to centralized environments within the course of each day and week. Many of us live within multiple paradigms, understanding (both consciously and subconsciously) the modes of behavior acceptable and supported within each paradigm. We each live in worlds that contain multiple cultures. I would suggest that this vision of America is the one which must operate in this last decade of the 20th century and into the 21st century. A foreign dignitary visiting the United States recently remarked that the America of the 1990s is in fact the world in microcosm. He said: "If America is successful in bringing its people together, maybe the world has a chance." These are our questions of the 21st century. Can we bring the American people together, and if we can, does that mean that the world has a chance?

This concept is particularly important for Asian American groups whose population base in the United States is still relatively small. Each is attempting to preserve its own cultural symbols, practices and arts while also attempting to live in and adapt to American systems. Many people who have come to this country from Asia did not come to leave their culture, but rather came because the political and economic strife of their country did not support their culture. They wish to bring their economic and cultural context to the United States, where our freedoms provide an environment in which their cultures can survive. They come here, hoping for support, but they see the omnipresent mass culture impacting upon their lives and most particularly on the values, ethics and arts of their children. Newly-arrived immigrant families seem to be "assimilating" more quickly, or in other words, "leaving their culture behind" more urgently. Newly-arrived groups look to public agencies for support, but meet a reluctance to change by those in policy-making positions. Yet the urgency of their concerns is created not by the calendar of arts politics but by the imperative of cultural survival. Cultural equity becomes a matter of utmost importance when "the sands of our cultures are slipping through our fingers."

As one reviews the adverse role that public policy in the arts has had on newly-arrived groups throughout American history, one might be prone to suggest that Asian cultural traditions would be better off in a society in which government were "neutral" about culture, and did not impose public intervention. Throughout history, each of America's cultural and ethnic communities has persevered to maintain its own traditions, often attempting to counteract the actions of the government or other public systems. Public policies have encouraged and at times even mandated the genocide of various Native American nations, the separation of the African American family through the slavery system, prohibitions against speaking our native tongues in the public school system, and the destruction of Japanese American cultural materials in the concentration camps of World War II. Yet communities have established their own internal structures, without public assistance, to support cultural preservation through churches, social centers and fraternal organizations, and have responded with their own political initiatives to counteract "no-choice" and English-Only initiatives.

The large increase in the Asian American population has, in recent years, increased the awareness by government agencies, elected officials, and other arts policy-makers to our growing numbers, resulting in the appropriation of Asian American work into "mainstream" organizations and the encouragement of outreach programs and audience development programs. One example is the "workshopping" of Asian American plays at resident theatre companies, with the result that some have been produced on the "mainstage." Some might say that these centralized "mainstages" are where all the best work should be produced and that appropriation has resulted in greater cultural diversity. Yet many cultural groups have expressed concern regarding the issue of access versus control, as well as matters of cultural imperialism. Several years ago, most would have been pleased with the mere access to the facility, no matter who produced the work. Now, after a history of unfortunate experiences, Asian Americans are asking for control of their own cultures and cultural symbols. They've seen the work of the best Asian American playwrights "re-worked" by directors who don't understand their culture, and they've seen centuries-old Asian traditions trivialized by unknowing producers. In the visual arts, they are demanding that Asian American curators and institutions be involved in the selection of work for exhibitions and have central roles in the interpretation of those materials for their own and broader communities. Their concern is expressed in *An American Dialogue*:

> . . .when the content of one culture is left solely to another to express, without any consultation with that culture's community, then the result is usually distorted, unintentionally or by design. This outcome is even more likely—and more threatening—if the

two cultures are at odds: haves and have-nots, majority and minority, victor and vanquished. . . . In short, no culture can survive intact if its interpretation and transmission are controlled by people outside the culture.[6]

Responding to Cultural Diversity

To establish effective public arts policy to support culturally diverse communities will require recognition at each level of government of both the importance of the inclusion of Asian American audiences and artists in the "mainstream" of cultural activity within a community, as well as the support of culturally specific communities to preserve and present their own artistic work. *Our Many Voices* recommends a dual policy track which is based on the following conceptual framework:

1.　There is a fundamental right to culture—to honor each person's unique heritage, including the right to express and communicate, to practice customs, to be treated with respect.

2.　Cultural diversity is a positive social value, the source of our cultural vitality. It is a well of richness from which to draw new social forms and possibilities.

3.　Cultural life requires active participation, not just passive consumption of cultural products. Amateurs and professionals are equally weighted ends of a necessary continuum.

4.　No culture or active subculture can survive if its interpretation and transmission is controlled by someone outside the culture.

5.　In contemporary society, the concept of a "pure culture" is specious. Human society and behavior is varied and deeply textured, and present cultural practices have multiple cultural antecedents.

6.　Cultural equity demands the fair distribution of cultural resources and support throughout the society.[7]

How then can this be implemented in our various Asian American communities and at the national and state policy levels?

Our Many Voices goes on to recommend means by which new policies can be evaluated. The outcomes would be deemed a success if:

1. The amount of multicultural and culturally specific services is increased and the institutions that provide these services are strengthened.

2. The composition of the aggregate audience for the arts more closely reflects the demographic reality of Los Angeles.

3. The audiences for the arts are encouraged to explore the richness and diversity of Los Angeles' cultural heritage.

4. The ultimate criterion for success is the condition of choice:

   a. Is the control of the cultural symbolism held within the community?

   b. Do policy decisions increase the conditions of cultural choice?

   c. Is the public good kept in trust by these actions? Are the public facilities governed and used by, and accessible to, the many? Does public financing support the voices and aspirations of the many?[8]

It should be noted that these comments do not suggest a new tribalism. Rather, the suggestion of separation provides a basis from which we can then join together, as we must develop a common agenda with all people. Whether we "live on the hyphen" or not, we are all Americans, no matter what our national origins. We each live in communities and neighborhoods, and we each have a part to play in the cultural future of this country. We must find that common ground of working together. Racism is not a white person's disease, and sexism is not the exclusive domain of males. We all have misperceptions about one another and we need to dispel them as best we can to develop a truly multicultural society. These misperceptions are even greater about new immigrant groups from parts of the world we have learned little about from our schools, and from cultures which have not been incorporated into our arts institutions. It becomes therefore even more important that we learn about each other's values and cultures.

Our previous perceptions have often come from "old stories." Today, however, we must create and listen to the new stories. To take the final statement from *An American Dialogue*:

> Our job, then, is to make certain that the new stories that represent our common experiences are developed as creatively as we know how, and that they touch as many people as possible. If we succeed, our lasting legacy will be the work of those most creative among us—the artists who are best able to see beneath the surface of our actions and make order of our infinite complexity.[9]

Notes

1. National Task Force on Presenting and Touring the Performing Arts, *An American Dialogue* (Washington, D.C.: Association of Performing Arts Presenters, 1989).

2. Los Angeles 2000 Committee, *LA 2000: A City for the Future* (Los Angeles: Los Angeles 2000 Committee, 1987).

3. *Ibid.*

4. *Ibid.*

5. The 2000 Partnership, *Our Many Voices: A New Composition* (Los Angeles: The 2000 Partnership, n.d.).

6. National Task Force, *An American Dialogue*.

7. The 2000 Partnership, *Our Many Voices*.

8. *Ibid.*

9. National Task Force, *An American Dialogue*.

Is There a Future for Our Past?

Cultural Preservation Policy

Franklin S. Odo

DIRECTOR, ETHNIC STUDIES PROGRAM
UNIVERSITY OF HAWAI'I, MANOA

It is clear to everyone, by this time, that ethnicity, race and class play crucial roles in our world. The "rebalkanization" of Central Europe and the disintegration of the former Soviet Union are but two examples of a process in which ethnic groups—nearly ten thousand according to some estimates[1]—are asserting their rights to self-determination. Although definitions vary, ethnic groups tend to be unified by some combination of history, language, culture, gene pool and geography. Some, like the Kurds in the Middle East, form pockets of minority groups in several major nations. Others, like Native Hawaiians, are oppressed and dispossessed in their own, tiny and remote, ancestral lands. Still others, like the various Asians in America, are struggling to come to terms with the demands of acculturation and the sometimes countervailing forces of ethnic identity and cultural preservation.

In the complex and shifting ethnic and racial dynamics in the United States, there is increasing attention being paid to Asian Americans as the fastest growing racial group. Numbering approximately 1.5 million in 1970 (.7 percent of total U.S.), Asian Americans increased rapidly, just about doubling to 3.5 million (1.5 percent) in 1980 and 7.2 million (3 percent) in 1990. Assuming stable immigration and birth rates, there should be over 11 million in the year 2000 and between 15 and 20 million in 2010. Lest this appear to be too far in the future to apprehend, we might remember that children born in 1992 will (if accepted) be college freshmen in 2010.

Fear of a New "Yellow Peril"?

Recently, media images of Asian American "whiz kids" squeezing out other groups in competition for places in colleges and elsewhere have given rise to the fear of a new "Yellow Peril." This time around, however, there is a different cast to the old threat. The original version conjured up the specter of fanatic militarists in Japan leading hordes of Chinese against the bulwarks of Western civilization on the shores of the West Coast. This time, the menace comes from within: from the seemingly unstoppable Korean, Chinese, South and Southeast Asian youngsters who have a superhuman capacity for sheer study and preparation.

We have, to be sure, witnessed numerous variations on this ugly theme. Indeed, there is more than a hint of the image of the Chinese soldiers we faced during the Korean War whose capacities to do battle against American troops were disparaged as the mindless "Oriental" ability to accept propaganda, subsist on a handful of rice each day and embrace death as the supreme act of self-sacrifice. These qualities we ascribed to them helped rationalize our retreat southward as the media reinforced the images of massive numbers of Chinese in "human wave" attacks to overwhelm, temporarily, superior American troops. The Japanese attack on Pearl Harbor was a classic example, including for many, still, the image of Hawai'i residents of Japanese ancestry conducting espionage and sabotage on a massive scale.

In this wildly distorted and deterministic scenario, we are reassured that "we" ought not be expected to "compete"—that these antagonists have created an unfair arena; that the playing field is hardly level. It is an old theme, harking back to Chinese cigar wrappers in San Francisco Chinatown in the 1870s condemned for being "willing" to live in cubicles and subsist on rats. The same could be said of Japanese farmers in the Central Valley in the 1920s, sending wives and toddlers into the fields. How, it was reasonably asked, could decent white workers or farmers be expected to compete if it meant lowering living standards to levels long since discarded as unacceptable in our civilized world? Somehow, in the twisted logic of racism, the struggles and achievements of the oppressed can be turned against them—in ways reminiscent of the Nazi rationalizations for exterminating Jews. The notion of an international conspiracy of Jewish capitalist communists became useful in creating a scapegoat, no matter the oxymoronic nature of the allegations. The lesson is clear: the only thing worse than being labeled inferior and incompetent is appearing too competent.

In an interview with upscale *Town and Country*, sociologist E. Digby Baltzell discussed his ongoing battles with America's WASP establishment.[2] Baltzell had popularized the acronym WASP in the 1960s and continues to decry its demise. "Ethnicity and race are much deeper than we would ever have admitted 30 years ago—10 times as important as class. And the whole thing behind the Iron Curtain was ethnicity, wasn't it? I think that's appalling." Asked which group, assuming WASPs lose their grip on the U.S., would rise to power, Baltzell suggests the "post-Vietnam War wave of Asian-American immigrants."

But Asians in the United States, both foreign-born and American citizen alike, have been among the smallest of the identifiable "racial" groups. This will continue to be the case in spite of the fact that it is also the fastest growing of our racial groups. Even the projections for the year 2000, which suggest that the number of Asian Pacific Americans will climb to about ten million, suggest that this will be a mere 4 percent of the total American population, according to the Leadership Education for Asian Pacifics (LEAP) Feasibility Study.[3] The twin trajectories of increasing Asian Pacific numbers within a dramatically rising nonwhite population are producing both anxiety and anticipation, especially among those involved with allocation of resources and power. Under these conditions, the experience of Hawai'i, with an unbroken tradition of a population dominated, numerically, by people of color, may be more instructive than a casual look at the figures may warrant.

"Survival Needs" vs. "Access and Equity"

The sharp rise in numbers of Asian Pacific Americans and the unprecedented forms of diversity now manifest in the United States have evoked concerns over galvanizing these apparently irreconcilable constituencies into a unified force for political, economic and public policy advances. The LEAP Feasibility Study itself defines the polarities as between "Survival Needs versus Access and Equity" with the former being projected by refugee groups like the Hmong, Lao and Cambodians and the latter represented by more established groups like the fourth or fifth generation American-born Japanese and Chinese.

Survival needs, according to LEAP, include the following, by priority:

1. Problems with acculturation and assimilation

2. Need for job training programs and unemployment services

3. Serious concerns about youth-related problems, including youth gangs and delinquency

4. Need for the development of and education in language skills

5. Counseling service centers

6. Programs for the elderly

7. Establishment of mental health centers

8. Family resource centers

Access and equity issues, on the other hand, involve:

1. Discrimination issues, focusing on violence against Asians and growing anti-Asian sentiments

2. Economic issues, such as economic barriers imposed by the "model minority" myth and the "glass ceiling" syndrome

3. Concerns about education, principally admissions policies and equal access to universities

4. Empowerment issues, politically as well as economically and socially

5. Services for the elderly

6. Conflicts, such as cultural identity issues and concerns about the rate of intermarriage

7. Need for leadership development programs including those that address upward mobility and career development issues

8. Health and family resource services

9. Youth-related problems, including gangs and drugs

10. Low income medical services

The LEAP Study acknowledges that there is considerable overlap and that "it is merely a matter of degree as to how much each need is experienced within various subgroups. . .the needs of diverse Asian Pacifics can no long[er] exist in isolation of each other. The future well-being of each segment is necessary to the well-being and advancement of the community as a whole."[4] It will require careful discussions and extended negotiations to convince both "sides" that they do indeed have a common agenda and can work together for public policy advances. One likely arena that may not be immediately evident is the promotion and preservation of ethnic culture.

In considering the protection of cultural heritage, history and identity, it is presumed that ethnic groups privileged with power and elite status within any given society and any particular historical context, will extend their hegemony to this critical arena. Thus, in the United States, there is a clearly established hierarchy of cultural backgrounds and hierarchies within each ethnic culture as well. The long accepted symbols of "high culture"—European classical music and opera, the theater, art and history museums and the literary world—remain dominated by WASP notions of what constitutes a "canon." We have, to be sure, made progress in breaking down barriers to racial participation in many spheres of activity and there is plenty of evidence that more challenges are in the making.

Sports is an appropriate and useful metaphor for the gains and limitations of that progress; professional baseball, football and basketball include numerous multi-millionaires of color. We can see this change extended into privileged positions like the quarterback in football and with people of color on golf courses and in swimming pools—arenas kept lily-white until very recent times. But management and ownership are still extremely delicate subjects as the 1992 purchase of the Seattle Mariners major league baseball team by a Japanese capitalist indicates. And, as in athletics, the museums which epitomize the canonization of the experiences, art and artifacts deemed worthy of preservation, exhibition and interpretation, have been subject to enormous stresses in the wake of these demographic changes.

In an earlier era, African Americans formed their own Negro Leagues to provide venues for outstanding athletes locked out of racist institutions. Similarly, we are constructing separate and viable museums like the Japanese American National Museum in Los Angeles to provide access denied by traditional history museums. It would be unfortunate to interpret these new enterprises as necessary consequences of a mainstream elite incapable of embracing ethnic diversity and as continuations of the old Negro League phenomenon. These are, rather, new organizations serving dynamic manifestations of a new America coming into being, however awkwardly and reluctantly. There will be pressure and initiatives for more inclusive policies on the part of established institutions like the Smithsonian at the same time that new ethnic-based institutions are created. This latter development is part of a related social force in which hundreds of new historical museums and societies have mushroomed throughout the U.S. in the last two decades.

Preserving and Promoting Ethnic Cultures

One of the characteristics of this new America will be its aggressively plural nature with regard to points of view and promotion of cultural heritages. In the last section, this paper discusses policy recommendations dealing with ethnic culture promotion and preservation. Promoting ethnic cultures and traditions and preserving or perpetuating them are related concepts but they are not synonymous and need to be clearly distinguished. They are critical functions and most ethnic groups tend to pursue both simultaneously—but not necessarily by the same individuals or organizations and not necessarily for the same ends. For example, the various ethnic associations of merchants or attorneys or doctors or dentists may band together to promote business or protect their sense of identity but they do not necessarily preserve or perpetuate ethnic cultures or traditions. The same individuals might, however, belong to other organizations which do promote and preserve cultural traditions including martial arts, literature or music. Assuming that these efforts are of value, it may be helpful to examine some of the ways in which Asian Americans have thought about preserving their cultures and experiences.

The major Asian immigrant groups in the U.S. in the 19th century were the Chinese and Japanese, although there is evidence that Filipinos, for example, had been in Louisiana as early as the 18th century. In the 19th century, the decisive role in promoting Asian culture or civilization was played by political, business, intellectual and artistic mediators in the white West. Here, the dominant images alternated between ancient civilizations worthy of cultural respect and emulation and effete or barbaric obstacles to the advancement of Western civilization.[5] The rarity of Asian communities in the U.S. in the 1800s made it inevitable that American perceptions of these minority communities be based on the Asian models. This was so even though, by the turn of the century, there were sizable proportions of Chinese in Chinatowns of San Francisco and Honolulu and the 60,000 Japanese in the Territory of Hawai'i made up 40 percent of the population—a ratio which would remain for the next four decades.

The immigrant communities and their leaders worked to promote their own interests, of course, although the efforts sometimes merged with activities based in their homelands, as in the case of reform leaders from Qing China active in the Chinatown communities or the leaders of the San Francisco Six Companies who tried to deal with local politicians.[6] This was also the case with the Japanese Christian leaders in Hawai'i and the San Francisco area in the late 19th century.[7] In most of these cases, the leadership understood that the "American" perception of the Asian immigrant communities was absolutely based upon images of Asia (to a degree only hinted at by contemporary standards). In any case, the community leaders themselves were never far from the possibility of returning to Asia to live, and improving conditions in their native countries made good sense, especially when American racism directed at Asians was so commonplace and overt.[8]

Within the Asian immigrant communities, however, the picture looked very different. There, individuals and organizations actively promoted and practiced their cultural traditions. Asian language schools were almost mandatory for the American born for communication within the family, for employment in the community and for possible relocation to the country of ancestral origin. With language training came a host of activities and traditions including histories, music, games, stories, calligraphy, dance and sports. Many of these activities evolved into new forms as the immigrants adapted or adopted resources and material from their new environment. The Japanese in Kona, Hawai'i, for example, continued the tradition of *hanami*—viewing cherry blossoms with food, drink and merriment. Without cherry trees, however, they turned to their coffee trees in full bloom and spread mats under the pure white petals in the moonlight where they created a new version of an old tradition. They did this, too, with old folk melodies which they used to compose new *holehole bushi* lyrics which told of life, love, sex and work in Hawai'i.[9]

The second and third generations of Asian Americans were pushed and pulled into a monocultural and monolithic version of WASP America. In the process, many artifacts and experiences were irretrievably lost to storytellers and researchers who now try to recreate and analyze the development of these ethnic groups. World War II was an especially traumatic period when cultural practices and material possessions were jettisoned or confiscated. The 120,000 residents of Japanese ancestry were most affected, to be sure, but all Asian Americans were taught that close connections to Asia could be dangerous, that those connections could be cultural as well as political or economic. The fact that the first few hundreds of Japanese to be interned after Pearl Harbor were almost invariably Buddhist or Shinto priests, language school personnel, martial arts instructors or cultural leaders made this point with great effectiveness.

Now, when attempts are made to analyze the Asian American experience, there are large gaps in available sources and information. When, for example, the National Historical Publications and Records Commission of the National Archives provided a substantial grant for the survey of uncollected records of ethnic organizations in Hawai'i, we uncovered approximately two thousand linear feet of documents. These form the bulk of Okinawan, Japanese, Chinese and Filipino records extant but Korean and native Hawaiian sources remain to be surveyed. The survey was conducted in 1987-89, through the offices of the Hawai'i State Foundation on Culture and the Arts and implemented by the University of Hawai'i at Manoa's School of Library and Information Sciences and Ethnic Studies Program. While the results were gratifying in the variety and richness of documents uncovered, these records remain uncollected and unavailable for use by students and scholars. Worse, the survey made clear the vast amounts of material that, over the decades, have been discarded or have deteriorated. As a result, much of our social and cultural histories will never be recovered.

Some of these gaps are being plugged through the use of oral history techniques and these are immensely valuable.[10] In some cases, the use of oral history is the preferred methodology to generate personal and internal views or perspectives that are not routinely documented in writing. This is true for many individuals as well as for groups. Too often, however, it is the absence of other forms of evidence that forces us to resort to interviews in spite of limitations involving personal bias, the nature of memory and the problems, inherent in the technique itself.

When in, say, the year 2020, historians and other scholars of the Lao, Hmong, Vietnamese and Cambodian experience in America sift through the documentary evidence to provide the basic knowledge of which self-esteem, pride and cultural awareness are constructed, what will they find? They will be researching half a century of shared experiences in America since their involuntary removal from their homelands, and the second and third generations of Southeast Asians will be trying to recover languages, traditions, memories and values, the passing of which their own groups and, perhaps the whole society, will lament. They will be pleased to know that some "outsiders" thought enough of their lives to record some experiences.[11]

When pioneering film and video students attempted to capture their communities' experiences through moving images in the early 1970s, there was little in the way of encouragement or resources. Nevertheless, some of the most remarkable projects were among the earliest. Eddie Wong's insightful film on his father, *Wong Sin-saang*, remains a classic effort of a young and talented second generation Chinese American who had every opportunity to "make it" in the widest possible sense of the term. The son chose, instead, to focus on the need to demonstrate the validity and integrity of his family and community. He makes his father, a laundryman, come to life for us in ways that would never have been possible without this endeavor. "Mr. Wong" is revealed at work in day-to-day laundry activities; the mundane and endless actions are punctuated by the meaningless pleasantries of his customers. But at home, this seemingly colorless figure—just another laundryman—is transformed into a vital student of Chinese calligraphy and *tai chi chuan*, protecting his individual and ethnic identity in proud and dignified fashion.

Bob Nakamura's early film, *Wataridori—Birds of Passage*, is in the same genre: the work features three apparently ordinary Issei—Japanese immigrants in America, including the filmmaker's father. Nakamura takes the title to reflect on the image of Asian immigrants as sojourners; as people somehow devoid of the right to be acknowledged because they contemplated the possibility of returning to their homelands. But in America they formed families and communities and many sank deep roots into hostile soil. In the process, they took whatever they knew and transformed the culture, the knowledge, the values and the energy into the establishment of a new version of America. Nakamura's father is a gardener, and he is filmed on his daily rounds and as he reminisces about his life's work and meaning. The Chinese laundryman and Japanese gardener are the quintessential stereotyped male characters of early Asian America. Perhaps it was not coincidental or accidental that these two early and brilliant films came from sons who needed to provide the reality behind and beneath the stereotyped vacuum: to restore to the rest of society a capacity to appreciate its own humanity.

Fortunately for the new immigrants and refugees, there is a baseline expectation born of the efforts of Wong and Nakamura and a few others. Visual Communications is the company they helped to establish and "VC" continues to support filmmakers and videographers seeking to document the Asian American experience. Indeed, *Pak Bueng on Fire*, a film created by a Thai about Thai in Los Angeles, is certain to inspire other recently arrived Asians to continue this tradition. But for too many, these activities will be too little, too late—just as it was for the first and second generations of Chinese, Japanese, Korean and Filipino communities in America. This conclusion suggests policy directions which impact on current concerns of the apparently divided needs of established Asian American communities and the survival issues of post-1975 refugee Asians in America.

Staking Claims to Cultural Hegemony

The most important insight to be derived from this attempt to determine whether our past has a role in our future is that we need a deliberate and carefully delineated plan to preserve and perpetuate our diverse cultures. This is not simply a vision of better scholarship in the 21st century, although that would be an important goal in and of itself. It would be a critical attempt to engage all segments of Asian America in mutually reinforcing action programs to stake claims to cultural hegemony. Refugee groups cite "acculturation and assimilation" as their top priority. One of the "lessons" learned from previous generations of Asian Pacific Americans is the importance of dealing with the objectives and goals; especially the nature of the society into which we strive to assimilate. This is especially true in a period when many Americans of many ethnic backgrounds are raising identical concerns. What kind of America are we creating? What roles can Asian Pacific Americans play in the process— what resources and experiences and expertise do we have to contribute? How do we advance the causes of our own groups and communities as we relate to these larger issues?

First, we need to support the efforts of well-meaning individuals in all of the major institutions in American life from public schools to political parties to repositories of cultural heritage such as museums, that are wrestling with the need to address issues of cultural diversity. If for no other reason than financial survival, even the most powerful of the elite WASP institutions such as the Smithsonian are making ethnic and cultural pluralism a priority. The voices of progress in these institutions, including foundations, private corporations and universities are still relatively few and isolated. They must be supported in their struggle to bring their own institutions to the table. The immense resources, to which we as Asian Pacific Americans contribute through taxes, consumption and donation, need to be more equitably allocated so that the burden of supporting activities which empower and document does not fall only on the communities involved.

Second, we need to work on specific needs which cut across ethnicity and generation. All of the issues, on both sides of the spectrum noted in the LEAP Study, are amenable to resolution. One example: empowerment via education involving the youth. This is critical whether the discussion focuses on entry level jobs for refugee communities with 60 percent unemployment or "glass ceiling" problems for middle-class college graduates. In all cases, a knowledge of the racial, ethnic, economic and political terrains will be essential for individual and community progress. Knowing the history of the community; knowing the legal, educational, political and social service resources available locally, regionally and nationally; knowing the languages and cultural traditions of the ethnic group; knowing the problems from within the community itself and its multiple perspectives; all of these have policy implications.

Every scholar with Asian American Studies ties or policy-maker with an Asian American constituency can develop a relationship with one or another of these issues whether labor or labor union related, housing, pre-school education, secondary school co-curricular, political party platform development, family conflict resolution or many others.

It would be fascinating, for example, to take second generation Japanese American Nisei beyond the history of the legal victory (at the U.S. Supreme Court in 1927) to retain language schools and the intra-ethnic dialogues, often bitter, about the advisability of continuing such education, into the advocacy of cultural retention programs for recent immigrant groups or for the Hawaiian language immersion programs. Or to take second generation Korean Americans beyond the fascinating history of immigrant nationalist movements to liberate Korea from Japan prior to World War II to the political conditions confronting Southeast Asians looking to their own homelands. The possibilities are nearly endless; the potential for advancement is great.

Finally, we need to support the institutions which attempt to deal specifically with these issues: the Asian Law Caucus, Na Loio no na Kanaka (Lawyers for the People, in Hawai'i), Asian American Journalists Association, Visual Communications, National Asian American Telecommunications Association, Association of Asian American Studies, Leadership Education for Asian Pacifics, National Asian Pacific American Bar Association, etc.

The Hawai'i example has been cited as one which may be especially instructive in the decades to come. Hawai'i has always had a majority of people of color but it has always, since the early 1800s, been subject to the arbitrary demands of European and American hegemony. As part of the United States since 1898, it has always been subject to the demands of American racism as well. In spite of these conditions, considerable gains were possible and the forging of multiethnic communities of interest, however fragile or temporal, were possible. But if there is any lesson to be learned from the Hawai'i example, it would be that progress required careful planning and sustained effort and sacrifice for modest gain.[12] None of the vaunted progress made by Asian Pacific Americans in Hawai'i came solely or primarily by virtue of numbers; and the immediate future is clouded by anxieties felt by those—especially the Japanese Americans—who have achieved modest levels of power in the public sector.

We need to consider the possibility and potential of combining the issues of empowerment with the imperative of cultural preservation. This is the single strategy with the power of incorporating the wide diversity of ethnic, generation and class groups among Asian Americans. It would also suggest a means by which all Americans might find some common ground to develop a unified vision of a new society, embracing the diversity which now threatens to rend it asunder.

Notes

1. Elise Boulding, "Ethnicity and New Constitutive Orders," in *From Chaos to Order*, edited by Hisakazu Usui and Takeo Uchida (Tokyo: Yushindo, 1991).

2. Interview with E. Digby Baltzell, *Town and Country* (June 1992), 42.

3. Leadership Education for Asian Pacifics (LEAP), *A Feasibility Study on Establishing an Asian Pacific American Public Policy Institute*, Los Angeles, 1991, Appendix C.

4. *Ibid.*, 4.

5. Richard Halloran, *Japan: Images and Realities* (New York: Random House, 1969); and Harold Isaacs, *Images of Asia* (New York: Torchbooks, 1972). For a useful summary, see Sucheta Mazumdar, "Asian American Studies and Asian Studies: Rethinking Roots," in *Asian Americans Comparative and Global Perspectives*, edited by Shirley Hune et al. (Pullman: Washington State University, 1991.)

6. Chinese Historical Society of America, *The Life, Influence and Role of the Chinese in the United States, 1776–1860* (San Francisco: Chinese Historical Society of America, 1976); Sucheng Chan, *Asian Americans: An Interpretative History* (Boston: Twayne, 1991).

7. Jiro Nakano, *Kona Echo* (Kona, Hawaii: Kona Historical Society, 1990); Yuji Ichioka, *The Issei: The World of the First Generation Japanese Immigrants 1885–1924* (New York: Free Press, 1988); Roland Kotani, *A Century of Struggle: The Japanese in Hawai'i* (Honolulu: Hawaii Hochi, 1985).

8. Sucheng Chan, *This Bittersweet Soil: The Chinese in California Agriculture, 1860–1910* (Berkeley: University of California Press, 1986); Ichioka, *The Issei*.

9. Franklin Odo and Kazuko Sinoto, *A Pictorial History of the Japanese in Hawai'i: 1885–1924* (Honolulu: Bishop Museum Press, 1985). For the Chinese counterpart, see Marlon Hom, *Songs of Gold Mountain: Cantonese Rhymes from San Francisco Chinatown* (Berkeley: University of California Press, 1987).

10. Akemi Kikumura, *Through Harsh Winters: The Life of a Japanese Immigrant Woman* (Novato, California: Chandler & Sharp, 1981); and Evelyn Nakano Glenn, *Issei, Nisei, War Bride: Three Generations of Japanese American Women in Domestic Service* (Philadelphia: Temple University Press, 1986); Craig Scharlin and Lilia Villanueva, *Philip Vera Cruz: A Personal History of*

Filipino Immigrants and the Farmworkers Movement (Los Angeles: UCLA Center for Labor Education and Research and UCLA Asian American Studies Center, 1992); and Peter Hyun, *Mansei!* (Honolulu: University of Hawaii Press, 1986).

11. Peter N. Kiang and Man Chak Ng, "Through Strength and Struggle: Boston's Asian American Student/Community/Labor Solidarity," *Amerasia Journal* 15:1 (1989); James Freeman, *Hearts of Sorrow: Vietnamese American Lives* (Stanford: Stanford University Press, 1989).

12. Noel Kent, *Hawai'i: Islands Under the Influence* (New York: Monthly Review, 1983); Roland Kotani, *A Century of Struggle*.

Making and Remaking
Asian Pacific America:

Immigration Policy

Bill Ong Hing

ASSOCIATE PROFESSOR OF LAW
STANFORD LAW SCHOOL

Asian Pacific Americans will continue to be the fastest growing ethnic group in the United States into the next millennium principally because of immigration. The demographic predictions for the year 2020 show that 54 percent of Asian Pacific Americans will be foreign born. This is consistent with census figures in 1980 and 1990 which revealed that except for Japanese Americans, every group was mostly comprised of those born abroad (e.g., Chinese, over 60 percent; Koreans, 80 percent; Asian Indians, 80 percent; Filipinos, over 70 percent; Vietnamese, 90 percent). These predictions also find support from current annual levels of immigration (e.g., Filipinos 60,000, Chinese 55,000, Koreans 30,000, Asian Indians 30,000, Pakistanis 9,700, Thais 8,900). In 1992, 50,000 Southeast Asian refugees were admitted. And a trend in increased immigration from Japan has developed as well. During the 1980s, Asian Pacific immigration totaled about two million to help account for the 108 percent increase during the decade (from approximately 3.8 million to 7.3 million).

Beyond numbers, there is every reason to believe that immigration and refugee policies will continue to shape the Asian Pacific American profile in terms of where people live, gender ratios, employment and income profiles, and even social and political life.

Understanding How Immigration Policy
Shapes Asian Pacific America

The 1965 amendments to the Immigration and Nationality Act set the stage for the development of Asian Pacific America as we know it today.[1] Its emphasis on family reunification (ironically not intended to benefit Asian immigration) provided the basis for growth. Family categories offered many more visas (80 percent of all preference and 100 percent of immediate relative, nonquota visas were designated for family reunification) and less stringent visa requirements. A relationship as spouse, parent, child or sibling is all that was necessary. In the occupational categories, on the other hand, a certification from the Department of Labor was needed to show that no qualified American worker could fill the position an immigrant was offered. Today, 80 to 90 percent of the immigration from most Asian Pacific nations is in the family categories. But that was not always the case.

Filipinos, Asian Indians, and Koreans are the best examples of how the 1965 amendments were used to transform Asian immigration. In the late 1960s, about 45 percent of Filipino immigrants entered in the professional and 55 percent in the family unity categories. Within a few years, however, family networks developed that enabled naturalized citizens to take advantage of reunification categories. By 1976 Filipino immigration in the occupational categories dropped to about 21 percent. And by 1990, just over 8 percent came from the occupational categories compared to 88 percent in the family categories. About 64 percent of all Koreans entered in family categories in 1969 compared to over 90 percent by 1990. For Asian Indians, the figures were 27 percent in 1969 and about 90 percent in 1990. In the late 1960s and early 1970s, Koreans and Asian Indians also took advantage of the nonpreference investor category. About 12 percent of all Koreans and 27 percent of Asian Indians entered as investors at that time. Investor visas became unavailable in 1978.

Here are some examples of how many Asians eventually used the family categories under the 1965 amendments:

Under the 1965 reforms immigrants essentially were categorized as immediate relatives of U.S. citizens or under the preference system. As immediate relatives they were not subject to quotas or numerical limitations. The category included the spouses and minor, unmarried children of citizens, as well as the parents of adult citizens. The preference system included seven categories. First preference: adult, unmarried sons and daughters of citizens. Second preference: spouses and unmarried sons and daughters of lawful permanent resident aliens. Permanent residents (green card holders) could petition for relatives only through this category. Third preference: members of the professions or those with exceptional ability in the sciences or the arts. Proof from the Department of Labor that the immigrant would not be displacing an available worker was required for third and sixth preference. Fourth preference: married sons and daughters of citizens. Fifth preference: siblings of adult citizens. Sixth preference: skilled or unskilled workers, of which there was a shortage of employable and willing workers in the United States. Seventh preference: persons fleeing from a Communist-dominated country, a country of the Middle East, or who were uprooted by a natural catastrophe. Seventh preference was eliminated in 1980, but not until after about 14,000 Chinese from mainland China entered in the category.

Here are some examples of how the immigration system worked between 1965 and 1990:

■ A Korean woman who had married a U.S. serviceman (presumably a citizen) could immigrate in the immediate relative category, thereby becoming a lawful permanent resident of the United States. After three years of marriage, she could apply for naturalization and become a citizen. She could then petition for her parents under the immediate relative category, and also for siblings under the fifth preference. Once her parents immigrated, they, as lawful permanent residents, could petition for other unmarried sons and daughters under the second preference. Married siblings entering under the fifth preference could be accompanied by spouses and minor, unmarried children.

■ A doctor or engineer from India could immigrate under the third preference as a professional. He/she could be accompanied by a spouse and unmarried, minor children. After five years of permanent residence, the doctor/engineer could apply for naturalization, and upon obtaining citizenship could petition for parents under the immediate relative category, siblings under the fifth preference, and married sons and daughters under the fourth preference (who could also bring their spouses and minor, unmarried children). The same scenario is possible even if the first Indian immigrant in this family had entered as a nonpreference investor when such visas were available.

■ A nurse from the Philippines might be able to immigrate under the third preference. After qualifying for citizenship five years later, she could petition for her parents. Her parents could petition for other unmarried sons and daughters under the second preference or the nurse could petition for these siblings under the fifth preference. If the son or daughter married on a visit to the Philippines, that spouse could then be petitioned for under the second preference.

■ A Chinese American citizen might marry a foreign student from Taiwan. The student would then be able to become an immigrant under the immediate relative category. After three years of marriage to a citizen, naturalization opens immigration possibilities for parents under the immediate relative category and siblings under the fifth preference.

Gender ratios are affected by immigration as well. Today, more women than men immigrate from the Philippines, China, Korea, and Japan. For example, about 60 percent of Filipino and 55 percent of Korean immigrants in 1990 were women. This has contributed to census findings that the Chinese, Japanese, Filipino, and Korean American communities are predominantly female. The Asian Indian community has a very even gender ratio, in part because about the same number of men as women immigrate each year from India.

There is every reason to believe that many Asian women (particularly Koreans, Filipinos, and Japanese) immigrate because they perceive relatively progressive views on gender equality in the United States. This is interrelated to the fact that many women from Korea and the Philippines were able to qualify for employment categories as nurses and in other medical fields. Marriages between women and U.S. servicemen in these countries also contributed to a larger share of immigrant women.

The employment profile of various Asian Pacific communities also has its roots in immigration policy. The fifth of the preference visas that were set aside for employment categories under the 1965 amendments provided a window for many Asians to immigrate who did not have specific relatives in the United States. The proportion of professionals in every Asian Pacific community increased as a result. And even after more began using the family categories, the actual number of immigrants who identified themselves as professionals or managers remained high.

Some observers, who note fewer professionals among Chinese immigrants for example, contend that after the initial influx of professionals in the late 1960s and early 1970s, poorer, working-class Chinese began entering. But this is only part of the story. The proportion who enter in professional and occupational categories did decrease over time in part because a 1976 law required all professionals to first secure a job offer from an employer. The absolute number of professionals and executives, however, has increased. In 1969, for example, a total of 3,499 immigrated from mainland China, Taiwan and Hong Kong. In 1983 the total had jumped to 8,524. Thus, the smaller percentage merely reflects the increased use of family categories. The proportion of those who enter in professional and occupational categories from Taiwan is also much higher than for those from mainland China (28 percent to 5 percent in 1989). And though more than twice as many born in mainland China entered in 1989 (32,272 to 13,974), Taiwan had more occupational immigrants (3,842 to 1,599). Large numbers of professionals continue to enter from the Philippines, Korea, and India as well. Over 6,500 Indian immigrants who designate their prior occupation as professionals or managers enter annually.

Immigration policies influence residential preferences as well. Historical recruitment of Asian and Pacific immigrants to work in the fields, on the railroads, and in service industries in the West Coast established a residential pattern that has continued for some time. However, in recent years, more and more Asian immigrants are settling in other parts of the country. Since 1967, New York City has attracted more Chinese immigrants than San Francisco and Oakland combined, and more than 17 percent of Chinese Americans reside in New York State. Almost 23 percent of Korean Americans live in the Northeast, 19.2 percent in the South, and 13.7 percent in the Midwest. Thirty-five percent of Asian Indians live in the Northeast and about 24 percent in the

South. Asian Indians and Filipinos are the largest Asian American communities in New Jersey and Illinois. Relatedly, working class immigrants who are able to enter in the family categories have helped to sustain Chinatowns and develop residential enclaves among Koreans, Filipinos, and Asian Indians. Koreans have also established small business enclaves in places like New York, Chicago, Washington, D.C., and, of course, Los Angeles.

The 134.8 percent growth rate of Vietnamese Americans between 1980 and 1990 (261,729 to 614,547) makes them the fastest growing Asian Pacific group. The development of Southeast Asian communities in the United States is related more to refugee policies than to standard immigration admission criteria. Take its current size. Of the 18,000 who immigrated by 1974, many were the spouses of American businessmen and military personnel who had been stationed in Vietnam. But a dramatic upsurge in new arrivals began after 1975, with 125,000 admitted immediately after the troops pulled out of Southeast Asia. By 1980 more than 400,000 additional refugees were welcomed from Vietnam, Laos, and Cambodia, approximately 90 percent of whom were from Vietnam. Although the 1980 Refugee Act established new controls, the flow of refugees continued due to persistent humanitarian pressure on the United States. After a second, sizable wave entered in 1980, the flow of new entries declined steadily. In 1984, 40,604 Vietnamese refugees entered, then the average dropped to about 22,000 until 1988 when 17,626 were admitted. So by 1988, 540,700 Vietnamese refugees had arrived. By October 1991, 18,280 Amerasians (mostly from Vietnam) arrived along with another 44,071 relatives. Eventually as many as 80,000 to 100,000 Amerasians and their relatives may enter. As a result of these entrants, over 90 percent of the Vietnamese population is foreign born, the highest percentage of all Asian American groups.

Refugee policies also affect gender ratios. In 1980 there were 108.5 Vietnamese men per one hundred Vietnamese women, compared to 94.5 per one hundred in the general population. This ratio is not as skewed as those for initial waves of Filipinos and Chinese which were much more male-dominated. The refugee policy that enabled Vietnamese to enter after 1975 under unique circumstances contributed to greater balance. Rather than fleeing individually, those departing Vietnam have done their best to keep their families intact. Roughly 45 percent of recent arrivals are women.

Another policy was to resettle refugees across the country in order to lessen the economic and social impact on just a few areas, and to avoid ghettoization. Although many refugees moved after their initial placement, refugees have become widely dispersed. By 1990, over 54 percent of the Vietnamese resided in the West, but 27.4 percent were in the South, almost 10 percent in the Northeast, and 8.5 percent in the Midwest. More of them lived in the South and Midwest than Filipinos and Japanese.

The goal of preventing ethnic enclaves ignored the dynamics of Vietnamese culture and perhaps even basic psychology. The need for ethnically based social, cultural, and economic support among refugees was either seriously misjudged or coldly ignored. Although enclaves provided an historical means for the mainstream to keep an eye on Asian immigrants, those established by Chinese, Filipino, and Japanese immigrants played key roles in easing their adjustment to American society. The need for a stable support system may be even more crucial for Southeast Asians, whose experience has been profoundly unsettling. Politically persecuted, unexpectedly driven from their homes, their hopes dashed, these refugees not surprisingly turned to the past for sustenance.

In doing so they turned to each other, and despite numerous obstacles have been remarkably successful in developing their own communities. They have, for example, transformed San Francisco's red-light district near Union Square into a bustling hub of Vietnamese hotels, residences, and small businesses. Vietnamese Americans have likewise helped to develop a "booming" wholesale district out of Skid Row in Los Angeles and altered the downtown areas of San Jose and Santa Ana, California, as well as a section of the Washington, D.C., suburb of Arlington, Virginia.

Nationwide, 64 percent of all Southeast Asian households headed by refugees arriving after 1980 are on public assistance, three times the rate of African Americans and four times that of Latinos. Not surprisingly, groups such as the Vietnamese have been accused of developing a welfare mentality, and the government has responded in knee-jerk fashion. Their relatively low rate of labor-force participation has in fact led many Vietnamese refugees to depend on government assistance. But much of this dependency is due to a system that creates disincentives to work. Policy-makers have urged state and local resettlement agencies to expeditiously assist refugees with job placement. Under the 1980 Refugee Act, refugees were given 36-month stipends of special refugee cash, medical assistance programs, and other support services. But in 1982 amendments to the act reduced the stipends to 18 months to pressure refugees to become economically independent more quickly. These changes came with the entry of the poorer, less-educated, and more devastated second wave of refugees. After 1982, most programs stressed employment-enhancing services such as vocational, English-language, and job development training. Most refugees are unable to acquire the skills that would qualify them for anything other than minimum-wage jobs in 18 months. They were, nonetheless, constrained to take these positions in the absence of continued public assistance.

Restrictions on federal assistance thus help to account for increased Vietnamese American concentration in entry-level, minimum-wage jobs requiring little formal education or mastery of English. For many refugees, in fact, these types of jobs and the poverty that results are unavoidable. Indeed, figures show that in 1979, a striking 35.1 percent of Vietnamese families were living below the poverty level. And by 1985 the figure had risen to an astonishing 50 percent for all Southeast Asian refugees.

Amendments to the Law in 1990

After 1990 reforms, immigration visas are distributed under two preference systems, one for family reunification and the other for employment. The immediate relative category (spouses, unmarried children, and parents of adult citizens) continues to remain unlimited and outside of any of the numerically restricted preference systems. In the family preferences, first preference is for unmarried adult sons and daughters of citizens. Second preference is the only category under which lawful permanent residents of the United States can petition for relatives. There are two subcategories: (1) the 2A category for the spouses and children (unmarried and under 21), and (2) the 2B category for unmarried sons and daughters (age 21 and over). Third preference is reserved for the married sons and daughters of United States citizens. And fourth preference is for brothers and sisters of adult citizens. Only United States citizens, not lawful permanent residents or noncitizen nationals, can petition for married sons and daughters and for siblings.

The law now provides several categories for employment-based immigrant visas. First preference is for immigrants with extraordinary ability (such as in the sciences, arts, education, business or athletics), outstanding professors and researchers, and certain executives and managers of multinational companies. Second preference is for members of the professions holding advanced degrees or for those of exceptional ability. Third preference is for skilled workers, professionals, and other workers. Fourth preference is for special immigrants (except returning lawful permanent residents and former citizens). Fifth preference is a category for investors whose investments are to each create at least ten new jobs.

Persons who immigrate to the United States under the preference systems are subject to two types of numerical limitations: a worldwide numerical cap and a country or territorial limit.

At least 226,000 family preference category visas are available annually on a worldwide basis. While in theory the worldwide quota can be increased to a cap of 465,000 annually through 1994, and 480,000 thereafter, the level will not likely be much more than 226,000. This is because the family preference category level is determined by subtracting the number of immediate relative entrants—generally well over 200,000 annually—from the cap (465,000 or 480,000), with an absolute floor of 226,000. Assuming that 226,000 is the operative figure, this means that in a given year, a maximum of 226,000 persons can immigrate to the United States under the first, second, third, and fourth preferences. A separate worldwide numerical limitation of 140,000 is set aside for employment-based immigrants.

In addition to the worldwide numerical limitations, the law also provides an annual limitation of visas per country of 7 percent of the worldwide quotas. Thus, assuming a 226,000 worldwide family visa numerical limitation and 140,000 for employment visas, 7 percent of the total (366,000) is 25,620 for each country. But 75 percent of the visas issued for spouses and children of lawful permanent residents (family second preference "2A") are not counted against each country's quota.

Note that the visa of any immigrant born in a colony or other dependent area of a country is charged to that country. However, Hong Kong, which will become part of the People's Republic of China in 1997, is treated as a separate foreign state for purposes of its annual visa allotment (i.e., 25,620), except that through the end of fiscal year 1993 its annual quota is set at 10,000 preference visas.

Considerations for the Future

The confluence of social, political, and economic conditions in Asia and the Pacific region will continue to drive immigration to the United States for many more decades. And U.S. policies will continue to shape the profiles of Asian and Pacific communities here. As the prospects of immigration during the next several decades are appraised, these are the types of issues that have to be kept in mind:

■ *Impact of 1990 reforms.* Asian Pacific immigrants comprise almost half of all legal immigrants today, mostly entering in the family reunification categories. The 1990 reforms did not reduce the number of visas available to family immigrants. In fact it added some numbers for families and added large numbers for employment categories. Asian Pacific immigrants are likely to continue taking advantage of the family preference system. And as in the late 1960s and early 1970s, they will likely use the employment categories and new investor category to create further bases for future family migration. For example, interest in emigration remains high among Chinese professionals. Taiwan's politically volatile environment has contributed to the desire of the educated class to look for residential options elsewhere, and the stability of the United States and its longstanding anti-Communist philosophy appeals to them. Similarly, the impending return of Hong Kong to mainland China's jurisdiction in 1997 has provided a strong impetus for its elite to look to the United States. And the Tiananmen Square massacre in June 1989 significantly accelerated emigration from Hong Kong. But there are analogous sociopolitical considerations for Filipinos, Asian Indians, and Koreans. And Japanese have also demonstrated a slow but steady increase in immigration in recent years, particularly among women.

■ *Gender ratios.* The special interest in immigration that has been demonstrated by Korean, Filipino, Chinese, and Japanese women is likely to continue, especially because of the increase in employment-based visas and the perception of gender equality in the United States.

■ *Working-class immigrants.* A continued influx of working-class and service-class immigrants will also continue to enter in family preference categories. This will continue to impact not only the employment profile of communities, but also such things as the viability of residential enclaves—not only Chinatowns, but also Koreatowns, Little Manilas, and Asian Indian ghettos.

■ *Southeast Asians.* In spite of large numbers of refugees that continue to flee Southeast Asia and occupy refugee camps in Asia, the United States has gradually reduced the number of refugee slots to Southeast Asians since the Refugee Act of 1980. The admission of up to 35,000 refugees from Southeast Asia was allocated in 1990, and another 22,000 spots were reserved for relatives of refugees already in the United States under the Orderly Departure Program. But this is a far cry from the 525,000 that were admitted between 1975 and 1980. Following the pattern set by other Asian Americans, small but increasing numbers of Vietnamese are entering in family reunification categories. In order to take full advantage of these categories, U.S. citizenship is required, and most Vietnamese have been residents long enough to qualify. Some do so to demonstrate allegiance, others recognize that, as citizens, they may petition for more relatives. Though about 38 percent of the first wave of Vietnamese were naturalized by 1984, the rate for the second wave is significantly lower. In 1983 roughly 3,300 entered in the family categories, and by 1988 more than 4,000 had. These figures do not approach those of the other large Asian American communities for family category admissions (with the exception of the Japanese). Nonrefugee admission is likely to remain low because in the absence of normal diplomatic ties between the United States and Vietnam, Vietnamese nationals attempting to obtain exit permits face tremendous difficulties. After an immigration petition is filed by a resident on behalf of a relative in Vietnam, the Vietnamese government must approve it. In 1984 only 3,700 immigrants were allowed under the Orderly Departure Program. More than half a million cases are currently backlogged. As a result, sizable growth of the Vietnamese American community exclusively through existing nonrefugee categories is unlikely.

■ *Other Asians.* Aside from the larger Asian Pacific groups mentioned—Chinese, Filipinos, Japanese, Koreans, Vietnamese, and Asian Indians—as well as other groups alluded too, such as Laotians and Cambodians, other Asian Pacific countries send at least a few thousand immigrants to the United States each year. Annual admissions of Indonesians (3,500), Malaysians (1,800), Pakistanis (9,700), Thais (8,900), Tongans (1,400), and Samoans (700) contribute to growing communities that have become part of the Asian Pacific patchwork.

■ *Political backlash.* As always, immigration and refugee policies in the near and distant future will respond to economic and social pressures. The 1990 reforms put into place the concept of a ceiling on preference visas, which could be extended to the immediate relative category given strong xenophobia or nativism. While some might label as extreme the anti-immigrant of color sentiment of someone like presidential candidate Patrick Buchanan, are his views really that different from that of the mainstream's given the popularity of English-Only initiatives across the nation? We also kid ourselves if we think this sentiment is aimed solely at Latin immigration. Consider only the experiences of Chinese in Monterey Park and the widespread upsurge in anti-Asian violence. Public opinion polls reveal that the general population does not hold Asian Americans in very high esteem. In one national survey which ascertained attitudes towards 15 different ethnic groups, no European ethnic group received lower than 53 percent positive rating, and no Asian group received higher than a 47 positive rating. Conducted before recent Japan bashing, Japanese were considered to be the minority group that had contributed the most (47 percent), followed by African Americans, Chinese, Mexicans, Koreans, Vietnamese, Puerto Ricans, Haitians, and Cubans. In a separate poll that focused on refugees, only 21 percent believed that Southeast Asian refugees should be encouraged to move into their community. Nearly half believed that Southeast Asians should have settled in other Asian countries, and one-fourth believed that "America has too many Asians in its population." Other polls continue to show that much of the public regards Asians as sinister, suspicious, and foreign. Thus, the threat of a serious backlash against Asian Pacific Americans that could negatively impact immigration laws is always real.

Asian Pacific America has been shaped by immigration and refugee policies. The profiles of the communities we know today are reflective of the 1965 amendments and a variety of refugee policies. The reforms in 1990 in all likelihood will continue the opportunities of the past 27 years, particularly in family reunification categories, but also open new doors with the expansion of employment-based numbers and the renewed availability of an investors category. Only if anti-immigrant, or specifically anti-Asian, sentiment carries the day will the course set in 1965 be obstructed.

Notes

1. A much more detailed analysis of how immigration and refugee policies shape the demographic and social profiles of various Asian Pacific communities can be found in my book *Making and Remaking Asian America Through Immigration Policy* (Stanford: Stanford University Press, 1992).

Work Issues Facing
Asian Pacific Americans:

Labor Policy

Paul Ong

Associate Professor, UCLA Graduate School of
Architecture and Urban Planning

Suzanne J. Hee

UCLA Asian American Studies Center

Over the next three decades, the Asian Pacific American labor force will triple to nearly ten million. How well Asian Pacific Americans fare in the labor market will directly define the economic well-being of this population. Despite a high number of self-employed, the vast majority of Asian Pacific Americans make a living through wage and salary work.[1] This paper explores the factors that will determine outcomes in the 21st century.

The following analysis uses data from both the projections for 2020 and the Current Population Survey (CPS). The CPS is a national monthly survey of 57,000 to 59,500 households, and is used to collect information on labor market conditions, particularly the unemployment rate. The March survey, which produces the Annual Demographic Profile, contains extensive information on work experiences and earnings for the previous year. Since 1989, the CPS has included Asian Pacific Americans as a separate racial category. We pooled the survey for 1989, 1990, and 1991 to get a reasonable sample of Asian Pacific Americans.[2] Income data are adjusted to 1990 dollars, and the reported statistics on earnings and hourly wages are the weighted average for the three years (1988, 1989, and 1990). Statistics on the labor market status (e.g., labor force participation rates) are for the survey week.

Labor Force Projections

Based on the projections for 2020 and current information on labor force participation rates, we expect that the Asian Pacific American labor force[3] will increase from about 3.2 million in 1990 to 8.6 million to 10.2 million in 2020. The population projections are discussed elsewhere. Our labor force participation rates (LFPRs) are based on the patterns for 1989 and 1991. For those between 15 and 64, the male Asian Pacific American LFPR was 77 percent. This is below the 84 percent rate for male non-Hispanic Whites.[4] Differences in the age profile accounts for very little of the disparity. When we age-adjust, the participation rates are 78 percent for Asian Pacific American males and 84 percent for non-Hispanic white males.[5] The gap in LFPRs is due to a substantially lower rate for younger Asian Pacific American adults who are much more likely to be attending school. For females the unadjusted rates are 62 percent for Asian Pacific Americans and 68 percent for non-Hispanic Whites, and the respective age-adjusted rates are 60 percent and 69 percent. The gap between Asian Pacific American females and non-Hispanic white females is also due to diferrence among young adults.

We use two alternative sets of LFPRs to estimate the Asian Pacific American labor force in 2020.[6] The first, and more conservative, assumption is that the rates will remain constant over time. This produces a very low projection. It is more likely that the LFPRs for Asian Pacific American females will increase over time given that there has been a long-term secular increase in LFPRs among all females over the last several decades. The same changes in social norms and employment opportunities that will draw an increasing number of females into the labor force will also affect Asian Pacific American females. Moreover, acculturation of immigrant Asian Pacific American females will work in the same direction. Our second assumption is that by 2020, the LFPRs for Asian Pacific American males will remain constant, and that the Asian Pacific American females will close half of the LFPR gap with their male counterparts.

A low projection of Asian Pacific Americans is derived by combining our conservative assumption regarding labor force participation rates with the low population projection. The low population estimate places the population for Asian Pacific Americans ages 15 to 64 in the year 2020 at 12.4 million. Of that number, there will be approximately 8.6 million in the labor market in the year 2020. A high projection of the Asian Pacific American labor force uses our second assumption regarding labor force participation rates (increased female labor force participation rate) and the high population projection. For the high estimate, the Asian Pacific American population (ages 15 to 64) for the year 2020 is 13.8 million. Of these people, 10.2 million are estimated to be in the labor force in 2020. We believe that the most likely net increase in the Asian Pacific American labor force will be between six and seven million over the next three decades, approximately a tripling of the Asian Pacific American labor force. This projection is in line with the most recent Bureau of Labor Statistics (BLS) projections. The BLS numbers are for 2005 only. According to this series, the number of Asian/other workers increases by 3.1 million during the 15-year period between 1990 and 2005.[7] This is a little less than half the increase we calculated for the 30-year time period using the higher LFPRs and population projections.

TABLE 1. Asian Pacific American Labor Force

AGE	1990	2020 LOW	2020 HIGH	Lo Growth Rate	Hi Growth Rate
Males					
25-34	580,000	1,169,000	1,342,000	101 %	131 %
35-44	543,000	1,246,000	1,358,000	129 %	150 %
45-54	324,000	1,113,000	1,176,000	244 %	263 %
55-64	163,000	752,000	777,000	361 %	377 %
Total	1,610,000	4,280,000	4,653,000	166 %	189 %
Females					
25-34	387,000	922,000	1,203,000	138 %	211 %
35-44	400,000	980,000	1,222,000	145 %	206 %
45-54	234,000	842,000	1,041,000	260 %	345 %
55-64	136,000	532,000	694,000	291 %	410 %
Total	1,157,000	3,276,000	4,160,000	183 %	260 %

Table 1 provides a breakdown of the growth of the labor force by ten-year age groups and by gender. Although all age-gender groups will grow substantially, the highest growth rates are for the males and females between the ages of 55 and 64.

Over the next three decades, changes in the composition of the Asian Pacific American labor force by nativity will parallel the shift in the adult working-age Asian Pacific American (25 to 64) population. This population will still be dominated by immigrants, but the U.S.-born population will grow at a much faster rate. In 1990, 80 percent of the adult Asian Pacific Americans were foreign born, but by 2020, the percentage will drop. The low projection places the figure at 73 percent, the middle projection places the figure at 72 percent, and the high projection places the figure at 74 percent. In terms of growth rates, the U.S.-born adult population will grow approximately twice as fast as the foreign-born adult population.[8] There is another important distinction between the two groups: the U.S. born will be younger than the foreign born. The median age for foreign-born adults for the low projection is 45 years as compared to 35 years for U.S.-born Asian Pacific American adults. The respective number for the middle projection are 45 years and 35 years; and for the high projection, the numbers are 44 years and 34 years.

Educational Attainment

One of the most important indications of the quality of the Asian Pacific American labor force is educational attainment. One of the most interesting statistics is the relatively high proportion of the Asian Pacific American population with four or more years of higher education (see table 2). Compared to non-Hispanic white males, the education level for Asian Pacific American males between the ages of 25 to 64 is considerably greater. The percent of Asian Pacific American males with college attainment is 48 percent while that of non-Hispanic Whites is 29 percent. The educational attainment level for Asian Pacific American females is also greater than that of non-Hispanic white females: 38 percent and 23 percent, respectively. This high rate of attainment is the product of two factors. The first is that Asian Pacific Americans who are educated in the United States (both native born and immigrants who come here as children or students) tend to complete more years of education. For example, for those between 19 and 24 years old, 53 percent of Asian Pacific Americans attend school, while only 35 percent of non-Hispanic Whites do. The second factor is that modern immigration has been biased towards those with higher education, particularly those in the professional, scientific, medical, and engineering fields. This was initially the product of the occupational quotas set aside by the 1965 Immigration Act. Although new restrictions on occupation-based entry were put into place in the mid-1970s, the highly educated continued to be overrepresented. The few who entered through occupational quotas were joined by the highly educated who were sponsored by highly-educated relatives who had immigrated earlier.

Table 2. Educational Attainment by Ethnicity, Age, and Gender
Asian Pacific American and Non-Hispanic White Adults, 25-64

AGE	LT HS	HS	Some College	College
Non-Hispanic White Males Total	13 %	38 %	20 %	29 %
Asian Pacific American Males Total	13 %	24 %	15 %	48 %
Non-Hispanic White Females Total	13 %	44 %	21 %	23 %
Asian Pacific American Females Total	19 %	29 %	14 %	38 %

It is likely that Asian Pacific Americans will be an even more highly educated population in 2020. Asian Pacific American college enrollment will in all probability increase in the future, although not without greater competition and friction with the non-Hispanic white applicants for scarce positions in the top colleges and universities. Future immigration will also be biased towards those with a college education because the 1990 Immigration Act has renewed and expanded the preference given to those with higher education.

Despite the high percentage of Asian Pacific Americans with college educations, there continues to be a sizable population with very little formal education. The population of Asian Pacific Americans with less than a high school education is three percentage points higher than that of non-Hispanic Whites. The vast majority of this Asian Pacific American subpopulation tends to be immigrants.

Labor Market Barriers

Current labor market outcomes indicate that the full incorporation of Asian Pacific American workers into the U.S. economy will be hindered by two problems. One, although the Asian Pacific American labor force will be a very educated labor force, several barriers hinder Asian Pacific Americans from attaining concomitant wage and occupational status. Two, there is a sizable number of Asian Pacific Americans who are low-wage workers.

The income-to-education disparity can be seen in the statistics on hourly wages.[9] As indicated earlier, Asian Pacific Americans are more likely to be college educated. The average years of education for Asian Pacific American male workers is 14.1, and 13.9 years for female workers. The corresponding numbers for non-Hispanic Whites are 13.6 and 13.5, about a half year lower than the Asian Pacific American averages. Nonetheless, average hourly wages for Asian Pacific American males are $15.40, and $15.90 for non-Hispanic white males. The same pattern occurs in annual earnings: $31,500 for Asian Pacific American males and $34,000 for non-Hispanic white males. Interestingly, a comparison of wages and earnings for female workers reveals a disadvantage for Asian Pacific Americans based on gender rather than race. Asian Pacific American female workers make on the average $12.10 per hour and $22,000 per year, while non-Hispanic white females workers make on the average $11.10 per hour and $19,400 per year. Although there is a lack of racial disparity among females, Asian Pacific American and non-Hispanic white females are both disadvantaged compared to their male counterparts. Some of the disadvantages experienced by Asian Pacific American male and female workers can be attributed to discrimination in the form of a "glass ceiling," which is a barrier that keeps Asian Pacific Americans from obtaining higher management positions.[10] The glass ceiling means that Asian Pacific Americans can see these management positions within their reach, yet there is an obstacle that keeps them from obtaining them. This kind of barrier is of great concern in the community. Although many Asian Pacific Americans are qualified and competent for higher management positions, they are often stereotyped as not aggressive, inarticulate in the English language, and too technical to become managers.

The impact of the glass ceiling can be seen in the percentage of workers in the professional category versus those in the executive/management category. Because of the higher educational attainment, Asian Pacific American males are more likely to be in a professional occupation than non-Hispanic white males—23 percent versus 14 percent.[11] This is roughly a three-to-two ratio in favor of Asian Pacific American males. However, Asian Pacific American males lag behind in the executive and management positions—14 percent versus 17 percent for non-Hispanic white males. In other words, non-Hispanic white males enjoy a three-to-two advantage. Clearly, many Asian Pacific American males are able to move into the professional category, but enjoy considerably less success in moving above that level. Asian Pacific American females also suffer from a similar problem. Although 17 percent are professional, only 12 percent are executives or managers.

The second main problem experienced by Asian Pacific American workers is that many are trapped in low-wage work. Among Asian Pacific American males, 12 percent make less that $6.00 per hour and 20 percent earn less than $15,000 per year. The corresponding statistics for non-Hispanic white males are 9 percent and 14 percent. Among Asian Pacific American females, 21 percent fall into the low hourly wage category and 39 percent fall into the low annual earnings. For non-Hispanic white female workers, 22 percent are in the low hourly wage category and 41 percent earn under $15,000 per year.

Most of the Asian Pacific American low-wage workers are immigrants with little formal education, limited English language ability, and skills that are not transferable to the U.S. labor market. Many end up in the ethnic subeconomy, which is heavily concentrated in the low-skill service sector. Consequently, it is not surprising that Asian Pacific American males are overrepresented in the occupational category that includes food service—12 percent versus 4 percent for non-Hispanic white males. For Asian Pacific American females, the figure is 14 percent and for non-Hispanic white females the figure is 12 percent.

Contribution to the U.S. Economy

Despite the barriers mentioned above, the rapidly expanding Asian Pacific American labor force will contribute to the U.S. economy in two ways: (1) by providing workers at a time when the growth in the total labor supply is slowing, and (2) by providing desperately needed skills. The Bureau of Labor Statistics projects that over the next decade and a half the growth rate in the GNP (gross national product) will slow in a large part because the population growth will slow.[12] In this larger context, the growth of the Asian Pacific American labor force emerges as a disproportionately larger share of the future net increase in the total labor supply. According to the BLS projections for the 1990-2005 periods, Asians will make up about 12 percent of the net increase in the total labor force.[13] Since our projections are in line with those by the BLS, we expect that Asian Pacific Americans will continue to contribute disproportionately to the growth of the labor force during the 2005-2020 time period. Without this contribution, the U.S. economy would experience an even greater slowdown in the GNP growth.

Asian Pacific Americans will also contribute to the U.S. economy by supplying a large share of the badly needed high-skilled labor. One way to maintain the economic growth, particularly in per capita terms, in the face of a slowing in the growth of the labor supply is to increase the productivity of workers. Moreover, increasing international competition will also place pressure on the United States to increase labor productivity. In this context, post-secondary education and training become critical factors in stimulating growth and increasing our competitiveness in the global economy.[14] It is projected that the professional and technical occupations will experience the greatest demand and growth over the next decade and a half.[15] However, it is not likely that the U.S. will face a problem in filling the higher skilled positions given the current crisis in our educational system. Not only are our public schools failing to provide a meaningful education to our children, particularly inner-city, minority youths, but our colleges and universities are experiencing difficulties in attracting students into the scientific and engineering fields.

Given the educational patterns discussed earlier, there is no question that Asian Pacific Americans will play a central role in providing much of the needed highly educated labor. Even today, Asian Pacific Americans make up a disproportionate share of the highly-skilled labor in our high-technology industries whose vitality is crucial to the United States economy. Asian Pacific Americans will increase their contributions in these fields over the next three decades.

International Dimensions

The very same competitive forces that increase the contribution of Asian Pacific American workers to the U.S. economy will unfortunately generate social tensions. The international movement of Asians, particularly the highly educated, will reemerge as an international dispute. This is not an entirely new issue. In the late 1960s and early 1970s when the United States attracted large numbers of college university graduates from the Third World, developing countries accused this nation of "Brain Drain," the systematic siphoning of the most talented workers, while at the same time perpetuating underdevelopment. This particular debate waned, in large part, because Third World nations were unable to absorb the growing number of highly educated people. The accusations were based more on national pride than on economic reality. Today, however, many of these countries, particularly in the Far East, are at a stage of development where they can absorb and greatly benefit from a highly-skilled, technical labor force. The loss of those with college and university training has real economic effects. Consequently, the charges of "Brain Drain" will be resurrected by nations pursuing development that is dependent on high technology.

The "new" debate is not likely to be one-sided. Within the United States, there is a growing concern that Asian countries are too successful in re-attracting highly-educated labor.[16] The fear is not the loss of individual workers, but rather that returning Asians accelerate the transfer of advanced technologies, which ultimately undermines this country's competitive edge. This concern is not without foundation. Unlike early decades when a vast majority of foreign students remained in the U.S. after graduating, an increasing number of them are choosing to return. Moreover, there are some notable individuals with years of work experience in the United States who have relocated to Asia to help develop new industries. The potential payoff of this reverse migration is so great that Asian countries have implemented recruitment programs in the U.S.

Several factors contribute to the reverse migration. The newly industrialized economies now have the resources to pay globally competitive salaries, and have the scientific and technical infrastructure that allows the highly educated to continue their career. At the same time, there is a sense that the United States is not the land of the unlimited opportunity. Certainly the existence of the glass ceiling is causing some Asian Pacific Americans to reconsider the pursuit of their career goals in the U.S. These factors are likely to become more prominent in the future, thus generating greater incentives for highly-educated workers to remigrate.

In reality, reverse migration plays a small role in the transfer of technology. Other factors such as overseas investment, joint international ventures, and global licensing agreements play much larger roles. Even with the growth of reverse migration, immigration to the United States will greatly outnumber emigration by several folds. The U.S. will continue to be a net gainer in the international movement of people. Despite this, the fear of the loss of technology will add to the anti-Asian hostilities.

Policy Options

Although the size and characteristics of the Asian Pacific American labor force in 2020 will be determined by factors beyond the scope of this paper (demographic and economic forces, and immigration laws and policies), there are nevertheless three crucial policy issues within the labor market arena: (1) anti-discrimination laws, (2) anti-poverty programs, and (3) international trade and linkage. Eliminating the discrimatory barriers described earlier means battling unfair practices that limit employment and promotional opportunities for Asian Pacific workers. The problems facing Asian Pacific Americans are forcing a redefinition of Civil Rights because the types of discrimination encountered by Asian Pacific Americans are not merely racial, but cultural and language-based as well. We need policies that, along with providing equal opportunity, combat Asian Pacific American poverty by helping workers escape low-wage work. In Los Angeles, for example, the Asian Pacific American poverty rate is two times as high as the non-Hispanic white poverty rate,[17] and low-wage work contributes to this disparity. One of the most effective strategies to overcome this problem is to provide skills and

English-language training to adult immigrants. The domestic problems are great, but our policy concerns should also address international issues. There is no question that over the next three decades, the global economy will become more integrated. We should have policies that enable Asian Pacific Americans to play a constructive role in promoting this integration along a non-conflictual path.

Notes

1. Fourteen percent were self-employed or unpaid family members. The remaining 86 percent worked either in the private or governmental sector.

2. For example, the sample used to calculate wages includes 2,135 Asian Pacific American males and 1,980 females. The actual number of unique individuals is about two-thirds of the sample size because the CPS retains a proportion of the March sample over a two-year period.

3. The labor force is defined as the sum of those with a job and those actively seeking employment.

4. We use non-Hispanic Whites rather than Whites as our own comparison group. A significant number of Latinos are classified as Whites, and since they have work experiences that are very different than the work experiences of non-Hispanic Whites, statistics for all Whites tends to be different than for just non-Hispanic Whites.

5. We use the age distribution by five-year grouping for the total population to adjust the labor force participation rate.

6. The rates are estimates for ten five-year groups (e.g., 15 to 19, 20 to 24, etc.).

7. Howard Fullerton, "Labor Force Projections: The Baby Boom Moves On," *Monthly Labor Review* (November 1991), 33.

8. The respective rates are 266 percent and 135 percent according to the low projection; 267 percent and 127 percent according to the middle projection; and 281 percent and 161 percent according to the high projection.

9. The statistics for wages are calculated for those who worked at least 100 hours in the previous year, and were between the ages of 25 and 64.

10. See United States Commission on Civil Rights, *Civil Rights Issues Facing Asian Americans in the 1990s*, Washington, D.C., February 1992, 131–135.

11. These figures are calculated for wage and salary workers, and exclude the self-employed.

12. Norman Sanders, "The U.S. Economy into the 21st Century," *Monthly Labor Review* (November 1991), 13–30.

13. Fullerton, "Labor Force Projections," 36.

14. Ronald Kutscher, "New BLS Project Wins: Findings and Implications," *Monthly Labor Review* (November 1991), 10.

15. George Silvestric and John Lukasiewicz, "Occupational Employment Projections," *Monthly Labor Review* (November 1991), 65.

16. Paul Ong, Lucie Cheng, and Leslie Evans, "The Migration of Highly Educated Asians," *International Educator* (Fall 1991), 26–29.

17. Paul Ong and Evelyn Blumenberg, "Racial and Ethnic Inequality in Los Angeles: Two Decades of Neglect," unpublished report, UCLA Graduate School of Architecture and Urban Planning, 1992.

Legal and Civil Rights Issues in 2020:
Civil Rights Policy

William R. Tamayo

MANAGING ATTORNEY
ASIAN LAW CAUCUS
SAN FRANCISCO, CALIFORNIA

An examination or projection as to the legal and civil rights issues that will likely exist as a result of the increase in the Asian Pacific American population requires, at the outset, a premise for the assertion that the social category will be relevant in the year 2020.

Furthermore, this analysis rests on an assumption that our collective goal as defenders of civil rights is to ensure that the experiment of democracy known as the United States can live up to the ideals it professes to uphold: equality, full opportunity, inclusion, democratic rights, and respect for civil rights.

This analysis as presented rests on the following premises and assumptions about life in 2020:

1. Racism against nonwhites will still be an integral component of the United States economy and cultural life both institutionally and socially;

2. While legal forms of blatant racism will likely remain unlawful, a national consensus for a coherent or uniform remedy for the social impact of centuries of systemic racism will still be lacking;

3. "Asian Pacific American," as a category created by and asserted in response to racism, will still be relevant both as

a political vehicle and as a category to measure the impact of inequality; and

4. Immigration from Asia will likely be from the "developing" Asian countries, e.g., Philippines, India, China, Korea, many of which still are undergoing massive upheavals around issues of civil liberties, democracy, labor rights, and freedom of movement.

Initial demographic projections assert that the Asian Pacific American population in the year 2020 will be 18–20 million, representing a near tripling of the 1990 population. Immigration from Asia will be a major source of this growth. Thus, the majority of the community will likely be foreign born, and a significant portion non-citizens. This "foreign-born" characteristic combined with a relatively small voting bloc will still leave Asian Pacific Americans in a weak political position to make civil rights gains or to implement civil rights agendas on a national scale, but may be able to impact or sway local elections and activities.

The State of the World in 2020

Without a doubt, a projection of legal and civil rights issues must consider the state of the world in 2020—its economic health, its environmental health, whether peace or wars dominate the political landscape, and whether massive migration of labor (especially from Asia) to countries of real and perceived opportunities will continue.[1] Should political and economic instability and upheavals continue in the sending countries and other Asian nations, it can be expected that immigration—legally and illegally—from Asia will continue. As of January 1992, over 1.5 million persons from Asian countries (representing 53.2 percent of the worldwide list) were on visa waiting lists, with the Philippines (472,714) leading all countries worldwide.[2] (The top seven sending countries are all Asian nations except for Mexico, which ranks second in the numbers of its citizens registered for visas.)[3] This number does not even begin to include the numbers of relatives who will migrate as "immediate relatives"[4] of United States residents, a number which could, at least for some countries, represent twice as much as those on the preference waiting list.[5]

Some countries worth close observation for students of demography and migration include Burma, Thailand, Pakistan and Indonesia. As more and more movements for democracy demand changes but are met with resistance (in the form of violence and repression) from existing governments, and as economies in Asia fail to meet the basic needs of the vast majority of the population, there will be steady streams of migration from these countries.

At the same time, attempts to develop East Asia into a major "economic union," similar to the European Economic Community, could and are alleged to lead to greater prosperity throughout the region. Consequently, this could conceivably reduce the need for workers to migrate from Asia to the United States, and affect immigration projections.[6]

On the other hand, the state of the U.S. economy and its ability to "absorb" newer immigrants will pose issues. That is, other "Western" or capitalist countries could be the recipient of the new migrations of Asian labor. As evidenced by migrations in the late 1980s and early 1990s, Asian workers are also migrating to England, Western Europe, Middle East, Australia, and Canada.

Not surprisingly, however, this massive migration of Asians and others has precipitated a resurgence and growth of anti-immigrant and racist movements represented in spontaneous outbursts and uprisings of white youths to organized and well-financed electoral movements, e.g., "Le Pen" in France and anti-immigrant movements in Germany in 1992. Reminiscent of anti-immigrant movements that dotted the history of the United States[7] and that were forerunners to fascist and neo-fascist movements in Western Europe in the 20th century, these movements have, unfortunately, gained wider acceptance among white Americans and Europeans. Institutional support through government and private parties has similarly created a more fearful climate and pressed civil rights advocates.

Nevertheless, it is likely that given the projections for the Asian Pacific American population in 2020, any analysis on the civil and legal rights issue of that year will be impacted by perceptions both in fact and fiction, that there will be even more persons of Asian descent migrating to the United States. The fear of more "yellow and brown hordes" being absorbed into an unstable and declining economy will have great social implications.

The State of the U.S. Economy and Social Relations

The national state of social relations, particularly around such a fundamental issue as racism, will greatly determine the civil rights agenda of Asian Pacific Americans. The social issues, however, are inextricably intertwined with the health of the U.S. economy and with the willingness of leaders to put forth and to finance a progressive social rights agenda. Unfortunately, the experiences of 1992 and the 12 previous years when national leadership "planned" social policy based on "racial polarization" rather than "racial inclusiveness and unity" do not give ground for optimism. This catering to a "white, native-born consensus" based on some notion of preserving a perceived birthright has been at the cornerstone of social policies negatively affecting civil rights, immigration policy, and labor policy. The disturbing rise of explicitly racist and pro-violence organizations, the rise of similarly inclined politicians (and the frightening followers), and the failure of national leadership to quell this growth lays fundamental problems for all racial minorities including Asian Pacific Americans. Aside from catering to traditions of racism, these proponents have also taken on the bashing of immigrants (read: nonwhite immigrants) as part of their crusade. Proposed measures from militarizing the U.S.-Mexico border, to increased immigration raids in Asian and Latino communities, to outright denials of labor protections to immigrants have been part of these proponents' arsenal.

If the United States economy is relatively healthy in 2020, then racial relations should be improved.[8] However, increased economic instability combined with racist and nativist appeals by national figures will lead to continued divisiveness and set the stage for increasing legal and civil rights issues for Asian Pacific Americans and other nonwhite communities.

Simultaneously, the relationships of our community to its allies in the broader civil rights community will determine the agenda. Given the near tripling of our population by 2020, the concerns of the community will have to be part of a broader national civil rights agenda. *That agenda will have to take on an internationalist perspective based on full civil and democratic rights for all regardless of race, national origin, and immigration status if it is to adequately address the civil rights concerns of largely immigrant, nonwhite communities.* In addition, it will be incumbent on civil rights leadership to build viable and operational multiracial and multicultural coalitions with matching agendas.

Inherent to forging the relations of the civil rights coalition is a grappling with a lingering issue of whether Asian Pacific Americans will "be used" by Whites against other minority groups, and whether other minority groups, i.e., Blacks and Latinos, will view Asian Pacific Americans (or some ethnic groups) as indistinguishable from a political and economic view from Whites (who will presumably still direct most major corporations and be the majority of elected officials in 2020). Professor Mari Matsuda warned that Asian Pacific Americans had better understand the fundamental characteristics that tie people of color within the social dynamics of U.S. society lest they be used as buffers between Whites and other communities of color.[9] Inherent in that relation, however, is an incumbent duty for Asian Pacific Americans to stand with their brothers and sisters of color in addressing all issues of racism together in both time and place.

Legal Issues for Asian Pacific Americans

Asian Pacific Americans as workers, women, gays and lesbians, consumers, immigrants, non-citizens, and general members of U.S. society will be loaded with a myriad of legal problems. Following, however, are particular legal issues which will likely emanate from the discrimination based on race, national origin, class, sex, and immigration status—categories of discrimination that are impacted by the existence of an Asian Pacific American category.

LABOR RIGHTS

Overwhelmingly, Asian Pacific Americans are working class, non-professional people (despite perceptions by the public and representations by the media). Recent immigrants and even those with residency over ten years overwhelmingly dominate the light manufacturing and service sectors and lower-paying positions in the medical and clerical industries.[10] The vast majority, similar to most Americans, are not represented by unions, and are not aware of their rights as workers. Thus, abuse of these workers from harassment, non-payment of overtime salaries, undercutting wages, and harsh working conditions in violation of labor laws, will likely continue. The attempts of certain industries to curb labor-law protections in the 1980s (often with Administration backing) serve as a harbinger of the types of labor battles that Asian workers will face in 2020. As international and domestic competition among industries heightens, it can be expected that various "cost-saving" measures will be utilized. The prospects for organized labor to rebound from its losses in the 1980s and 1990s and to be more inclusive of Asian Pacific American workers and their needs will also impact the landscape within which labor rights will be asserted.

Special attention will need to be given to the fact that the majority of Asian immigrants will be *women*. Aside from issues arising in other arenas, e.g., domestic violence, the fact that many of the immigrant workers will be women will also give rise to increasing attention to issues of sexual harassment, sex discrimination in employment, and employment of women in traditionally low-paid jobs, e.g., garment and service. The necessary components to setting the agenda for combatting this discrimination will, in part, have to be the empowerment of women of color within national women's organizations and unions and the effort of those organizations to be as aggressively inclusive as the times demand.

Furthermore, with its poverty rate being twice that of Whites, and with 50 percent of Southeast Asians living in poverty,[11] the community will have to grapple with the consequences of having a generation or two of our community virtually locked out of mainstream life. Poor educational performances, limited employment opportunities, and an increasing trend for youth to turn toward anti-social behavior as an economic necessity, will likely mark the life of refugees and their children.

THE GLASS CEILING AND APPROACHES TO AFFIRMATIVE ACTION

While the issue of the "glass ceiling," i.e., lack of promotion of racial minorities to management positions, and related issues of affirmative action have been on the agenda for the last few years, there is a strong likelihood that they will remain as issues three decades from now. The nearly three decades since the passage of Title VII of the Civil Rights Act of 1964 have clearly shown a glaring disparity between Congress' professed intent to eradicate discrimination and the harsh and stark reality created by decades of inequality. For while some minorities have been promoted to positions in management, management in corporations does not even begin to mirror the demographic profile of the working community. Hopefully, the Civil Rights Act of 1991 will have created a more favorable legal climate within which programs for aggressive affirmative action will find their way to general acceptance. However, if there is a continued polarization, and in view of the fact that the existing Supreme Court has conservative members who will likely be serving on the court for two or three more decades, the prospects for favorable anti-discrimination legal precedents appears dim. Thus, the Asian Pacific American legal and civil rights community will need to develop more creative approaches—both legally and legislatively.

On another front, Asian Pacific Americans will have to articulate a clearer approach to affirmative action and will have to answer some hard questions regarding the collective applicability of affirmative action to a community which has distinct ethnic communities with varied histories in the United States. Some of the questions include: Will recent immigrants be able to claim that they inherit the impact of decades of discrimination against other Asian groups and thus are entitled to affirmative action remedies? When there is underrepresentation of some Asian Pacific Americans, e.g., Filipino Americans, in certain jobs or college admission slots, but not of other groups, e.g., Japanese Americans, is this a cause for complaint? Will the relatively more affluent position of Asian Americans relative to other minority groups, i.e., Blacks and Latinos, render the claims for affirmative action less meaningful, particularly since the bulk of Asians migrated in more recent years when laws against discrimination have already been passed?

IMMIGRANT RIGHTS

Given the overwhelming immigrant character of our community and the expected increase past the year 2020, expanding and protecting the rights of immigrants—documented and undocumented—to be free from discriminatory treatment will fill the civil rights agenda. The onslaught upon the rights of immigrants will likely come in these forms, as our history shows:

- attempts to curb Asian and other immigration through legislation aimed at decreasing family unity;[12]

- further restrictions on the due process rights of immigrants in court and administrative proceedings so as to expedite deportation;

- legal and quasi-legal restrictions on the rights of immigrants (both documented and undocumented) to public benefits and social services (assuming both will still exist in 2020);

- increased use of force in restricting immigration and enforcing immigration laws;

- the building of more immigration detention centers in order to incarcerate immigrants and deprive them of access to legal representation and social services;

- the growth of xenophobic movements expressed through violence, legislation, media, etc.;

- curbs on the numbers of refugees admitted from war-torn, politically unstable, or economically devastated countries.

Defenders of immigrants rights in our community will be forced to strengthen with even greater fervor the internationalist, humanitarian, and pro-civil rights moorings upon which to analyze and critique the above expressions of anti-immigrant sentiments.[13] Furthermore, the issues will require an astute and thorough understanding of the political economy of the sending nations that prompts this massive migration. The political instability of the sending nations will have to be addressed as we attempt to seek refugee protections or "safe haven" status for those fleeing persecution from those countries.

Inherent to this responsibility will be the task of working more closely with other immigrant communities that will similarly be impacted by U.S. foreign policy considerations, political upheaval in sending countries, and the response of the U.S. government. The commonalities for seeking a more unified agenda to address these civil rights concerns will be more vivid.

One major issue that appears likely for addressing will be the increasing demands of certain U.S. industries for already-trained skilled workers from abroad rather than investing in the existing workforce through job training and better education. While some in our community will view this avenue for migration as a positive opening to increase immigration, it raises substantial public policy questions, and asks the Asian Pacific American community where it stands on the issue of protecting and improving the domestic workforce through corporate and governmental investment. Asian Pacific American leaders will have to demand, as will other communities, especially those communities of color hardest hit by the callous indifference to improving the education and job skills of U.S. workers, that government and business look first to retraining the domestic labor force before seeking skilled labor from abroad. Simultaneously, however, knowing well that much of that skilled immigrant labor will enter into the social dynamics of U.S. racism and xenophobia, and employment discrimination or abuse, we will have to defend their rights as immigrants and workers.

LANGUAGE RIGHTS

Short of English becoming the universal language of the world (God forbid!), our community will be filled with "language minorities," i.e., non- or limited-English-speaking communities. The issue becomes more complex since our community shares no common language, but instead is a polyglot of languages and dialects, each with a distinct historical development. Nevertheless, lack of access to services, lack of access to the ballot, and discrimination in employment because of being a language minority will likely be issues in 2020. The successful effort to have the bilingual voting materials provisions of the Voting Rights Act reauthorized in 1992 (to be valid until 2007) will hopefully create more favorable conditions for their maintenance and expansion in 2020.

"English-Only" rules in the workplace,[14] or terminations from or denials of employment based on accent discrimination will likely continue in view of the increasing and constant immigration from Asian countries. It could be expected that there will be legislative, referendum, or initiative measures that will be introduced to make English the "official language" of the United States or of various states in order to present some alleged "uniformity" in communication which will supposedly improve relations. Asian Pacific American civil rights advocates will have to respond to these thinly guised racist and exclusionary attempts to further disempower and disenfranchise language minority communities. Again, it will be incumbent for Asian Pacific Americans to be active players in insuring that the broader civil rights community places the defense of language minorities on its agenda of action.

Hate Violence

Disturbingly and unfortunately, hate violence will likely be an issue in 2020 unless there is a major turnaround in the approach to social problems. The increasing polarization of the country around race, compounded by the fierce international competition in business and by decreasing economic and employment opportunities, have laid the seeds for increasing hate crimes and violence. Asian Pacific American advocates will continue to press states to enact laws allowing the prosecution of acts of violence as "hate crimes" (which enhance the sentences), and to press local prosecutors and state attorneys general to bring cases against the perpetrators.

On a national scale, these advocates will have to pierce and thoroughly discredit the "racialized patriotism" which serves as the cornerstone or rationale for a perceived duty to bash persons of Asian descent whether they be foreign-born or eighth-generation Americans. This daunting task will also require demands for quick and responsive action from federal officials and from United States and Asian corporate officials to denounce acts of anti-Asian violence.

Voting Rights

Asian Pacific Americans on a national scale actively participated in the redistricting process for the first time in 1991-92. While not all proposed plans were adopted, Asian Pacific Americans served notice on legislatures and city councils that we were stepping forward to defend our rights under the Voting Rights Act, and placed into the public record the historical discrimination suffered by Asian Pacific Americans in voting. While Asians in 1992 were 10 percent of the California population, there had been no Asians in the state legislature for 11 years. Asians were 3 percent of the national population, but less than 1 percent of the House of Representatives. In 2020, with an expected Asian Pacific American national population of 5-6 percent, and a California population of 15-20 percent, ensuring adequate representation at all electoral levels will be a major civil rights concern. Challenges to at-large election schemes which have historically served to exclude minorities from city councils, boards of supervisors, and school boards, will be needed.

Is There Power in Numbers?

Although Asians will number 20 million in 2020, we will likely still represent only 5-6 percent of the national population. In some states, e.g., California, we could likely be 15-20 percent of the population. Adding to this factor are projections that there will be no racial group that constitutes a majority. Perhaps Washington, D.C., will finally give some favorable attention to this population. However, articulating a civil rights agenda for Asian Pacific Americans will necessitate a conscious summation of the collective experiences garnered as a distinctly created racial group. Our community of 2020 will have a qualitatively different proportionate ethnic make-up than that in 1992 as the waves of immigrants from various Asian nations make their way to these shores. Our collective American experience in the number of years may be limited, but factors such as racial violence and anti-immigrant hostilities will intensify that experience. Civil rights advocates will have to harness the lessons of the past, and present the commonalities that mandate working under a common civil rights agenda.

Like other communities of color, and like the rest of the general U.S. population, our community hopes that 2020 will not be a year when the issues of racial polarization, xenophobia, and discrimination dominate the social relations of our country. The ideal that we call "United States democracy" has yet to be fully realized for the vast majority, but especially for those communities legally and socially marginalized because of their immigration status, race or national origin. Unfortunately, the years of professed belief from the federal government and from the national social agenda of the late 1960s in "full equality" and "full remedies" to address centuries of societal discrimination are still, when placed against the backdrop of United States history, an aberration and an exception to the rule. The escalation of racism throughout the 1980s and 1990s serves as a painful reminder that our work to build a nation committed to full rights and opportunity remains.

At the same time, years of common experience have provided valuable insights and produced new coalitions in the civil rights arena. It will be incumbent upon advocates for civil rights to extrapolate the lessons from history in order to articulate a more relevant and more effective agenda.

Notes

1. "Figures are far from precise—partly because of poor monitoring, partly because of illegal immigration—but 4 million to 5 million workers from South and east Asia probably work abroad." "Asia Supplies the World with Workers," *The Economist*, reprinted in *San Francisco Chronicle* (September 21, 1988).

2. U.S. Department of State, *Visa Bulletin* 7:9A (1992).

3. *Ibid.* As of January 1992, following the Philippines, the next six countries have the following registered: Mexico (466,684), India (254,049), China, mainland-born (181,143), China, Taiwan-born (122,284), Korea (118,949), and Vietnam (109,276).

4. "Immediate relatives" are defined as parents, spouses, and unmarried minor children under 21, and are exempt from the preference waiting lists.

5. For example, approximately 40,000 Filipinos (twice the number allowed under the preference system) entered as immediate relatives of U.S. citizens annually for the past three years.

6. Workers from the Philippines, Korea, Pakistan, India, Bangladesh, and Thailand already migrate all over the world. In 1985 approximately 460,000 Filipinos, 200,000 Koreans, 230,000 Pakistanis, 160,000 Indians, 80,000 Bangladeshis, and 70,000 Thais worked abroad. The United States is but one of dozens of countries to which they migrate for employment. See "Asia Supplies the World with Workers."

7. For a review of anti-Asian immigration laws and policies, see William R. Tamayo, "Asian Americans and Present U.S. Immigration Policies: A Legacy of Asian Exclusion," in *Asian Americans and the Supreme Court*, edited by Hyung-Chan Kim (Westport, Connecticut: Greenwood Press, 1992), 1105–1130.

8. It's no accident that the Civil Rights Act of 1964, the Voting Rights Act of 1965, and the Immigration Act of 1965 were enacted during a period when the U.S. economy was generally healthy, and the unemployment rate was relatively low. Many believe that the Immigration Act of 1965 was designed to increase immigration from Asian and Latin American countries. However, its proponents perceived it as a measure to increase European immigration, and assumed that Asian immigration under the act would be minimal. See Tamayo, "Asian Americans and Present U.S. Immigration Policies."

9. Mari Matusda, "We Will Not Be Used," *Asian Law Caucus Reporter* (Spring 1990).

10. The impact of the proposed North American Free Trade Agreement (Canada, United States, and Mexico) and other measures on the export of light manufacturing jobs, e.g., electornics and garment, will also have to be taken into consideration.

11. W. O'Hare and J. Felt, "Asian Americans: Fastest Growing Minority Group," Population Reference Bureau, February 1991.

12. Section 141 of the Immigration Act of 1990 provides for the establishment of a nine-member Commission on Legal Immigration Reform to review and evaluate the impact of the 1990 Act. Its first report is due on September 30, 1994, and its final annual report, including findings and recommendations with respect to legal immigration, is due September 30, 1997. Particular issues that the Commission will address include:

a. Family reunification-based immigration;

b. The impact of immigration and the implementation of the employment-based and diversity programs on labor needs, employment, and other economic and domestic conditions in the United States;

c. The social, demographic, and natural resources impact of immigration;

d. The impact of immigration on the foreign policy and national security interests of the United States;

e. The impact of per-country immigration levels on family-sponsored immigration;

f. The impact of the numerical limitation on the adjustment of status of aliens granted asylum;

g. The impact of the numerical limitations on the admission of non-immigrants under Section 214 (g) of the Immigration and Nationality Act (H categories);

h. The impact of the diversity program including the characteristics of the individuals admitted and how such characteristics compare to the characteristics of family-sponsored immigrants and employment-based immigrants.

The nine members appointed are:

Lawrence Fuchs, Ph.D., former Executive Director of the Select Commission on Immigration & Refugee Policy (which eventually led to the passage of IRCA 1986); Professor, Brandeis University

Cardinal Bernard Law, Boston, Massachusetts

Harold Ezell, former INS Western Regional Commissioner (1981–89), former executive for Der Wienerschnitzel

Nelson Merced, member, Massachusetts legislature

Richard Estrada, the Federation for American Immigration Reform (FAIR)

Robert Hill, lawyer, Graham & James

Bruce Morrison, former member of Congress from Connecticut, former chair of House Subcommittee on Immigration, Refugees and International Law, co-author of 1990 Act

Warren Leiden, Executive Director, American Immigration Lawyers Association

Legislation is pending in the 1992 Congress to expand the Commission to 13 members (S. 3090). Thus far, no Asian Pacific Americans have been appointed.

13. For an elaboration of various immigrant rights concerns for the Asian American community, see William R. Tamayo, "Broadening the Asian Interests in United States Immigration Policy," *Asian American Policy Review*, Harvard University (Spring 1991).

14. "English-Only" rules have been implemented in the medical industry which is overwhelmingly dependent on nurses and nursing assistants from the Philippines.

The Case of the
Southeast Asian Refugees:
Policy for a
Community "At-Risk"

Ngoan Le

*DEPUTY ADMINISTRATOR, DIVISION OF PLANNING
AND COMMUNITY SERVICES
ILLINOIS STATE DEPARTMENT OF PUBLIC AID

The popular stereotype of Asian Americans is one of a self-sufficient community whose average income is higher than that of other racial groups in the United States. This image often obscures the fact that a significant number of Asian Americans live below the poverty level.

The majority of Asian Americans living below poverty are Southeast Asian refugees. The term "Southeast Asian refugee" refers to persons originally from Cambodia, Laos and Vietnam and is preferred over the term "Indochinese," which is found to be offensive by some Southeast Asian refugees. The term "refugee" used here serves to distinguish the Cambodians, Laotians and Vietnamese from other ethnic communities also from Southeast Asia such as Thai, Filipino or Malaysian. The distinction is important because while most other Southeast Asians and Asian Americans generally came to this country as immigrants, Cambodians, Laotians and Vietnamese arrived here as refugees.

Within the Southeast Asian refugee population, there are also minority populations such as the Hmong from Laos and the ethnic Chinese

* For identification purposes only

from Vietnam. Each majority and minority population has a distinct history, language and culture. The purpose of referencing all of these groups as "Southeast Asian refugees" is appropriate only because they do share the common experience of being refugees; they arrived in the U.S. at roughly the same time, and they share some similarity in their "American experience."

This paper will profile this community, examine some data suggestive of this population's being economically and socially at risk, and make recommendations for both the Asian American community and the American community at large for actions to improve the conditions of this population.[1]

Profile of the Southeast Asian Refugee Communities

WHY ARE THE SOUTHEAST ASIANS IN THE U.S.?

Contrary to the experience of other Asian Americans who immigrated to the U.S. for a variety of economic reasons, Southeast Asians have been resettled in the U.S. as part of a worldwide rescue effort.

As the result of constant warfare and systematic persecution of individuals with differing political or religious beliefs, the communist governments that came to power in 1975 killed and imprisoned countless Cambodians, Laotians and Vietnamese. Millions had to flee to seek refuge elsewhere. A significant number who attempted to escape lost their lives crossing hostile borders and the South China Sea in unseaworthy boats. Southeast Asian countries such as Thailand, Malaysia, and the Philippines offered temporary asylum. Few of these countries, however, have resettled any refugees permanently for fear of retribution from the governments of Cambodia, Laos and Vietnam, as well as for reasons of limited resources.

Many other countries of the world offered permanent asylum for Southeast Asians. The United States resettled the largest number among all nations, even though it ranks only fifth among all countries in terms of ratio of refugees resettled per total population.

WHEN DID THE SOUTHEAST ASIANS ARRIVE IN THE U.S.?

In the U.S., the rescue of Southeast Asian refugees was initially thought to be a one-time crisis intervention following the communist takeover in 1975. That this was thought to be a short-term process can be seen in classification of the Indochinese Resettlement Assistance Act of 1975 as a "sunset" law, scheduled for termination by 1977. The subsequent continuing flow of refugees prompted the passage of the historic Refugee Act of 1980, which, for the first time, defined who could be admitted to this country as a "refugee," and established the framework under which the federal refugee assistance program operates. Through the Refugee Act, the number of refugees to be admitted each year is determined by the worldwide refugee need and by the ability of the U.S. to absorb and provide for these individuals. Reauthorization of the Refugee Act occurred in 1984, 1986, 1989 and 1992.

Because so many of the refugees fleeing Cambodia, Laos, and Vietnam lost their lives in their attempts to escape and because those who survived created tremendous political, social and economic pressures in the countries of first asylum, the Orderly Departure Program was established in 1979 to create a mechanism through which a limited number of Southeast Asians (primarily Vietnamese) could leave and be admitted to the U.S. through legal immigration channels.

In 1988, Congressman Robert J. Mrzarek of New York, a Vietnam veteran, introduced the Amerasian Homecoming Act to speed up the process to admit Amerasians and their families to the U.S. Amerasians are children of Vietnamese mothers and U.S. citizens. In many instances these children were abandoned by their fathers. By April 1992, a total of 62,351 Amerasians and their families were resettled in the U.S.

In 1989, the U.S. State Department negotiated and signed an agreement with the Vietnamese government allowing the release of political prisoners from "reeducation camps" to be resettled in the U.S. As of June 1992, an estimated 50,000 former Vietnamese political prisoners and their families were admitted to the U.S. under this program; among them are religious leaders, former government officials and military servicemen.

Data from the U.S. State Department indicate that by September 1991, Southeast Asians constituted the largest group of refugees worldwide admitted to the U.S. since 1975. Roughly 29 percent of the Southeast Asians arrived in the U.S. during 1980 and 1981. From 1975 to 1979, approximately 90 percent of all refugee arrivals were Vietnamese; a small number of Laotians arrived in 1976. The majority of Laotians and Cambodians arrived after 1980. Because Cambodians were considered "displaced persons" rather than "refugees" by Thailand, the country of first asylum, the number of Cambodians admitted to the U.S. was reduced substantially by the late 1980s. Only those qualified as immigrants and "humanitarian parolees" arrived after 1987.

The conditions and temporal variations of arrival are important in understanding the development of communities relative to the length of residence in the U.S. While the first wave of Southeast Asians generally was composed of individuals considered to be the "elite" in their countries of origin, those arriving in subsequent years represent a wider range of socioeconomic backgrounds. The "late arrivals" also tend to have been exposed to more trauma in their home countries because of persecution and imprisonment. Their escape attempts were more dangerous, and their stays in refugee camps were longer because of the difficulty in obtaining permanent asylum.

	TABLE 1: National Origins of Refugees by Year of Arrival (Fiscal years 1975-1987)			
	Total No. SE Asians Resettled	Percentage of Resettled		
		Cambodians	Laotians	Vietnamese
1975	135,000	3.5	0.6	95.0
1976	15,000	7.6	70.3	22.1
1977	7,000	11.5	15.4	73.1
1978	20,574	6.4	39.2	54.4
1979	76,521	7.4	37.4	55.1
1980	163,799	9.6	33.3	57.1
1981	131,139	20.5	14.6	65.0
1982	73,522	27.8	13.0	59.1
1983	39,408	33.8	7.4	58.8
1984	51,960	38.2	13.8	47.9
1985	59,970	38.5	10.6	50.9
1986	45,450	22.2	28.4	49.3
1987	40,112	4.8	38.9	56.3

Source: David Haines (1989); data collected by Linda Gordon (1987) and Office of Refugee Resettlement (1987).

Where and How Many Cambodians, Laotians, and Vietnamese Are in the U.S. Today?

According to the 1990 census, the total number of Americans who trace their ancestry to the countries of Cambodia, Laos and Vietnam is 1,1001,054. This figure includes the number of arrivals as refugees, immigrants, and children born in the U.S. It is estimated that a significant number of individuals from these three countries may choose to identify themselves as ethnic Chinese, therefore contributing to the undercount of Southeast Asian refugees in the U.S. The Southeast Asian refugee population thus accounts for 13 percent of the total Asian American population, and ranks third only after Chinese Americans (1,645,472) and Filipinos (1,406,770). Individually, the 1990 census identifies 614,547 Vietnamese, 147,411 Cambodians, and 239,096 Laotians—including 90,082 Hmong.

It is important to note that the distribution of each ethnic community differs somewhat. While California has roughly 45 percent of all Cambodians, Laotians and Vietnamese, the secondary areas of concentration of each of these communities reflect that there are unique patterns of re-

TABLE 2: The Ten States with 76 Percent
of the Southeast Asians in the U.S.

State	Total Number
California	453,363
Texas	85,029
Washington	36,724
Minnesota	36,459
Massachusetts	33,732
Virginia	27,178
Pennsylvania	23,788
Wisconsin	23,010
New York	22,619
Florida	20,379

Source: Bureau of the Census, *1990 Census Report*

settlement. The differences may be due to variations in community support systems and in opportunities for community development in different parts of the U.S. To this end, the East Coast seems to be the destination of preference for Cambodians since five of the top ten states with the largest concentration of Cambodians are Massachusetts, Pennsylvania, Virginia, New York and Rhode Island. The Laotians, on the other hand, choose the Midwest, with Minnesota, Wisconsin and Michigan comprising the largest contiguous states with a significant concentration of Laotians. For the Vietnamese the Gulf states (Texas, Louisiana and Florida) are their second favorite locations.[2]

GENERAL CHARACTERISTICS OF THE SOUTHEAST ASIANS

As mentioned in the introduction, to refer to Southeast Asian refugees as a group would be similar to describing Asian Americans as one homogeneous ethnic/racial block. Even the refugee experience is widely different among Southeast Asian groups. Vietnamese generally left their home country by boat, while Cambodians and Laotians walked across the border to Thailand. The survival rate of those who attempted escapes was determined by homeland conditions, escape routes, the receptivity of the countries of first asylum, and the safety afforded to the refugees during their stay in refugee camps.

The characteristics of Southeast Asians in the U.S. consequently reflect those of the survivors. Among Cambodians, for example, 12.2 percent were found to be widowed. Data collected during the early years of Southeast Asian refugee resettlement in the U.S. provide some general images of these communities. A large percentage of Vietnamese, ethnic Chinese, and Lao was from urban areas. The Hmong, on the other hand, came primarily from rural areas, as did about 50 percent of the Cambodians.

Selective data points out that Vietnamese tend to be the best educated and more proficient in the English language. More Vietnamese are professionals and technicians. They also have smaller households and the lowest fertility rate. On the opposite side are the Hmong, who have high illiteracy rates, large households, very high fertility rates, and the highest percentages of individuals with farming and fishing skills.

The Cambodians and Laotians have more diversified populations, e.g., coming from both urban and rural areas, and one third being illiterate in their native languages. Their household sizes are fairly large and the fertility rates, while lower than those of the Hmong, are still significantly higher than the U.S. average of 1.8.

In reviewing the data profiling each major ethnic community below, it is critical to understand that these data were collected from a specific site in the U.S. for the populations arriving prior to 1983. Perhaps nearly 50 percent of Southeast Asians came after 1983 or were born in the U.S. Therefore, this selective data provides a glimpse of these populations which may need modification to reflect current national profiles. For example, a significant number of political prisoners arrived after 1989, which should alter the percentage of individuals from Vietnam whose previous occupation was related to the military services.

Data collected by the Office of Refugee Resettlement by September 1991 indicates that about 55 percent of Southeast Asians are males while 45 percent are females. The median age of those arriving as refugees was 28. Approximately 2 percent were pre-schoolers (this count does not include children born in the U.S.), while 21 percent were between the ages of 6-17, and an additional 19 percent were young adults between the ages 18-24. Those 65 or older constituted 3.5 percent. Altogether 60 percent were considered in the prime working age of 18-44.

Close to one third of the Southeast Asians are of school age, indicating the tremendous impact this population has on the education system in their communities of residence. The population within the age group 18-24 may also impact the vocational training or higher education systems. The majority, however, are of working age and should contribute to the general labor force in the U.S.[4]

Analysis of the At-Risk Nature
of the Southeast Asian Refugee Population

SOCIOECONOMIC INDICATORS

It is rather evident from the data above that Southeast Asian refugees face barriers preventing them from achieving successful adaptation to American society. Extremely high rates of illiteracy in their own native language, in the case of the Hmong, or low levels of formal education in the homeland signify that Cambodians, Lao, and Hmong must overcome greater educational gaps to achieve minimum levels of English language

TABLE 3: General Characteristics by Ethnicity

	Chinese	Hmong	Cambodian	Lao	Vietnamese
California, 1977					
Mean education (yrs.)	5.9		8.0	3.6	9.7
Some English: speaking	48.0 %		49.0 %	49.0 %	74.0 %
English: reading	47.0 %		49.0 %	50.0 %	74.0 %
Five sites, 1982 (1978-82 arrivals only)					
Education: at least some college	3.6 %			5.1 %	13.8 %
No formal education	6.5 %			21.0 %	1.6 %
Households with at least one person with "some" English at arrival	47.0 %			46.0 %	68.0 %
San Diego, 1983					
% illiterate in native language	17.6 %	70.8 %	34.2 %	26.6 %	1.0 %
Years of education	6.7	1.6	5.0	4.9	9.8
% urban	95.4 %	8.3 %	46.3 %	79.1 %	94.0 %
Months in Refugee Camps	10.3	34.3	25.5	23.0	7.8
Household size	5.8	8.7	8.3	6.3	5.5
Close family member lost	0.5	1.0	1.7		0.6
% widowed	2.3 %	3.5 %	12.2 %		1.0 %
Total fertility rate	4.7	11.9	7.4	6.6	3.4
Previous occupation:					
% white collar	12.2 %	5.0 %	7.1 %		33.1 %
% sales	38.8 %	2.0 %	14.2 %		18.8 %
% blue collar	27.6 %	2.0 %	8.0 %		10.5 %
% military	6.1 %	31.3 %	15.9 %		25.6 %

and vocational skills than other refugees. Without these they cannot compete for jobs with salaries to support their large households. Lack of English language fluency has direct impact on a Southeast Asian refugee's ability to enroll in vocational training programs, or to pursue higher education. High fertility rates further exacerbate the difficult economic conditions and limit prospects for making economic improvement in the United States.

The study conducted by Ruben G. Rumbaut in San Diego found that household sizes of Southeast Asian families were significantly larger than the average U.S. household size of 2.7. The Hmong have the largest household size with an average of 8.8 persons; Cambodians average 8.7 persons; and Vietnamese households average 5.5 individuals. In contrasting nuclear family size against household size, the researchers found that the nuclear family is smaller for refugees than the U.S. population, averaging from 3.4 for Hmong to 4.0 for Cambodians. The larger household size versus nuclear family can be interpreted to mean: (a) the refugees continue to maintain the traditional extended family structure of multiple generations under one roof; and/or (b) there is an economic necessity to combine many families or single individuals within a household to pool income, especially in areas such as California where housing costs are prohibitively high.

Further analysis of household data shows that significant percentages of the Cambodian households (26.6 percent) are headed by women.

For Hmong families, approximately 16.7 percent were headed by women, as were 8.6 percent of Vietnamese families.[5]

Many refugee families coming from rural areas (e.g., the Hmong) would have the additional adjustment problem of leaping economically and socially from a primarily primitive agrarian culture to a post-industrialized society where economic forces and social interactions all move at a rapid pace. Those formerly rural residents who are resettled in Los Angeles, Chicago, New York, and Philadelphia have the extra burden of adapting to life in poor neighborhoods, where crime can be rampant and competition for such resources as affordable housing can create tensions among the needy populations already concentrated in the same geographic area.

Southeast Asians with professional credentials may no longer be employed in the same professions here since it is not unusual that their credentials are not accepted in the U.S. The large percentage of military personnel may also mean that there are significant numbers of Southeast Asians with skills for which there is no longer a market. There are exceptions, such as the case of former pilots who could combine their previous training and experience with English language training to secure commercial work. However, very few can successfully make this type of transition easily. The majority must learn new skills or upgrade their training to be more marketable in the new economic environment.

ECONOMIC INDICATORS

Dependence on Public Assistance.[6] Because the overwhelming majority of refugees from Southeast Asia arrived in the United States with little or no possessions, limited English skills and few transferable skills, Congress authorized, through the Refugee Act of 1980, an assistance program to help families and individuals overcome barriers to successful integration in the U.S.

Food, clothing, shelter, and transportation during the first 30 days following arrival in the U.S., cash grants and medical assistance up to the first 36 months in the U.S., and English language training and vocational training, job placement, counseling, and mental health services were made available through a variety of agencies and organizations.

Refugees from Southeast Asia, as with other refugee populations, are generally discouraged from applying for public assistance; in fact, most were instructed to find work as quickly as possible. The multitude of problems experienced by this population, however, indicated a need for a transition period for moving from dependency to self-sufficiency. The most recently available data on the welfare dependency rate measures only the period during which the federal government reimbursed states for cash grants and medical assistance expenses incurred at the state level. Data from the report to Congress for the 1991 fiscal year estimated the welfare-dependency rate of Southeast Asians in the first 12 months of their resettlement in the U.S. to be about 45 percent for Vietnamese, 44 percent for Laotians (including Hmong), and close to 100 percent for Cambodians.

These estimates fluctuate from one year to another, reflecting the special populations arriving each year. For example, the high rate of dependency for Vietnamese during the fiscal year 1991 may be due to the high proportion of Amerasians admitted in that year. Additionally, these estimates must be understood from the limitation that reports on welfare dependency are not consistent from state to state. One state may choose

TABLE 4: States with the Highest Dependency Rates,
All Refugee Populations (FY 1988, 1989)

State	Dependency Rates (%) at the End of 24 Months
California	78.9
Hawaii	76.8
Minnesota	69.1
Wisconsin	69.1
Ohio	62.9
Montana	61.3
Delaware	57.9
Washington	55.1
Oregon	50.1
Massachusetts	45.2

Source: Department of Health and Human Services, Office of Refugee Resettlement (1991).

to include a particular federal assistance program, such as Supplemental Security Income (SSI), while others may not. The dependency rate reported here also does not measure accurately the variable of arrival date. Consequently, if a large percentage of refugees arrived in the last two quarters of the fiscal year, the dependency rate reported actually reflects a six-month welfare utilization rate, rather than a whole year.

As a point of comparison, during the same fiscal year 1991, welfare utilization rate for immigrants from the former Soviet Union is 50 percent, for Afghans 45 percent, for Ethiopians 30 percent, and for Iranians 34 percent. Dependency rates also differ from one geographic region to another. Among the total of 183,717 refugees arriving in the U.S. between fiscal years 1988 and 1989, 43 percent were Southeast Asian.

Some states with high welfare-dependency rates are states with large concentrations of Southeast Asians. High levels of welfare dependency indicate that large numbers of Southeast Asians are living below the poverty level.

Income/Occupational Status.[7] The annual survey conducted by the Office of Refugee Resettlement measured the economic progress of Southeast Asian refugees for the first five years after resettlement. Ac-

TABLE 5: Previous and Current Occupational Status (%)		
Occupation	In Country of Origin	In U.S.
Professional/Managerial	9.4	1.4
Sales/Clerical	26.2	16.2
Total, White Collar	**35.6**	**17.6**
Skilled	13.8	24.4
Semi-Skilled	3.5	35.4
Laborers	0.0	4.3
Total, Blue Collar	**17.3**	**64.0**
Service Workers	7.7	17.7
Farming, Fishing	39.4	0.6

Source: Refugee Resettlement Program (1992).

cording to this survey for fiscal year 1991, 37 percent of the 1986 arrivals were participating in the labor force by 1991 as compared with 66 percent for the U.S. population. The first year arrivals' labor participation rate is 23 percent.

For those able to find work, the employment retention rates improve each succeeding year, in spite of the fact that the majority of Southeast Asians had to make major occupational changes upon resettlement. For those surveyed in the five-year study, 36 percent had white collar jobs in their countries of origin, but only 18 percent had white collar jobs in the U.S., largely in sales or clerical positions. The majority, 64 percent, held blue collar jobs. For the 39.4 percent who were once farmers and fishermen, only 0.6 percent work in such occupations now.

For those in the labor force, the average wage earned during the first five years is estimated at $209.20 per week, or $5.23 per hour. The relatively low wages for the first five years and the fairly large family sizes may explain why Southeast Asians continue to have to rely on public assistance. For those households with employed individuals, it takes more than two income earners to be economically independent. Households with more than six members and close to two individuals employed would still need some public assistance. Ability to speak English appears to be a major determinant regarding job acquisition and retention. The larger the number of individuals in a family who can speak English fluently, the higher the family employment rate.

HEALTH AND MENTAL HEALTH INDICATORS

What separates a refugee from an immigrant is the impetus and the conditions for leaving their country of origin. For refugees, a decision to leave is normally based on survival, yet escape from the homeland is equally life-threatening. For those fortunate enough to survive the escape, they must often face complete lack of control over their lives during their stay in the refugee camps. The experience of loss, whether of loved ones, ancestral homes, or country, remains with them for the rest of their lives. The impact of such experiences may not be felt or exhibited until years later when the immediate needs for shelter, clothing, and food are met.

Most studies on mental health and psychological adaptation document the deep depression experienced by refugees. For Cambodians in

TABLE 6: English Speakers and Job Acquisition

	Household Receiving Assistance	Household with Jobs & Assistance	Household with Jobs Only
Average household size	5.1	6.0	4.4
Number of wage earners	0	1.7	2.1
% with at least one fluent	7.5	21.7	29.3
% with children under 16	45.6	25.1	18.0

Source: Refugee Resettlement Program (1992).

particular, post-traumatic stress syndrome is a common experience for many adults and children who survived the "Killing Fields." The Sudden Death Syndrome, experienced primarily by Hmong, is a phenomenon where physically healthy young men die in their sleep. These experiences serve as indicators that many refugees must confront both the stress of adaptation to their new lives in the U.S. as well as the painful memories of their losses and trauma.

Studies have shown that the mental health of individual refugees is predicated upon the conditions which preceded their arrival in the U.S. and the conditions in the communities of resettlement. Ruben Rumbaut's study, "Mental Health and the Refugee Experience," conducted in 1985, found that 65.8 percent of Cambodians had lost at least one family member, 83.3 percent were separated from their family, and 76.3 percent could not communicate with families left behind. For Vietnamese, on the other hand, 42 percent reported having a family member jailed by the government in power, 30 percent were assaulted during their escape, and 39.5 percent had lost family members.[8]

Over 73 percent of all Southeast Asians surveyed in this study experienced fear of being killed during their escape attempts, and more than half were without food while escaping.

The trauma experienced by the refugees were often exacerbated by life in the refugee camps. At their best, these camps provided a transient respite with a subsistence level of food and some social or educational programs. At their worst, such as the border camps in Thailand or the holding centers in Hong Kong, the refugee camps were detention centers keeping refugees inside barbed wire compounds with minimal provisions of security, food, and shelter. These facilities became breeding grounds for hopelessness, anger, depression, and social problems. The longer the refugees stayed in these camps, the more difficult their adjustment tended to be upon arrival in the U.S.

Among the multiple barriers preventing Southeast Asians from seeking jobs, health problems were cited by 56.8 percent of those age 44 and older as the major barrier, according to the FY92 Refugee Resettlement Report to Congress.

The Center for Disease Control of the Public Health Services, Department of Health and Human Services, is charged with providing health screening to detect problems considered a possible threat to U.S. public health. The Center has identified for states working with Southeast Asian refugees that priority areas for health screening and follow-up care include tuberculosis, hepatitis B, anemia, malnutrition, and hearing, vision, and dental problems. These areas of concern indicate that poor health care, or the absence of health care systems in home countries and refugee camps, have generated unique problems for refugees requiring special attention.

SOCIAL PROBLEMS

In February 1989, *The Los Angeles Times* commissioned an extensive survey on the Vietnamese community in Orange County where an estimated 100,000 Vietnamese reside. Findings from this survey show that 41 percent of Vietnamese considered gangs and crime as the most serious problem facing the community in Orange County.[9]

The Vietnamese concerns, however, are widely shared. Reports from community leaders indicate that there are widespread juvenile delinquency problems among all Southeast Asian communities. Children as young as 12 or 13 are reported to be engaging in gang-like activities. This problem has received more attention in recent years but there is still no adequate research to understand the cause and magnitude of the problem. Suffice it to say that juvenile delinquency and criminal activities are common to most communities on the lower end of the economic social strata. For refugee youth, the inability to catch up with their peers in schools and their sense of alienation from their families due to cultural gaps no doubt contribute significantly to this rebellion against institutions and law and order.

Other social problems such as drug and alcohol abuse also surfaced as major concerns in Southeast Asian communities. To a large degree, these problems again have not been adequately studied to determine their impact on family and community life. It may be plausible to speculate that the trauma experienced by refugees plays a role in drug and alcohol abuse.

The Los Angeles Times survey also reported that the Vietnamese consider "assimilation" as their second most serious concern, even greater than their concern for jobs. This may reflect the fact that the community sees itself as still being very isolated due to little opportunity for interaction with the larger community and because of limited English proficiency.

Special populations such as Amerasians and former political prisoners have greater needs than other refugee populations because of the hardships experienced prior to their arrival in this country. While there are limited assistance programs, the magnitude of their needs deserves more attention and creative solutions.

Among the Hmong population, the tradition of early marriage for young women in their early teens has presented a cultural, social and economic dilemma for the community and for the new generation of Hmong in particular. These early marriages prevent teenagers from finishing their education, and with early pregnancy, the prospect for continuing their education or improving their economic conditions becomes even more difficult. Challenging this tradition, on the other hand, would mean questioning cultural values and practices of the Hmong people, who have already experienced great losses. Such clashes involving cultural values and practices also manifest themselves in the increasing rates of domestic violence and divorce among all the Southeast Asian populations. Family breakdowns can also result from role changes, or from difficulties confronting couples who have been separated for a number of years—especially in the case of former political prisoners.

Prospects for the Southeast Asian
Refugee Community

The data presented above suggest some of the challenges confronting Southeast Asian refugees in their quest to become full participants and productive citizens in their adopted land.

Economic survival depends not only on their ability to acquire new skills and achieve a level of English competency, but also on their capacity to overcome social and cultural barriers preventing them from realizing their full potential. For the first generation of refugees, these problems may seem insurmountable. There are also, however, indications that for some in this first generation, the prospect can be rather promising.

The Office of Refugee Resettlement has been able to examine the income gains of Southeast Asians after the first five years by collecting data from the Internal Revenue Service for those individuals arriving between the years of 1975 and 1979. This was possible because a block of Social Security numbers was given to these Southeast Asians at that time. These data reveal that after ten years, the average income of those arriving in 1975 is $17,092. At this level, the 1975 arrivals had achieved an income equal to the average U.S. resident. Again, it is important to note that refugees arriving in this country in 1975 were primarily the Vietnamese "elite" who generally had some English proficiency, a high level of education, and an urban background. Their experience therefore cannot be seen as representative for the larger percentage of refugees arriving in later years.[10]

The report from the Bureau of the Census shows that between 1982 to 1987, the number of businesses owned by individuals identifying themselves as Vietnamese increased 414 percent, from 4,989 businesses in 1982 to 25,671 businesses in 1987 with the reported receipts of $532,200,000 in 1982 to $1,361,000,000 in 1987. This increase is more remarkable when compared to the 87 percent increase for all Asian American populations, and 14 percent for all U.S. firms during the same period.[11] It appears that the Vietnamese have contributed, through self-employment, to expanding the economy by meeting the needs created by the new population. Through such expansion, they created jobs for themselves and for the local labor force. These entrepreneurial activities promoted new commercial areas, showing that the Vietnamese community can serve as a viable economic force. In some cases, Vietnamese refugees revitalized inner city neighborhoods in Chicago, Illinois, and Arlington, Virginia. In other locations, entire new ethnic commercial centers, such as Westminster for the Vietnamese and Long Beach for the Cambodians, created new cultural centers in areas where Asians were once invisible.

Annual reports on scholastic performance of the Southeast Asian refugee children point to a long list of valedictorians and academic contest winners. Glowing as these reports are, they should not mask the high drop-out rate among other Southeast Asian youth who arrived in the U.S. after having their education disrupted. These young people have not been able to catch up with their peers because of lost time as well as their limited English proficiency.

The portrait of the Southeast Asians, thus, is a community of extremes. The success of some seems extraordinary in view of the obstacles they must overcome. The failure of others who have not achieved economic self-sufficiency or overcome the social, cultural and language barriers exasperates both the individuals who have survived the worst horrors, as well as their community leaders, who struggle to establish a place for their people in this highly competitive and pluralistic society.

The success of some young Southeast Asian professionals and the alienation and despair of other young Southeast Asian gang members demonstrates the wide range of prospects for Cambodians, Laotians and Vietnamese in the U.S. The implications of this profile of extremes point to the need to view these communities as not homogeneous, but rather as consisting of multiple subgroups defined by ethnicities, and socioeconomic backgrounds, different experiences before and after arrival, and different potentials for development.

Policy Implications

Public and private institutions concerned with alleviating poverty must not overlook the Southeast Asian communities, whose problems may be hidden through lumping together with other Asian Americans who have achieved a relative degree of economic success. This misperception may deny opportunities for Southeast Asians to work on their own problems and to improve the conditions of less fortunate community members.

The lack of knowledge about conditions in Southeast Asian communities is presently not limited to public and private institutions working on poverty issues. Asian American and Southeast Asian communities and leaders also need to be more informed. While the annual report to Congress prepared by the Office of Refugee Resettlement yields important data on the background and economic progress of Southeast Asians, further studies are necessary to understand the reasons for the shortcomings and to explore strategies and programs which could help those communities gain economic and social self-sufficiency. A new generation of young Southeast Asian social scientists should be employed to conduct research studies to provide cultural and linguistic insight into these issues.

Of utmost importance is the need to begin working more closely and directly with families living in poverty to help find better prospects for their economic survival. Programs are needed for the adult populations, as well as for the next generations, to avoid development of a cycle of poverty. Social problems associated with poverty are severe enough to warrant immediate actions by policy-makers. The youth delinquency problem and gang-like activities must be dealt with through prevention programs.

To this end, the leadership of Southeast Asian communities needs to be equipped with appropriate skills and knowledge of the economic and social problems confronting members of their communities. The success of community leaders in solving these problems is crucial to the success of the community as a whole. The investment of resources in refugee community organizations is a crucial means in a long-term strategy for responding to the needs of the less fortunate.

Additionally, because of their economic conditions, Southeast Asians generally live among other ethnic and minority populations who face many of the same social and economic barriers. For this reason, interethnic and interracial relations skills must be developed by and for community leaders to build a climate of tolerance and acceptance. Otherwise, there will be interethnic tensions due to the perceptions of others that the refugees are receiving preferential treatment or are competing with others for limited resources. Southeast Asians could become useful bridge builders between communities of different economic and social backgrounds, because of their unique experience in which many who were once "the haves" are now "the have-nots."

Specific Action/Policy Recommendations

ECONOMIC AND SOCIAL ADJUSTMENT

- Congress and the administration should provide adequate funding to at least maintain the level of assistance provided to new arrivals. Loss of funding allocated through the Office of Refugee Resettlement would result in decreasing levels of services and create undue pressure at the state and local levels, where resources are limited.

- The coordination of services among federal, state, and local government and with the private sector, including Southeast Asian self-help organizations, is critical to the successful integration of Southeast Asians in the U.S. Policies and funding decisions affecting these various sectors must be made with the intent to maintain and build on the crucial role of each type of institution, rather than giving particular institutions more control in the initial resettlement effort.

- Private foundations and corporations should provide more resources to programs addressing the multiple needs of this at-risk population.

- Programs addressing family needs must be developed to prevent further breakdown and the escalation of existing problems. Gang prevention, family counseling, and early pregnancy prevention are urgent needs calling for immediate attention.

EDUCATION AND TRAINING

- Employment and training programs must take into consideration the unique language and skill transfer needs of the Southeast Asians. Professionals and skilled workers should be provided opportunities for retraining or upgrading their skills. Those without transferable skills should be placed in programs promoting employment and training simultaneously.

- Additional English classes should be provided for the adult population. Long waiting periods for enrollment in language classes in major urban areas prolong the integration process both economically and socially.

- Funding to support K-12 education institutions serving this at-risk population must be restored in order for public schools to continue providing necessary remedial and early intervention programs critical to the needs of Southeast Asian youth.

HEALTH AND MENTAL HEALTH

- Public education and preventative programs, such as health screening to address communicable diseases and good health care habits, must be expanded. The use of community organizations and culturally and linguistically appropriate methods are crucial to eradicate existing health problems and teach better health care practices.

- Special efforts to recruit and train Southeast Asians to work in the fields of public health and mental health are very much needed to ensure that bicultural and bilingual professionals and para-professionals are available to work with communities and to provide direct services to individuals in need of counseling and intervention.

- Funding for mental health services is also crucial to meet the needs of those experiencing post-traumatic stress syndrome and adaptation crises. Community resources for addressing the needs, such as cultural events and the role of religious leaders, must be recognized and supported.

Notes

1. The two major sources of information for this paper are the *Fiscal Year 1991 Report of the Office of Refugee Resettlement to Congress, Refugee Resettlement Program, Report to Congress,* U.S. Department of Health and Human Services, Office of Refugee Resettlement, DHHS, Washington, D.C., January 31, 1992; and the book edited by David Haines, *Refugees as Immigrant: Cambodians, Laotians, and Vietnamese in America* (Totowa, New Jersey: Rowman and Littlefield, 1989).

2. U.S. Census Bureau, *U.S. Census Report* (Washington, D.C.: U.S. Census Bureau, 1990).

3. See David Haines, ed., *Refugees as Immigrants.* The San Diego data derive from Ruben Rumbaut, "Mental Health and the Refugee Experience: A Comparative Study of Southeast Asian Refugees," in *Southeast Asian Mental Health: Treatment, Prevention, Services, Training and Research,* edited by Tom C. Owan (Rockville, Maryland: National Institute of Mental Health, 1985), 441; and Ruben Rumbaut and John F. Weeks, "Fertility and Adaptation: Indochinese Refugees in the U.S.," *International Migration Review* (1986), 445. The 1982 five site survey is from Nathan Caplan, John K. Whitmore, and Quang Bui, *Southeast Asian Refugee Self-Sufficiency Study: Final Report* (Ann Arbor: Institute for Social Research,1985), 46, 48, 57, and 70. The data for California are from Jacqueline Aames et al., *Indochinese Refugee Self-Sufficiency in California: A Survey and Analysis of the Vietnamese, Cambodians and Lao and the Agencies That Serve Them. Report Submitted to the California State Department of Health, State of California* (Sacramento,1977), 16, 106, and 107.

4. *Fiscal Year 1991 Report,* Office of Refugee Resettlement.

5. Ruben Rumbaut, "Southeast Asian Refugees in San Diego County: A Statistical Profile." Report prepared for IHARP (Indochinese Health and Adaptation Research Project), Department of Sociology, University of California, San Diego, 1984.

6. Office of Refugee Resettlement, *Fiscal Year 1991 Report.*

7. *Ibid.*

8. Ruben Rumbaut, "Mental Health and the Refugee Experience."

9. Steve Emmons and David Reyes, "Gangs, Crimes Feared Most by Vietnamese," *Los Angeles Times* (February 5, 1989).

10. U.S. Department of Health and Human Services, Office of Refugee Resettlement, *Refugee Resettlement Program, Report to Congress,* DHHS, Washington, D.C., January 31, 1992; January 31, 1991; and January 31, 1990.

11. United States Department of Commerce, Bureau of the Census, Economics and Statistics Administrations, "Business Firms Owned by Asian Americans, Pacific Islanders, American Indians and Alaska Natives Increased 87 Percent Over Five Years, Census Shows," Washington, D.C., August 2, 1991.

Empowering Our Communities:

Political Policy

Stewart Kwoh

PRESIDENT AND EXECUTIVE DIRECTOR
ASIAN PACIFIC AMERICAN LEGAL CENTER
LOS ANGELES, CALIFORNIA

Mindy Hui

ASIAN PACIFIC AMERICAN LEGAL CENTER
LOS ANGELES, CALIFORNIA

How much influence will the increasing Asian Pacific American population have on the political empowerment of our communities? By the year 2020 Asian Pacific Americans will number 18 to 20 million nationally and seven to eight million in California alone. Even during the next ten years, our population will leap to ten million or more nationally.

Political empowerment should be defined not only by the number of Asian Pacific Americans who hold elected offices, but also by the ability of our communities to influence the outcome of elections and the development, passage and implementation of policies which benefit our people. Looking at political empowerment from this perspective allows us to gauge our success by broader criteria.

Significant research and community-wide dialogue on our empowerment strategies have been lacking. What we can learn from the experiences of other U.S. ethnic groups? One of the strategic debates in the African American community has been what to do about their perceived or actual decreasing political clout, while the number of elected African American officials has dramatically increased over the past 20 years. Latinos also will be able to elect more representatives to local and statewide offices in the 1990s, yet will this translate into favorable policies affording opportunities for a group that is destined to be the largest ethnic group in the U.S. in the next century? What lessons does the Jewish American experience have for Asian Pacific Americans? Jewish Americans have been successful both in electing many Jewish Americans to public office and in influencing U.S. policies on Israel and other issues. As Asian Pacific Americans work for our own political empowerment, we will need a far deeper understanding of the experiences of other ethnic groups. A comprehensive understanding of these experiences will assist in a comprehensive political empowerment strategy. There are also many unique characteristics of the Asian Pacific American community which require close scrutiny.

Responding to the Complexities
of a Changing Community

What are the characteristics of our population that will advance or impede this political empowerment? What are the challenges and barriers facing us in the coming decades? Seven population characteristics will directly affect our political involvement:

1. Our population will continue to be fueled by new immigration. In Los Angeles, site of the largest population concentration of Asian Pacific Americans in the U.S., two-thirds of our population is foreign born. While our rate of citizenship naturalization is higher than that of Latinos, Asian newcomers will not be able to vote if they remain permanent residents.

2. Our population is concentrated in immigrant centers like Koreatown, Chinatown and others, but there is also a significant degree of dispersal. The dispersal is greater than that of Latinos and African Americans. The ethnic bloc vote, then, may be possible for our community, but we will have less influence than other minorities because our population is more dispersed and because our concentrations tend to consist of newer immigrants.

3. Our population has a broad range of income strata. While our community has a much larger percentage of poor than is commonly believed (about 15 percent nationally), we have very significant middle income and higher income strata. The potential for class conflict in formulating policies for our community is apparent. There is also a significant ability for some in our community to donate hefty amounts to political campaigns. In fact, in most large populations centers, Asian Pacific Americans contribute to candidates in amounts greater than our proportion of the total population. A reconciliation between these varied interests is a significant challenge in the development of a viable political strategy.

4. Thus far, all Asian Pacific Americans who hold office have been elected by a majority of non-Asian voters. Our politicians have succeeded only by being able to "cross over" to non-Asians for support. The ability to have multi-group appeal and respond to a cross-section of residents is a major strength of our office holders. However, the number of our elected officials remains small, so the question is whether this process will continue to occur at a snail's pace or whether it can be accelerated.

5. Our population has few political organizations that have sufficient numbers of staff or funding to conduct major campaigns. While some local organizations have launched successful voter registration drives, few have the capability for mounting sustained and sophisticated campaigns. There is currently no equivalent within our community to the South West Voter Registration Project.

6. The population centers of Asian Pacific Americans tend to be close to or intertwined with population centers of other minority groups. The implications of this situation means that Asian Pacific American candidates must build

coalitions with other minority populations if they are to have a chance of winning. It also means that the use of voting rights laws will have to deal with greater complexities than in the past, which have largely dealt with a majority and a minority population (e.g., African Americans in the South).

7.   Voter registration data for various Asian Pacific ethnic groups indicate that less than 25 percent of age-eligible Asian Pacific Americans are registered to vote and that members of our community are affiliated with both the Democratic and Republican parties. This split means a more difficult time in developing an Asian Pacific bloc vote to win partisan elections.

The above characteristics reveal the complexity of the Asian Pacific American population and the challenges facing us in mobilizing our community politically. Perhaps one conclusion is clear—population growth will enhance the potential for political empowerment for our community, but developing this potential will certainly not be easy. That potential will only be realized by providing a level playing field in the voting process and by organizing in the community at a significantly greater level than in the past.

Overcoming Structural Barriers:
Redistricting and the Voting Process

Asian Pacific Americans also confront structural challenges and barriers to political empowerment. Although many of the overt legal barriers to citizenship and voting have been removed over the past 40 years, several structural impediments continue to frustrate the political aspirations of Asian Pacific Americans.

One of the important structural barriers limiting our political participation is the unfairness in redistricting. Redistricting is the process of drawing political boundaries for elections. It plays a fundamental role in determining the political strength of a community of interest. When a community of interest is maintained intact in one district, that community's voting strength is greatly enhanced. A single official is held accountable to that community, and services are easier to come by. However, when a community is fragmented into several different districts, its overall voting strength is diluted. When a crucial issue for the community arises and the community demands accountability from an elected official, the official can divert the problem to his counterpart in an adjacent district. This practice can go on indefinitely until the issue is dead, or members of the community give up in frustration.

The legal basis for fair reapportionment is the Federal Voting Rights Act of 1965, 42 U.S.C. 1971 et seq. (1988) Section 2. It prohibits any voting practice or procedure "imposed or applied by any State or political subdivision in a manner which results in the denial of the abridgement of the right of any citizen of the United States to vote on account of race or color" or language minority status. Plaintiffs can establish a Section 2 violation by a showing of discriminatory intent, or by a showing of discriminatory effect, based on the totality of the circumstances. In addition, in *Garza* v. *County of Los Angeles*, 918 F.2d 763 (9th Cir. 1990), cert. denied, 111 S. Ct. 578 (1991), the court found that Los Angeles County intentionally discriminated against the Latino community in redrawing district lines. The court ruled that the County was aware that its redistricting plan would continue to divide the Latino community and "further impair the ability of [minorities] to gain representation on the [government body]." Federal laws protect a minority community's voting rights and require that these communities be kept intact within single legislative districts, where possible.

Reapportionment is an important issue for the Asian Pacific community. Political empowerment is facilitated when a community's voting power is not divided arbitrarily. A strong, legally defensible reapportionment scheme can strengthen the minority voters' voice and forces elected officials to become more responsive to their community issues.

In 1991, Asian Pacific Americans in key cities of the U.S. were signficantly involved in redistricting. The valuable experiences of this first-time participation have just begun to be summarized. California redistricting was a mixed success for Asian Pacific Americans. In northern and southern California, there was unprecedented Asian Pacific American involvement at hearings and significant coalitions. In addition, the Coalition of Asian Pacific Americans for Fair Reapportionment (CAPAFR) was able to work with Latinos and other minorities.

In Los Angeles, CAPAFR focused on the three largest Asian Pacific core regions in Los Angeles County: San Gabriel Valley, the South Bay, and Central Los Angeles. Due to lack of resources to develop redistricting plans for all areas, CAPAFR focused locally on the city of Los Angeles and at the state level on the Assembly districts, the smaller of State legislative districts. In California, an Assembly district consists of about 370,000 residents, while a Senate district has approximately 740,000 residents. In contrast, a Congressional district can have as many as 573,000 residents.

The highest Asian Pacific population concentration in Southern California's state assembly is 28 percent in San Gabriel Valley's district 49, which includes the cities of Monterey Park, Rosemead, San Gabriel and Alhambra. CAPAFR was able to keep this Asian Pacific community intact in the state's final redistricting plan, having been split into three districts in the 1981 redistricting plan.

Reapportionment does not necessarily mean a zero-sum game where there are winners and losers among minority groups. San Gabriel Valley CAPAFR was able to work out and agree upon a plan with the San Gabriel Valley Latino Redistricting Committee. (Asians are second only to Latinos as the largest minority group in that region.) This success was partly due to the negotiating efforts of community leaders, common interests and a commitment to follow through with future projects such as voter registration and resolution of Asian-Latino student conflicts in the district.

Another political structural barrier involves the voting process. Much of our Asian Pacific American population is college educated, either in their former countries or in the United States. However, they have limited English proficiency. For this reason, bilingual ballots are necessary for members of our community to participate in the electoral process. In the past, the benchmark for providing bilingual ballots was 5 percent of the total voting age population. However, based on this guideline, many large counties, such as Los Angeles, with substantial numbers of language minority citizens, were not covered. Los Angeles County alone has a total population of nearly 9 million and covers an area of 4,063 square miles, which is larger than the state of Delaware and Rhode Island combined.

Language diversity exists among Asian Pacific Americans. Several

Asian Pacific ethnic groups have more than 10,000 persons requiring bilingual ballots. However, according to the former federal 5 percent benchmark, an ethnic group would need to have 450,000 persons requiring bilingual ballots before the guidelines would take effect.

In the summer of 1992, Asian Pacific Americans achieved a victory with the signing into law of a 15-year extension to the bilingual provisions of the Voting Rights Act of 1965, introduced by Senator Simon of Illinois. Under the new law, voting materials are required in jurisdictions which reach the 5 percent threshold as well as jurisdictions with at least 10,000 voting-age, single language, limited English proficient citizens. Los Angeles will now provide multilingual assistance in six languages: English, Spanish, Chinese, Tagalog, Japanese and Vietnamese. Bilingual ballots will enable many limited English proficient citizens to take part in the political process.

Although barriers such as unfair redistricting and inaccessibility to bilingual ballots may at first seem insurmountable, this is not the case. Significant lobbying by Asian Pacific American groups such as the Japanese American Citizens League, Organization of Chinese Americans, Chinese American Citizens Alliance, the National Asian Pacific American Legal Consortium, and the National Asian Pacific American Bar Association gave a big boost to the legislation. Progress was also made through efforts at coalition building with other ethnic communities. For example, Asian groups worked closely with the Mexican American Legal Defense and Education Fund (MALDEF) and other key Latino organizations to advocate for the passage of bilingual ballot provisions. In addition, the Latino's community victory in *Garza* v. *County of Los Angeles* has raised the hopes for all ethnic groups for legal remedies against government bodies that violate the political rights of minority communities.

Asian Pacific Americans were active in redistricting efforts in New York, Los Angeles, San Francisco and other Asian Pacific American key population centers of the United States. We have also become more sophisticated in advocating legislative changes. Fair redistricting and access to bilingual ballots will help to remove structural barriers facing our community. These measures alone will not get Asian Pacific Americans elected but will help to create the basis for political empowerment.

The Need for a
Comprehensive Approach to Empowerment

Exciting, attracting and mobilizing the Asian Pacific American voter will be the long-term key to political empowerment. Asian Pacific Americans must adopt a comprehensive approach to political empowerment involving the development of candidates, voter registration, and coalition building. Today, Asian Pacific Americans account for almost 10 percent of California's population, but until recently there were no legislators of Asian Pacific heritage among the 120 Assembly and Senate representatives. Congressman Robert Matsui recently reported that while we may be 10 percent of California's population we are only 2 percent of the electorate. In most communities, less than 25 percent of Asian Pacific Americans over age 18 are registered to vote.

A comprehensive approach to empowerment involves five components:

1. Talented Asian Pacific American candidates must be encouraged to run for office, and supported by our community. A strong emphasis on local elections and appealing to a cross-section of voters will develop the base for chances at higher elective offices.

2. Voting must be increased through a variety of strategies, such as expanded nonpartisan and partisan voter registration drives, citizenship campaigns, and get-out-the-vote mobilizations.

3. Newly won voting rights such as bilingual ballot provisions must be fully utilized to encourage political participation.

4. Donors must get "a bigger bang for their buck" by working with the community to identify issues and then influencing the candidate to support these measures.

5. Grassroots organizing and coalition politics must be encouraged, both within the Asian Pacific community and with other ethnic groups. Debate and resolution over the

"agenda"—or significant rallying issues—for Asian Pacific Americans must be a cornerstone of such organizing, for the fragmentation within the communities cannot be solved with organizing techniques alone.

Understanding the unique characteristics of the Asian Pacific American population, removing structural barriers to voting, and finding ways to excite our voters are key steps to unlocking the potential for our influence in American politics. In the aftermath of the Los Angeles civil unrest, where over 3,500 Asian Pacific Americans lost stores and a few lost their lives, many have questioned whether politicians and police simply abandoned the victims. Substantial assistance has been lacking. Perhaps this tragedy will send a strong signal to our communities that political empowerment is not a luxury; it is a necessity.

Out of the Melting Pot and Into the Fire:

Race Relations Policy

Michael Omi

ASSISTANT PROFESSOR, ASIAN AMERICAN STUDIES
UNIVERSITY OF CALIFORNIA, BERKELEY

In 1947, then New York Governor Thomas E. Dewey declared that "New York City is not a melting pot, it's a boiling pot." Thirty-five years later, it is an apt description of Los Angeles and other major American cities. Patterns of residential segregation, the inequitable distribution of public goods and services, and capital flight from core urban areas all provide the backdrop for increasing incidents of racial conflict and violence. And what is increasingly evident is that such racial tensions are no longer intelligible, if indeed they ever were, within the framework of a "black/white" paradigm of race relations.

Despite this quite obvious observation, the prevailing race relations literature continues to retain an exclusive black/white focus. A look at recent popular books by Andrew Hacker, the Edsalls, and Studs Terkel[1] suggests that when scholars and journalists talk about race relations, they mean relations between African Americans and Whites. Such biracial theorizing misses the complex nature of race relations in the post-civil rights era and is unable to grasp the patterns of conflict and accommodation among several increasingly large racial/ethnic groups. In most major cities, for example, Whites have fled to surrounding suburban rings, leaving the inner city the site of turf battles between different racial minorities.

Confronting this reality, political analysts have had to reexamine the utility of various models of race relations, or, as is more often the case, attempt to make the facts fit within the existing black/white paradigm.

While the latter option is a meaningless exercise, a contemporary response to Marvin Gaye's troubling question "What's going on?" is not easy to frame.

The recent riots in Los Angeles may serve to broaden our racial outlook. Journalist Tim Rutten described the devastation in the immediate wake of the Rodney King decision as "the nation's first multi-ethnic urban riot, one that involved not simply the traditional antagonism of one race toward another, but the mutual hostility, indifference, and willingness to loot of several different racial and ethnic groups."[2] Indeed, if only for a fleeting moment, the Los Angeles riots served to focus media attention on generally neglected racial/ethnic subjects—Korean, Guatemalan, Salvadoran, Chicano—who were both victims and victimizers. Given the contemporary and projected patterns of immigration, it is precisely these groups which will shape the patterns of race relations in a state such as California.

What impact will the tremendous projected growth and increasing visibility of Asian Americans over the next several decades have on racial/ethnic relations in the United States? I believe that it will challenge existing paradigms of race relations, reveal new patterns of "racialization" with respect to individual/collective identity and political organization, and fuel disturbing trends in racial politics.

The Limits of Existing Race Relations Theory

For most of the 20th century, the dominant conception of American race relations has been that of assimilation.[3] It has been a popularly accepted understanding that different racial/ethnic groups over time would lose their cultural distinctiveness and become what mainstream social scientists have called "Anglo-conformists." From the vantage point of this perspective, structural boundaries would recede and groups would neither be segregated nor marginalized in residential life, the labor market, and politics.

The assimilationist framework has been the dominant paradigm in interpreting the historical experiences of Asian Americans. At the turn of the century, it was used as a justification for Asian exclusion, the rationale being that Asians were unassimilable and a significant racial threat to the white population on the West Coast.[4] In the 1950s, it was used as a gauge by which to measure the degree of "separateness" of

Chinese Americans and as a plea for the shedding of "difference."[5] In the late 1960s, in the midst of ghetto rebellions and the emergence of Asian American consciousness, it was used to illustrate the successful integration of Japanese Americans into the mainstream of American life.[6] Currently, however, the paradigm's continued usefulness in explaining patterns of social/cultural/ political consciousness and organization among Asian Americans is questionable.

The assimilationist perspective has assumed a zero-sum relationship between assimilation and the retention of ethnicity. To become more "Americanized," therefore, meant that one was less "Asian." By contrast, recent scholarship on Japanese Americans has suggested that they have been able to maintain high levels of ethnic consciousness and ethnic community involvement, while simultaneously becoming structurally assimilated into the dominant society.[7]

Another challenge to the assimilationist framework is the fact that the new wave of post-1965 Asian immigrants have had an unprecedented opportunity to develop "private cultures" within the broader American culture. In sharp contrast to the pre-1965 immigrants, they have been able to maintain more comprehensive links with their respective homelands. Some of these connections have been shaped by the video revolution and the global dissemination of popular culture. The proliferation of video stores in Asian American communities allow new Asian immigrants to view the latest tapes from Manila, Seoul, or Hong Kong— "soap operas," dramas, musicals, and soft-core pornography. In addition, independent television stations in selected markets regularly broadcast ethnic programming, keeping their audiences "current" in news and popular culture.

New Asian American immigrants maintain their connection to the homeland not merely through electronic means, but through trans-Pacific travel as well. Quick and relatively affordable, air travel has made the borders and boundaries which separate Asia and the mainland United States more fluid. This has allowed new Asian American immigrants to shuttle back-and-forth to meet family obligations, vacation, or to allow their children a periodic immersion into their respective language and culture. Such a situation contrasts sharply with the pre-1965 Asian immigrants who were more divorced from their homelands and faced forced assimilation in the immediate postwar period.

New Asian communities are emerging, on an unprecedented scale.

They are not small, dingy, urban enclaves like the Chinatowns and Japantowns of recent memory, nor are they a product of restrictive covenants or other mechanisms of ghettoization. They are a product of the demand for ethnic goods and services, and, in many instances, are testimony to the infusion of Asian capital here in the U.S. A "Little Saigon" has arisen in Westminster in Orange County, California, featuring dozens of mini-malls and a large-scale shopping center with huge, gleaming white Buddhist figures gracing the entrance. And when one is in Monterey Park, California, whose population is well over 50 percent Asian, it is not clear *who* is assimilating into *what*.

In suggesting that the new immigrant communities do not face a stark choice between assimilation and the maintenance of ethnic identity and organization, I do not wish to imply that no transformation exists. Clearly what is interesting to examine is the manner in which a *new* distinct identity and culture is shaped, contested, and continually re-formed. Tran Van Ngoc, 45, a former helicopter pilot in Vietnam who now works as a computer technician in Southern California, articulates the seemingly unconscious nature of this process, and the confusion it engenders:

> We are Vietnamese but we are not Vietnamese. Living in a new country, we change and we don't even know it. Our thoughts are different and we don't even know it. Sometimes I try to deny that I am Americanized, but I have changed.[8]

The growth and persistence of private cultures poses a challenge to the smooth trajectory of incorporation into the dominant culture predicted by the assimilationist paradigm. In many respects, the limits of the assimilationist model are rooted in its emergence as an analysis of the historical incorporation of succeeding waves of white European immigrants. By contrast, an alternative perspective would have to account for distinct trajectories of incorporation, exclusion, and social/ cultural autonomy, and not take assimilation as an inevitable outcome or desirable goal. Such an alternative view of race relations, I would argue, first needs to confront and challenge the prevailing concepts of race.

Racial Formation and the Concept of Racialization

For the most part, contemporary social science has explicitly rejected biologistic notions of race in favor of approaches which stress the *social construction* of race. But while it has elevated the idea of race as a socio-historical concept, much of contemporary social science nonetheless slips into a kind of objectivism about racial identity and racial meaning. In many empirical studies, race is simply treated as an independent variable requiring little or no elaboration. Such studies can intriguingly correlate race and poverty, race and heart disease, or race and residential patterns, but in so doing render unproblematic the concept of race itself.

In contrast to this approach, *racial formation* theory[9] treats race as a fluid, unstable, and "decentered" complex of social meanings constantly being transformed by political conflict. Relations between "races," therefore, fundamentally transform what races are about. Central to the discussion at hand is the construction of racial identity and meaning which Howard Winant and I call *racialization*.

The concept of racialization signifies the extension of racial meaning to a previously racially unclassified relationship, social practice, or group. A historical example would be the consolidation of the racial category of *black* in the United States from Africans whose specific identity was Ibo, Yoruba, or Bakaongo among others. Parallel to this was, as historian Winthrop Jordan observes, the emergence of *white* as a term of self-identity evolving from earlier conceptions of *Christian, English,* and *free*.[10]

Asian Americans are undergoing unique and specific patterns of racialization which will deepen and intensify in the decades to come. In the post-civil rights era, they have been consolidated into a new racial category, have experienced the increasing significance of class divisions, and have been directly implicated in the overall politicization of race. This has, and will continue to have, profound effects on relations between Asian American ethnic groups, and between Asian Americans and other racial/ethnic groups.

Identity, Collective Consciousness, and Political Organization

The post-civil rights period has witnessed the rise of *panethnicity* as a phenomenon of racialization. Groups which were previously self-defined in terms of specific ethnic background, and which were marginalized by the seemingly more central dynamic of "black/white" relations, began to confront their own racial identity and status in a political environment of heightened racial consciousness and mobilization. Sociologists David Lopez and Yen Espiritu argue that such panethnic formation has become a crucial feature of contemporary ethnic change, "supplanting both assimilation and ethnic particularism as the direction of change for racial/ethnic minorities."[11]

Prior to the late-1960s, there were no "Asian Americans." In the wake of the civil rights movement, distinct Asian ethnic groups, primarily Chinese, Japanese, Filipino, and Korean Americans, began to frame and assert their common identity as Asian Americans. This political label reflected a similar historical experience of being subjected to exclusionary immigration laws, restrictive naturalization laws, labor market segregation, and patterns of ghettoization by a polity and culture which treated all Asians as alike.

The *racialization* of Asian Americans involved muting the profound cultural and linguistic differences, and minimizing the significant historical antagonisms, which had existed among the distinct nationalities and ethnic groups of Asian origin. In spite of enormous diversity, Asian American activists found this new political label a crucial rallying point for raising political consciousness about the problems of Asian ethnic communities and for asserting demands on state institutions. From a racialization perspective, Asian American panethnicity is driven by a dynamic relationship between the specific group being racialized and the state. The elites representing such groups find it advantageous to make political demands by using the numbers and resources which panethnic formations can mobilize. The state, in turn, can more easily manage claims by recognizing and responding to large blocs as opposed to dealing with the specific claims of a plethora of ethnically defined interest groups. In this context, conflicts occur over the precise definition and boundaries of various racially defined groups, and their adequate representation in census counts, reapportionment debates, and minority aid.

Panethnic consciousness and organization are, to a large extent, contextually and strategically determined. Different Asian American ethnic groups have found that there are times when it is advantageous to be in a panethnic "Asian Americans" bloc, and times when it is desirable to mobilize along particular ethnic lines.

The situational nature of this dynamic is illustrated by two examples. In an attempt to boost their political clout and benefits from land trust arrangements, native Hawaiians voted four-to-one in January 1990 to expand the definition of their people to anyone with a drop of Hawaiian "blood." Previously only those with at least 50 percent Hawaiian "blood" were eligible for certain benefits. By contrast, in June 1991 in San Francisco, Chinese American architects and engineers protested the inclusion of Asian Indians under the city's minority business enterprise law. Citing a Supreme Court ruling which requires cities to narrowly define which groups had suffered discrimination to justify specific affirmative action programs, Chinese Americans contended that Asian Indians should not be considered "Asian." At stake were obvious economic benefits accruing to designated "minority" businesses.

Such inclusionary/exclusionary debates make the very utility of the concept "Asian Americans" unclear. The irony is that the term came into vogue at precisely the historical moment when new Asian groups were entering the U.S. who would render the term problematic. The new post-1965 Asian immigrants, encompassing a diverse range of class origins, ethnic identities, and political orientations make it increasingly difficult to speak of a "shared" experience.

Such diversity between and within Asian American groups makes for interesting politics. Few can claim to speak for Asian Americans as a whole. Older organizations such as the Chinese Consolidated Benevolent Association cannot represent and articulate the needs of the increasingly diverse ethnic Chinese population in America. The second and third generation Asian Americans who founded many community-based organizations in the late 1960s and early 1970s are now in the demographic minority. Every group except Japanese Americans now has more foreign-born than native-born members. The estimated growth in the immigrant population suggests an emerging leadership gap between Asians on the basis of nativity status.

Differences also manifest themselves between Asian American ethnic groups as the result of distinct political agendas. Filipino "homeland" politics and the Japanese American movement for redress/reparations, for example, are issues which elicit little excitement or the potential for political mobilization outside of the ethnically specific community. In the wake of the L.A. riots, some Korean American leaders felt that other Asian American groups did not take a firm stand against the violence and property damage directed at Korean American small businesses. Bong Hwan Kim, executive director of the Korean Youth Center, said, "You can't deny the fact that among some [Chinese and Japanese Americans] there was an 'I-am-not-Korean mentality,' and then running for the hills."[12]

This, if anything, illustrates the situational nature of panethnic identity and organization, and the circumstances which can lead to its unraveling. Another source of potential difference lies in the increasing class stratification of Asian American communities.

The Increasing Significance of Class

The relative importance of class with respect to race is currently a central preoccupation in the race relations literature. When sociologist William Julius Wilson argued in 1978 that the contemporary life chances of individual African Americans "have more to do with their economic class position than with their day-to-day encounters with whites,"[13] he created a raging storm of a debate about the relative importance of race versus class in American life. At stake was discerning *the key factor* in determining life chances and the patterns of racial accommodation and conflict.

I would argue that correspondingly little attention has been given to the issue of class and contemporary Asian American communities. Research questions abound. What is the class structure of Asian American communities? How does it mirror, intersect, or diverge from the broader configuration of class stratification in the United States? What is the relationship of the distribution of status and power to economic class location in Asian American communities? What are the class bases for specific political mobilizations?

Suggesting these topics does not imply that no literature exists. Good work has indeed been done on political organization, the ethnic labor market, and the relationship of Asian Americans to the global economy.[14] However, what may be important to future research endeavors and policy initiatives is to understand the effects of race and class on the contemporary Asian American experience in a way which does not assert the primacy of one factor, nor treat each as an objectively distinct category with rigidly defined boundaries.

Korean-African American conflict in Los Angeles and other urban settings, for example, cannot be neatly framed in either purely class or racial terms. Such tragic conflict is overdetermined by an ensemble of factors involving the ghetto economy, patterns of small entrepreneurship, access to resources, and racial ideology in the United States and South Korea.

The recent U.S. Commission on Civil Rights report[15] on Asian Americans illustrates that racial discrimination is a problem which affects all classes in the Asian American community, although its effects vary widely by class strata. The problems encountered by a rich entrepreneur from Hong Kong and a recently arrived Hmong refugee are obviously distinct. The sites and types of discriminatory acts each is likely to encounter, and the range of *available responses* to them, differ by class location. Distinct class strata in the Asian American community experience a *differential racialization* in which race has been rendered more complex by class.

From a racialization perspective, much of the existing race/class debate suffers from the imposition of rigid categories and analyses which degenerate into dogmatic assertions of the primacy of one category over the other. I see the importance of analyzing racial and class divisions in a single unified framework—one which grasps the increasing significance of class for Asian Americans within a social order still highly structured by race. To do this, one would have abandoned any essentialist notions of race and class, and view them as different, and at times competing, modalities by which social actors see themselves and collective action is mobilized.[16]

In summary, the "increasing significance of class" does not necessarily suggest the "declining significance of race." However, a *differential racialization* has developed between and within different Asian American communities with important consequences for individual identity, collective consciousness, and political organization.

In the coming decades, there will be issues which unite Asian Americans, and issues which divide them. Redistricting and reapportionment debates, Asian American admissions in higher education, and anti-Asian violence are issues which cut across different Asian American ethnic groups and offer the potential for panethnic unity. On the other hand, class, nativity, and generational differences can manifest themselves in distinct political agendas. Many foreign-born Asians desperately need programs, such as English-acquisition and job-training programs which can ease their transition into the mainstream of American life. More "established" and resource-rich groups are less concerned with basic "survival issues" and instead emphasize mobility ones such as the "glass ceiling" in professional employment. In spite of these significant differences, I believe that panethnic consciousness will be an enduring feature of Asian American organization in the coming decades as political elites attempt to wield a range of disparate interests into a coherent political force. This may prove to be crucial in order to respond to disturbing trends in the prevailing political climate.

The Racialization of Politics

Last year, Megan Higoshi and other members of a mostly Japanese American Girl Scout troop were selling cookies outside of a suburban supermarket in Southern California. A man they approached simply replied, "I only buy from American girls."[17] Over 50 years after the bombing of Pearl Harbor, Japanese Americans are again victims of rising tensions between Japan and the United States. This should come as no surprise. The fate of Asian Americans has always been historically shaped by the prevailing state of U.S.-Asia relations.

The current state of relations is a rapidly deteriorating one. The "Buy American" craze continues despite the confusion created by multinational ownership, sourcing of parts and materials, and assembly. And the indicators of deteriorating relations are not purely economic, they are cultural as well. Examples like Baseball Commissioner Fay Vincent's objection to selling the Seattle Mariners to Nintendo, Michael Crichton's new thriller *Rising Sun*, and Ray Stevens' country hit, "Working for the Japanese" illustrate the cultural pervasiveness of anti-Japanese sentiments. Such sentiments have created an upsurge in random and organized acts of anti-Asian violence.[18]

More disturbing is the manner in which these sentiments seep into electoral politics. During the Senate campaign in New Hampshire, Democratic Senate candidate John Durkin accused his Republican opponent Bob Smith of accepting support from "Japs":

> The same Japs who planned and carried out a sneak attack on Dec. 7, 1941, are now planning a sneak attack on the voters of New Hampshire on Nov. 6, 1990. Here we have the Japs, they buy Rockefeller Center and are trying to turn the Rockettes into

geishas. That's bad enough. But here they're trying to buy a U.S. Senate seat.[19]

Durkin's analysis highlights a disturbing dimension of contemporary politics—the manner in which political issues are *racialized*. Political issues have been increasingly interpreted through a framework of racial meanings. Jesse Helms' come-from-behind Senate campaign in 1990, the late Lee Atwater's "Willie Horton" ad campaign for President Bush, and David Duke's surprising show of support in various Louisiana bids are all eloquent testimony to the fact that the *race card* can be effectively played and does win elections. "Racially coded" and racially explicit appeals have come to dominate electoral contests, and as such, there has been an increasing *racialization* of politics.

Much of this has taken the form of a concerted backlash to the perceived social impact of an increasingly diverse population. David Duke, during his declaration of candidacy in December 1991, argued that immigration should be a major issue in the presidential election. The time had come, he stated, to severely limit immigration into our society:

> What's happening is, we are unraveling. We're losing our way. This country is overwhelmingly European descent. It's overwhelmingly Christian. And if we lose our underpinning, I think we're going to lose the foundations of America.[20]

During his presidential campaign, Patrick Buchanan drew upon the assimilationist paradigm to weigh the social costs of integrating different groups:

> I think God made all people good. But if we had to take a million immigrants in, say Zulus next year, or Englishmen, and put them up in Virginia, what group would be easier to assimilate and would cause less problems for the people of Virginia?[21]

Other political initiatives are indicative of an overall intolerance towards diversity. U.S. English has recently begun a $1.6 million campaign against congressional representatives who oppose a House bill declaring English the official U.S. language. Norman Shumway, the organization's chairman and former Republican Congressman from California, says, "There are people coming to this country who feel they don't have to learn English, and we think that's a threat."[22] In addition to this, a growing number of businesses, ranging from hospitals to bottling plants, have implemented work rules which require their employees to speak English on the job. At the heart of these restrictions lurks the issue of race. Ed Chen, a lawyer for the ACLU, observes:

> For a lot of folks, language becomes a proxy for race or for immigrant status. It becomes a legitimate way of expressing concern about being overrun by hordes of Mexicans and Asians coming into the United States.[23]

The overall racialization of politics projects a grim vision of the future in which multiracial and multicultural diversity is openly resisted and legislated against, instead of celebrated.

Trends and Prospects

Some intriguing demographic shifts will occur in the years to come which will influence the nature of race relations between Asian Americans and other groups. The number of Asian Americans, which doubled in the last ten years, is expected, according to projections, to double again in 20 years to over 14 million. Although Asian Americans still tend to cluster in a few states and in urban centers like the Chinatowns of San Francisco and New York, they will increasingly be found in all parts of the country. According to the 1990 Census, some states have seen a dramatic growth in their Asian American population since the last count: Texas, up 165.5 percent (319,459); New Jersey, up 162 percent (272,521); and Rhode Island, up 245 percent (18,325).[24]

The Census also reveals that Asian Americans are increasingly likely to live in the suburbs. An interesting dimension of Asian American residential patterns in the post-civil rights period is that they are quite distinct from the patterns of "hypersegregation" which African Americans experience. An examination of the 16 largest cities in America found that Asian Americans were nearly half as likely to be residentially segregated from Whites as African Americans.[25] The growing "suburbanization" of Asian Americans, however, may bring with it a host of new problems as new Asian immigrants settle in areas and transform the established patterns of housing and consumption. In this regard, the political battles in Monterey Park over English-Only signs, development, and racial recomposition may prefigure the future.

In certain areas of the economy, Asian capital investment is growing and will continue to grow in the coming decades. It is estimated, for example, that Asians are starting a quarter to a third of all new electronics companies in California's Silicon Valley.[26] Recent changes in immigration laws may further stimulate investment. Under the Immigration Act of 1990, some 10,000 visas are reserved for wealthy foreign investors willing to invest a minimum of one million dollars and to create at least ten jobs for U.S. citizens. This has numerous states attempting to lure rich Asian immigrants as part of an economic development strategy.[27]

Despite their anticipated influence on economy and society, there has been, up to now, little attention given to Asian Americans and how they are affected by, and how they affect, the broader patterns of racial politics. The absence of a sustained scholarly and policy-oriented appraisal will become more glaring and untenable in the years to come. Currently a host of issues which cut to the heart of racial politics in the United States have been raised by, or centrally involved, Asian Americans:

- The question of bilingual education as articulated in the *Lau* v. *Nichols* decision.

- Immigration reform, particularly as it relates to the emphasis on family reunification, established in 1965.

- Affirmative action in a range of arenas, but particularly with respect to Asian admissions into institutions of higher learning.

- Reapportionment debates, particularly in California and New York in the face of the dramatically changing racial make-up of these states.

- Civil rights legislation as reflected in the disputed *Wards Cove* decision.

- Race and the performing arts as witnessed by the Jonathan Pryce/*Miss Saigon* controversy.

- And perhaps most immediately, interracial tensions in inner city communities of which the tragedy of African American-Korean relations in South Central is but one manifestation.

While analysts of race relations continue to focus almost exclusively on black/white relations, the reality is that Asian Americans have become a crucial barometer of the contemporary racial climate.

Indeed, an analysis of contemporary Asian American images—as a "model minority" and as a racial threat—reveals interesting dimensions of the very nature of racism in the United States. We tend to think of racism as hostility directed against those of a different skin color whom we believe to be "inferior"—in class and status terms, in intellectual ability, or in cultural orientation. This is coupled with structural forms of discrimination—in the job market, in politics, in residential patterns—and negative cultural representations. In the United States, African Americans are subject to this type of racism.

Asian Americans, however, are subject to a different form of racism. They are often the objects of *resentment* by other groups who perceive that they do "too well," that they unfairly secure wealth and other material resources and social advantages. This resentment has historically resulted in political disenfranchisement and exclusionary laws in the late-19th to early-20th century. We are seeing some of that today in the form of "English-Only" initiatives and more stringent curbs on immigration and foreign capital investment.

A political response from Asian Americans has emerged to this climate of increased intolerance, though it remains vague and in formation. Between Asian American ethnic groups, the degree of panethnic unity remains situationally defined. Between Asian Americans and other racial minority groups, there are issues which can potentially unite, and issues which threaten to divide. A common agenda around bilingual education, immigration reform, and employer discrimination against foreign-born or non-English speaking workers can seemingly be forged with Latino groups. These same issues, however, in an era of declining public resources and private opportunities, can be the basis for conflicts with African Americans. On the other hand, a shared concern for civil rights legislation and enforcement, equal opportunity in hiring and promotion decisions, and the economic reconstruction of our major cities can potentially unite Asian Americans with African Americans, as well as other racial minorities.

In an editorial reflecting on the meaning of the L.A. riots, Judy Ching-Chia Wong states:

The problems and experiences of Asian-Americans, African-Americans, Hispanics, etc., while sometimes similar, are not the same. Unless Asian-Americans learn to think and speak out as a group, we will continue to be caught in the middle, misunderstood and pummeled by both sides.[28]

Her assessment seems quite correct. In the worst case scenario, Asian Americans would increasingly be the victims of racial violence, while simultaneously being extolled and regarded by the media, political leaders, and the general populace as the shining exemplars of the assimilative capabilities of our society. In this context, Asian Americans will add a new and very troubling dimension to the continuing "American dilemma."

Notes

1. Andrew Hacker, *Two Nations: Black and White, Separate, Hostile, Unequal* (New York: Charles Scribner's Sons, 1992); Thomas Byrne Edsall and Mary D. Edsall, *Chain Reaction: The Impact of Race, Rights, and Taxes on American Politics* (New York: W. W. Norton, 1991); Studs Terkel, *Race: How Blacks and Whites Think and Feel about the American Obsession* (New York: New Press, 1992).

2. Tim Rutten, "A New Kind of Riot," *New York Review of Books* 39:11 (June 11, 1992), 52.

3. The most comprehensive explication of the assimilationist paradigm is Milton M. Gordon, *Assimilation in American Life* (New York: Oxford University Press, 1964).

4. Paul Takagi, "The Myth of 'Assimilation in American Life,' " *Amerasia Journal* 2 (1973), 149–158.

5. Rose Hum Lee, *The Chinese in the United States of America* (Hong Kong: Hong Kong University Press, 1960).

6. Harry H. L. Kitano, *Japanese Americans: The Evolution of a Subculture* (Englewood Cliffs, New Jersey: Prentice-Hall, 1969).

7. Stephen S. Fugita and David J. O'Brien, *Japanese American Ethnicity: The Persistence of Community* (Seattle: University of Washington Press, 1991).

8. Quoted in Seth Mydans, "Vietnamese, With Hearts across the Sea," *New York Times* (August 22, 1991), A16.

9. Michael Omi and Howard Winant, *Racial Formation in the United States: From the 1960s to the 1980s* (New York and London: Routledge, 1986).

10. Winthrop Jordan, *White Over Black: American Attitudes Toward the Negro, 1550–1812* (New York: Norton, 1968).

11. David Lopez and Yen Espiritu, "Panethnicity in the United States: A Theoretical Framework," *Ethnic and Racial Studies* 13 (1990), 198.

12. Quoted in L. A. Chung, "Asian Americans Frustrated in Trying to Respond to Rioting," *San Francisco Chronicle* (May 6, 1992), A4.

13. William Julius Wilson, *The Declining Significance of Race: Blacks and Changing American Institutions* (Chicago: University of Chicago Press, 1978), 1.

14. See, for example, Peter Kwong, *Chinatown, N.Y.: Labor and Politics, 1930–1950* (New York: Monthly Review Press, 1979); Ivan Light and Edna Bonacich, *Immigrant Entrepreneurs: Koreans in Los Angeles, 1965–1982* (Berkeley: University of California Press, 1988).

15. U.S. Commission on Civil Rights, *Civil Rights Issues Facing Asian Americans in the 1990s*, Washington, D.C., February 1992.

16. These comments can be extended to a consideration of gender as well. In many respects, racialization is a highly "gendered" process with women and men experiencing community, the labor market, and the "private, domestic" sphere in a distinct fashion. Racial ideology assigns distinct attributes to racialized men and women as endless versions of Madam Butterfly (from *M. Butterfly* to *Miss Saigon*) attest.

17. Quoted in Seth Mydans, "New Unease for Japanese-Americans," *New York Times* (March 4, 1992), A8.

18. See chapter 2, U.S. Commission on Civil Rights, *Civil Rights Issues Facing Asian Americans in the 1990s*.

19. "Opponent Calls Senate Candidate a Japanese Agent," *San Francisco Chronicle* (October 27, 1990), A8.

20. Quoted in Robin Toner, "Duke Takes His Anger into 1992 Race," *New York Times* (December 5, 1991), A14.

21. Buchanan made this comment on the ABC News program *This Week*. Quoted in Maureen Dowd, "Buchanan's Alternative: Not Kind and Gentle," *New York Times* (January 15, 1992), A12.

22. Quoted in Dan Levy, "U.S. English Goes National with Campaign," *San Francisco Chronicle* (July 9, 1992), A7.

23. Quoted in Seth Mydans, "Pressure for English-Only Job Rules Stirring a Sharp Debate Across U.S.," *New York Times* (August 8, 1990), A10.

24. Fox Butterfield, "Asians Spread Across a Land, and Help Change It," *New York Times* (February 24, 1991), A14.

25. Reynolds Farley and Walter R. Allen, *The Color Line and Quality of Life in America* (New York: Oxford University Press, 1989), 144–145.

26. Andrew Pollack, "Asian Immigrants New Leaders in Silicon Valley," *New York Times* (January 14, 1992), A1.

27. James Leung, "California Tries to Lure Rich Asian Immigrants," *San Francisco Chronicle* (February 11, 1991), A1.

28. Judy Ching-Chia Wong, "Victims of Both Races," *New York Times* (May 28, 1992), A15.

Asian Pacific Islanders and the "Glass Ceiling"— New Era of Civil Rights Activism?

Affirmative Action Policy

Henry Der

EXECUTIVE DIRECTOR, CHINESE FOR AFFIRMATIVE ACTION
SAN FRANCISCO, CALIFORNIA

Through education and the path laid down by the 1960s black civil rights movement, Asian Pacific Islanders have achieved entry-level employment in a broad range of businesses, occupations, and professions—telecommunications, finance, insurance, protective services, skilled construction, health care, the law—that had been traditionally closed to racial minorities. Now, three decades after the passage of the 1964 Civil Rights Act and federal enforcement of affirmative action regulations, Asian Pacific Islanders are in a position to carry the civil rights employment struggle into its next phase: challenging the racial make-up of corporate and public sector management.

The "glass ceiling"—promotional barriers against racial minorities and women—has stirred a sense of injustice and inequality among Asian Pacific Islanders. Numerous studies by scholars, governmental agencies, and non-profit organizations have documented the sparse representation of racial minorities and women in management positions. In its *Asian American Civil Rights Issues of the 1990s Report*, the U.S. Commission on Civil Rights cites the "glass ceiling" as one of five prevalent types of employment discrimination experienced by Asian Americans.[1] Reports have found that, among all racial groups including Whites, Asian Pacific Islander professionals face the worst chance of being advanced into management positions.[2] In its 1991 study of nine Fortune 500 corporations, the U.S. Department of Labor found that, "if there is not a glass ceiling, there certainly is a point beyond which racial minorities and women have not advanced in some companies."[3]

Frustrated and, at times, angry that they are not receiving promotional opportunities commensurate with their educational background and accomplishments in the workplace, some Asian Pacific Islanders argue that cracking the "glass ceiling" is the civil rights issue of the 1990s. They are shedding the image of the "silent" racial minority and openly aspiring for advancement into management and leadership roles. Asian Pacific Islanders have formed employee organizations, in part, to create a vehicle to voice their concerns about the lack of promotional opportunities.[4] Their impatience with cracking the "glass ceiling" suggests that the 1990s and beyond may constitute a new era of civil rights activism on the part of Asian Pacific Islanders.

Unlike their integration into entry-level employment, cracking the "glass ceiling" will not be an easy or simple task for Asian Pacific Islanders. Harsh criticism against race-based, affirmative action strategies remains unabated.[5] Notwithstanding the all-too-familiar pronouncement of equal employment policies, many corporate leaders have failed to take ownership or affirm the appointment of racial minority managers and administrators as an organizational responsiblity.[6] Socioeconomic differences within Asian Pacific Islander groups and between racial minorities underscore some of the limitations of affirmative action strategies. Racial minorities, women, and white males are all locked in a battle over a shrinking number of management and administrative jobs.

In order to understand and assess the likelihood of Asian Pacific Islander success to crack the "glass ceiling," I will examine some social and economic constraints that make the establishment and implementation of affirmative action promotional policies for Asian Pacific Islanders a challenging task. Specifically, I will discuss (1) socioeconomic differentials between Asian Pacific Islanders and black Americans that reinforce distrust of affirmative action policies favoring "advantaged" racial minorities over economically disadvantaged individuals; (2) population growth leading to possible fragmentation of Asian Pacific Islanders as a racial minority group; (3) higher tolerance level by Asian Pacific Islanders to endure racial discrimination, instead of pressing ahead for remedies. Then I will suggest strategies to enable Asian Pacific Islanders to more effectively crack the "glass ceiling."

More Help for the "Advantaged"?

Executive Order 11246 and its implementing regulations, issued by President Johnson in 1965, require federal contractors to provide equal employment opportunities through the implementation of affirmative action programs to recruit, hire, retain, and promote qualified racial minorities at every level of an employer's workforce. But for racial discrimination, qualified racial minorities would be represented at every level of a workforce in proportion to their respective representation in the labor force. Controlling for non-racial factors like education and geography, racial minorities should achieve roughly the same earnings level as their white male counterparts. Lower earnings and underrepresentation of racial minorities in the workforce signal the presence of discriminatory barriers.

In general, affirmative action has been an effective strategy for racial minorities to gain entry-level employment. Two-thirds of all Asian Pacific Islanders working full-time hold employment in largely white-collar occupations—professionals, technicians, managers, sales, and administrative support—compared to 57 percent Whites in the same occupations.[7] Between 1973 and 1982, the number of Blacks in professional, technical, managerial, and administrative positions increased by 57 percent, from 974,000 to 1,533,000, while the number of Whites in such positions increased by only 36 percent.[8]

William J. Wilson, Thomas Sowell, and Daniel C. Thompson observe, though, that significant civil rights employment gains made since the 1960s have benefitted mostly college-educated racial minorities.[9] Wilson argues that governmental efforts to eliminate traditional racial barriers through affirmative action have had the unintentional effect of contributing to the growing economic class divisions in the black community. These scholars view affirmative action programs as having aided only the already-advantaged or most advantaged of traditionally disadvantaged groups.

Though not direct targets of their criticism against affirmative action, many college-educated Asian Pacific Islanders, including the foreign born, have also taken advantage of affirmative action opportunities in the workplace. Thirty-nine percent of all Asian Pacific Islanders aged 25 and over have completed at least four years of college, almost double the rate of Whites.[10] To the extent that high educational attainment is equated with an "advantaged" status, Asian Pacific Islanders are popularly perceived as having leapfrogged over disadvantaged Blacks in the workplace.

In response to being labelled a "model minority," Asian Pacific Islanders point out that they still lag behind Whites economically.[11] The per capita income of Asian Pacific Islanders is lower than that of Whites; the poverty and unemployment rates of Asian Pacific Islanders are persistently higher.[12] In addition to the "glass ceiling," Asian Pacific Islanders consistently experience a lower earning return on education than white males at every educational attainment level. Such socioeconomic indicators reinforce the effects of past discrimination against Asian Pacific Islanders and the rationale for their inclusion in affirmative action employment programs. However, such comparisons with Whites have generally failed to dispel the perception that Asian Pacific Islanders are "advantaged."

The term "model minority" has been used implicitly, and at times explicitly, to chide black Americans and other racial minorities for alleged failures to pull themselves up by their own bootstraps. Racial minority community representatives have been understandably reluctant to draw socioeconomic comparisons among themselves. However, such comparisons are inevitable because, consciously or not, the economic plight of black Americans remains the standard by which America judges itself on achieving racial equality for its citizens.

If we reject outright the implicit and explicit value judgments associated with the use of "model minority," an objective comparison of Asian Pacific Islander and black socioeconomic characteristics indicate that, on average, Asian Pacific Islanders are better off than black Americans, in terms of higher individual and family median income, poverty and teenage unemployment rates that are respectively almost two-thirds and one-half lower, higher percentage of two or more earners per household, higher percentage of minority-owned businesses and doubling of the dollar amount of business receipts per firm.[13] The socioeconomic differentials between Asian Pacific Islanders and black Americans are almost as wide as the gap between white and black Americans. Relative to Whites, Asian Pacific Islanders are "disadvantaged"; but relative to black Americans, they are "advantaged."

The socioeconomic differentials between "advantaged" and "disadvantaged" racial minorities and within specific racial groups have led to calls for the reformulation of race-based affirmative action strategies. Dinesh D'Souza advocates the establishment of non-racial or socioeconomic affirmative action.[14] L. Ling-chi Wang insists that affirmative action programs must take into consideration race and class oppression, but also supports specific race-based remedies for black Americans.[15] Attri-buting the demise of black employment to the change of the American economy from being an industrial to a service- and information-oriented one, Wilson calls for the establishment of universal reform programs to promote economic growth and full employment so as to provide a larger number of job opportunities for the truly disadvantaged—the economic underclass and the least educated.

It is questionable whether any of these reforms will be any more effective than race-based affirmative action remedies in helping the truly disadvantaged.[16] Because today's economic competition and information-based society demands the employment of workers with high educational attainment levels and occupational skills, it is highly unlikely that employers will hire poorly educated individuals, especially racial minorities who lack certain occupational skills. Out of self-interest, employers will distribute affirmative action benefits only to those racial minorities who are educated and qualified. Wang's proposal is highly consistent with the freshman admission diversity policies at some highly selective universities, but would be perplexing, if not difficult, for an employer to implement, in terms of granting employment preferences based on an individual's current or past low-income status.

Race-based affirmative action employment policy, then, keeps the door open for educated racial minorities at the entry level and sets incentives for others to acquire more education. But it has not been used consistently or effectively to advance Asian Pacific Islanders into promotive positions.

The perception that Asian Pacific Islanders are "advantaged" does not accurately reflect their employment status. The strong work experience and educational background of Asian Pacific Islanders make them the true test case of how well the notion of meritocracy works in America. Proponents of meritocracy assert that, when compared to Whites, there are equal payoffs for qualified and educated racial minorities; education and other social factors, but not race, determine earnings.[17] The underrepresentation in management positions and lower median incomes of Asian Pacific Islanders, when compared to their white male counterparts, indicate that the payoff has not materialized for members of this racial minority group.

Yet, what is the likelihood that Asian Pacific Islanders can garner public sympathy and action to remedy this unequal employment condition? Employed, disillusioned, college-educated Asian Pacific Islanders may be stymied by promotional barriers in the workplace, but, in the public arena of competing social needs, their plight pales, in contrast to the social condition of chronically unemployed, economically disadvantaged racial minorities. Nationwide, there are slightly under one million poor Asian Pacific Islanders, but there are approximately ten million poor Blacks and 22 million poor Whites.[18] The growing number of poor and homeless people has had a greater impact on the American psyche than the comparative percentage of poor by racial group. Whereas there was an emotional edge in the early years of the civil rights movement to support racial minorities crossing and breaking the "color line" to achieve social justice, the "glass ceiling" problem has not evoked the same visceral response among the public, especially as it relates to Asian Pacific Islanders.

Race-based affirmative action strategies are also weak in adjudicating other competing social needs. Asian Pacific Islander women earn lower median incomes than both their Asian and white male counterparts, controlling for education. However, controlling for educational and occupational status when compared to white women, Asian Pacific Islander women do as well if not slightly better, in terms of earned median income.[19] Should Asian Pacific Islander women receive employment preferences over their male counterparts, but defer to white females? Unlike the normally larger numbers of jobs available at the entry level, both male and female Asian Pacific Islanders, other racial minorities, and white women find themselves at odds with each other over a shrinking number of administrative and managerial positions.[20] It is not clear who should be helped first.

Fragmentation of Asian Pacific Islanders

At the beginning of the 1960s civil rights movement, Asian Pacific Islanders were an inchoate racial minority group. An Asian Pacific Islander political consciousness had yet to be born. Immigrants from Asia came to America as Chinese, Filipinos, or Koreans. They did not bring with them an Asian Pacific Islander identity. They had little in common with Pacific Islanders, most of whom are native born. Language and cultural differences among all of these groups inhibited social or political interaction across ethnic lines. It would take the unfolding of the modern-day civil rights movement, enforcement of federal affirmative action regulations, and publicly funded social programs to help forge what has become a politically constructed racial minority group called "Asian Pacific Islanders."

The political advantages gained by a unified "Asian Pacific Islander" classification are tempered, however, by the complexities and potential difficulties in establishing employment policies to meet the needs of diverse Asian and Pacific Islander groups. Community representatives and scholars have reacted cautiously, if not negatively, toward certain "average" or "median" socioeconomic characteristics, attributed to Asian Pacific Islanders as a whole. They argue that, when compared to the socioeconomic characteristics of other racial minority groups, these "averages" and "medians" compromise public recognition of the social needs of economically disadvantaged Asian Pacific Islanders, thereby exacerbating the myth of the "model minority." They also fear that misinterpretation and misunderstanding of these "averages" and "medians" may lead to the demise of affirmative action remedies to benefit Asian Pacific Islanders.[21]

In addition to distinct social stratification within a specific Asian or Pacific Islander group, Asian Indians, Chinese, Japanese, Filipinos, and Koreans tend to be employed largely as white collar professionals, technicians, and administrative support workers. Employment barriers created by the "glass ceiling" are major challenges to members of these ethnic groups. They are more likely on average to earn higher wages, be better educated, and experience a lower poverty rate than other Asian Pacific Islander groups.[22]

In contrast, Vietnamese, Cambodians, Laotians, Hmongs, Hawaiians, Samoans, and other Pacific Islanders are more likely to be employed as blue-collar laborers, operators, service workers, and technicians. Low wages and substandard working conditions are dominant aspects of their employment. The acquisition of basic English, technological, and other occupational skills is vital to improve their economic status.

Established Asian groups—Chinese, Filipinos, Japanese, Asian Indians, and Koreans—constitute three-fourths of today's national Asian Pacific Islander population. The dominance and population percentage of these established Asian groups will diminish as more Southeast Asian and other Asian families become reunited in the U.S. The proliferation of language minority press and social institutions to serve the needs of these new immigrants will reinforce ethnic distinctiveness among these Asian and Pacific Islander groups, in contrast to the fostering of an inclusive Asian Pacific Islander identity. As some Asian Pacific Islander groups achieve a critical population mass, especially at the state and regional levels, they may seek to fragment and establish distinct affirmative action employment categories, separate from the unified Asian Pacific Islander category.[23]

Under federal law, employers are obligated to meet the employment needs of Asian Pacific Islanders, without making distinctions among the specific Asian and Pacific Islander groups. Mere compliance with the law may not satisfy the employment needs of these emerging groups. In occupational categories where Asian Pacific Islanders are well-represented, members of some established Asian groups—Chinese, Japanese, and Filipinos—generally dominate the level of Asian Pacific Islander representation. To what extent should employers be required to outreach, recruit, and give special consideration to members of non-established Asian and Pacific Islander groups? Will members of established Asian groups be tolerant of these preferential efforts for emerging groups?

Fundamentally, there have always been doubts about the inclusion of Asian Pacific Islanders as a protected group in affirmative action programs. Some scholars consider black Americans to be the quintessential minority group, better able than any other ethnic group with the exception of American Indians, to justify a claim for preferential treatment in employment.[24] The recent immigrant or refugee status of emerging Asian group members seemingly contradicts the historic oppression rationale for affirmative action inclusion.

Affirmative action proponents have always characterized race-based remedies and strategies as temporary interventions to overcome the effects of historic discrimination. Asian Pacific Islanders (or distinct subgroups) are likely to be the first racial minority group to demonstrate that affirmative action remedies are, in fact, temporary in nature. There is precedence for a specific Asian group, or Asian Pacific Islanders as a whole, to be excluded from affirmative action programs.[25]

With their strong representation in certain occupational categories, some may argue that Asian groups appear to have outgrown the need for affirmative action remedies. At what point should we state that some Asian groups have achieved equality in the workplace, while others have not? Should affirmative action coverage for Asian Pacific Islanders be withdrawn from some occupational categories but retained for others like management and administration?

Asian Pacific Islanders have historically spent much time to argue for their inclusion into affirmative action programs, but have not adequately assessed improvements in their socioeconomic status that are attributable to race-based affirmative action strategies. If Asian Pacific Islanders have transitioned out of affirmative action protection, it becomes critical to understand and acknowledge under what conditions equality has been achieved and to ask whether the same can be replicated to benefit Asian Pacific Islanders at the management level.

Temporary Tolerance of Discrimination: Lack of Action

One human resources expert has described the "glass ceiling" as the result of two cultures clashing: the Asian work style as contextual, indirect, inner-directed, and self-reliant; and the white male style as hierarchical, controlling, aggressive, and oriented toward win-lose outcomes.[26] It is not uncommon for Asian Pacific Islanders to describe themselves as being "non-aggressive" or "deferential."

Consequently, the lack of initiative to understand the demands of being a manager or desire to be promoted on the part of Asian Pacific Islanders has often been cited as a self-initiated barrier to advancement in the workplace, not the result of institutional barriers.[27]

Over the years, the number of race and national origin employment discrimination complaints filed by Asian Pacific Islanders with federal and state enforcement agencies has increased. Yet, these complaints barely constitute 1 percent of all complaints filed, proportionately less than the representation of Asian Pacific Islanders among racial minority groups protected by anti-discriminatory laws.[28] *Wards Cove Packing Co.* v. *Antonio* and *Wong* v. *Hampton* have been notable Asian Pacific Islander employment cases before the U.S. Supreme Court.[29] But, there has been a paucity of class action employment discrimination lawsuits filed by Asian Pacific Islanders in the last 28 years.[30] Notwithstanding some celebrated university tenure cases filed individually by Asian American faculty members, there has been no class action lawsuit in recent years involving an Asian Pacific Islander lead plaintiff who has sought to oppose promotional barriers in the workplace.[31]

As the national Asian Pacific Islander population continues to grow at a faster rate than all other racial groups, a critical mass of Asian Pacific Islanders willing to pursue legal complaints against discriminatory employment practices including the "glass ceiling" could emerge, but it is unlikely for a couple of reasons. First, there are greater personal risks involved, including retaliation, whenever a racial minority employee files a complaint alleging discriminatory promotional practices than when a non-employee files. Second, many public interest law firms impose income guidelines that preclude legal representation of employed racial minorities, especially those who earn salaries well above the poverty-level. The legal costs involved in pursuing time-consuming class action lawsuits have discouraged both potential clients and private attorneys from doing so. Third, paradoxically, the increase in the size of the Asian Pacific Islander workforce, due to the steady immigration of professionals, reinforces differences in how Asian Pacific Islanders and other racial minorities experience and react to racial discrimination.

Charles Hamilton and John Ogbu observe that ethnic immigrant groups, including Asians, come to America under three general circumstances: (1) they came voluntarily or by choice; (2) they perceive socioeconomic conditions in America to be an improvement over what they left behind; (3) while they may be oppressed and discriminated against, immigrant groups have not been dehumanized like black Americans.[32] In contrast, black Americans compare their social condition to that of Whites and find racism to be endemic and permanent.[33]

Immigrants expect to face racial discrimination in America. Within the context of survival in a new country, they strategically, and not culturally, resign themselves to tolerate temporarily unequal treatment and not to expect necessary government intervention to facilitate their transition into a higher socioeconomic status. According to Hamilton, whereas black Americans have had to engage in a continuous political struggle to demonstrate their humanity through the pursuit of anti-discriminatory remedies, immigrants have engaged themselves in an economic struggle first. Some reject the notion that Asian Pacific Islanders are "victims" and assert that members of this racial minority group have been successful in overcoming racism without government aid or affirmative action remedies.[34]

In contrast to black defiance toward racial discrimination, Asian Pacific Islanders, especially immigrants, hope that racial discrimination can be minimized by either ignoring it or focusing one's energy in another direction. That hope may be naive and premature. As Asian Pacific Islander employees develop tenure on the job and seek promotion opportunities, the impact of the "glass ceiling" will force a greater number of them than ever before to seek remedial assistance.

Foundation for Action

There has not been a shortage of strategies to crack the "glass ceiling." Seminars, conferences, and workshops on how to do so have become commonplace. Signs of organizational barriers are numerous: little or no acceptance of a multicultural workforce or of management ownership in promoting minorities, lack of management sensitivity, insufficient identification of talented minorities, lack of minority role models, lack of "informal" networks, inadequate performance evaluation system, insufficient opportunities for useful social interaction. The prescriptions to eradicate these barriers include: chief executive officer involvement in programs, establishment of goals and timetables to increase the number of minority managers, evaluation of managers on how well they reach their affirmative action goals, minority inclusion in succession plans, development and implementation of a career path process, establishment of a formal mentor program, creation of greater opportunities for senior managers to get to know talented minorities.[35]

The fierce competition for promotion opportunities forces Asian Pacific Islanders to explain, justify, and differentiate what unique qualities they as Asian Pacific Islanders may bring to leadership or management positions. Or stated in another way, what difference will they make as leaders or managers because they are Asian Pacific Islanders?

On an individual basis, Asian Pacific Islander employees have exhorted themselves to develop windows of opportunities, cultivate an inventory of skills and determine what needs to be done to market themselves within organizations, cultivate mentors, and develop informal and formal networks of support. In addition, some Asian Pacific Islander employees have identified the need to quantify their contributions to their employer, and where applicable, to involve themselves as a link in any Pacific Rim-related corporate activity.[36] Others simplistically suggest that the acquisition of new skills will help Asian Pacific Islanders vault these "glass ceiling" barriers.[37]

There are some limitations and pitfalls associated with these strategies. White males have long ago adopted many of these same strategies. Asian Pacific Islander adoption of these strategies does not necessarily propel them to the head of the waiting list for promotions, as white males are not standing still and are constantly honing their occupational skills and networks. Employers may be imposing undue pressure and unrealistic expectations on Asian Pacific Islanders in drawing a relationship between the right of qualified Asian Pacific Islanders to be promoted and their ability to cultivate Pacific Rim concerns. Informally or otherwise, white males do not feel compelled, nor are they expected, to associate themselves with a specific geographic market to demonstrate their worth to the employer or to justify the receipt of promotions. Asian Pacific Islanders face the distinct possibility of being stereotyped as being capable of increasing corporate profitability only through Pacific Rim-related activities.

The social and economic constraints discussed earlier—perception of being an "advantaged" minority, fragmentation among Asian and Pacific Islander groups, and reluctance to pursue legal remedies—motivate the consideration of other strategies. Asian Pacific Islander employees may want to consider strategies that more effectively enhance the realization of affirmative action promotional goals, increase public awareness of the different forms of discrimination against diverse Asian and Pacific Islander groups, and strengthen their role as managers who are capable of leading culturally diverse workforces.

First, Asian Pacific Islanders should develop strong employee organizations with clear goals to guide and monitor on a regular basis the implementation of affirmative action goals and timetables and to negotiate and secure a reasonably retaliatory-free framework in which to give direct feedback and advice on employer progress of achieving affirmative action goals. The presence of strong Asian Pacific Islander employee organizations constantly reinforces the need for employers to embrace and implement institution-wide practices and policies that eradicate the "glass ceiling."

Opponents of affirmative action frequently decry the competition and conflicts among racial minority groups over promotion opportunities. These critics perceive racial minority group members to be more interested in race than individual merit as the basis for promotional decisions. Such perceptions ignore the intense competition that occurs regularly among white males for promotions, much of which is not necessarily based on merit. Whether between racial minorities or between racial minorities and Whites, competition over a diminishing number of management positions is a reality in a rapidly changing workplace environment. In addition to ongoing efforts to emphasize their positive contributions to the workplace in a non-adversarial manner, Asian Pacific Islanders would benefit immensely from an organizational structure and support to focus and articulate objectively their employment aspirations. Otherwise, Asian Pacific Islander concerns become lost in the competition for promotions. These employee organizations should establish evaluation measures to assess the effectiveness of their monitoring, advisory, and advocacy role.

Second, Asian Pacific Islander employees in the workplace should seek out opportunities to inform and educate appropriate federal and state anti-discrimination officials about the different forms of promotion bias against members of this racial minority group. Enforcement officials also need to be sensitized about the employment needs of established and emerging Asian Pacific Islander groups.

The idiosyncratic nature of many managerial positions provides employers tremendous latitude in defining what is meant by leadership, communications, and interpersonal skills. Asian Pacific Islanders have reported that they have been assessed as lacking these skills, even though they may carry substantial workloads, communicate intelligibly, routinely train newly assigned management personnel, and are responsible for presentations before corporate executives or public bodies. Asian Pacific Islanders need to sensitize anti-discrimination officials to go beyond mere statistical analysis of racial minority representation in management positions and to achieve an understanding of how seemingly objective criteria are applied in a subjective manner, to the detriment of Asian Pacific Islander promotional aspirations.

Third, Asian Pacific Islanders should cultivate a heightened sense of social responsibility, interest, and ability to manage a culturally diverse workforce. Based on one's own experiences in coping with and overcoming racial discrimination, lessons learned need to be shared not just with fellow Asian Pacific Islander colleagues, but also with other racial minorities and disadvantaged group members so that respect for pluralism thrives in the workplace.

In the aftermath of the 1992 Los Angeles riots, middle-class Blacks became the target of introspection and self-criticism for possibly not doing enough to help all those left behind in the ghetto. Opposition to the U.S. Supreme Court nomination of Clarence Thomas strongly signalled a willingness on the part of racial minorities to look beyond race and scrutinize what an individual does with an opportunity. A similar challenge confronts educated Asian Pacific Islanders: how will Asian Pacific Islanders who achieve advancement through affirmative action programs aid and empower other racial minorities and the disadvantaged in the broadest sense? Asian Pacific Islanders in the workplace have the exciting challenge to define for themselves what they mean by "Asian Pacific Islander leadership." Clearly, such leadership means much more than fulfilling an affirmative action goal that results in self-gain. The civil rights movement envisioned affirmative action beneficiaries sharing skills, knowledge and experiences to enhance the public good and to assist all those who continue to experience racial discrimination.

The Next Phase of the Civil Rights Movement

Asian Pacific Islanders possess the educational and occupational background to carry the civil rights movement into its next phase of achieving the full integration of leadership positions in the workplace. I have discussed social and economic constraints that may prevent or delay Asian Pacific Islanders from fulfilling their management potential. Through the adoption of specific strategies that take advantage of organized actions, Asian Pacific Islanders can demonstrate that the utilization of affirmative action remedies benefits the individual recipient and the public good at the same time.

Notes

1. The other types of employment discrimination against Asian Americans, cited by the U.S. Commission on Civil Rights, include English-Only work rules, certification of foreign-trained professionals, discrimination caused by the Immigration Reform and Control Act, and employment discrimination against Asian American females.

2. Henry Der, Colleen Lye, and Howard Ting, *Broken Ladder: Asian Americans in City Government Reports* (San Francisco: Chinese for Affirmative Action, 1986, 1989, and 1992).

3. U.S. Department of Labor, *Glass Ceiling Initiative Report* (Washington, D.C.: U.S. Department of Labor, 1991).

4. Asian Pacific Islander employees at Avon Products, Pacific Gas and Electric Company, Pacific Bell, Levi Strauss, U.S. Forest Service, Internal Revenue Service, and University of California have formed in-house groups that promote cultural awareness and management sensitivity toward Asian Pacific Islander concerns.

5. Throughout the Reagan Administration, charges of reverse discrimination by white males slowed public employer compliance with court-ordered agreements to integrate police, fire, and other public departments in 51 local jurisdictions through the implementation of specific affirmative action goals and timetables. President Bush vetoed the Civil Rights Act of 1990, alleging repeatedly that affirmative action goals and timetables require the hiring and promotion of minorities and women on a "rigid quota" basis.

6. U.S. Department of Labor, *Pipelines of Progress: A Status Report on the Glass Ceiling* (Washington, D.C.: U.S. Department of Labor, 1992).

7. Claudine Bennett, *The Asian and Pacific Islander Population in the United States: March 1991 and 1990* (Washington, D.C.: U.S. Bureau of the Census, 1992).

8. U.S. Department of Labor statistics cited in William J. Wilson, *The Truly Disadvantaged: The Inner City, the Underclass, and Public Policy* (Chicago: University of Chicago Press, 1987).

9. William J. Wilson, *The Declining Significance of Race* (Chicago: University of Chicago Press, 1980); see also Thomas Sowell, *Civil Rights: Rhetoric or Reality* (New York: William Morrow, 1984); and Daniel C. Thompson, *A Black Elite* (New York: Greenwood Press, 1986).

10. Bennett, *The Asian and Pacific Islander Population.*

11. Bob H. Suzuki, "Asian Americans as the 'Model Minority'—Outdoing Whites? or Media Hype?" *Change,* American Association for Higher Education, Washington, D.C. (November–December 1989); and U.S. Commission on Civil Rights, *Civil Rights Issues Facing Asian Americans in the 1990s* (Washington, D.C.: U.S. Commission on Civil Rights, 1992).

12. Bennett, *The Asian and Pacific Islander Population.*

13. *Ibid.;* see also U.S. Department of Commerce, Economic Statistics Administration, U.S. Bureau of the Census, *1987 Survey of Minority-Owned*

Business Enterprises (Washington, D.C.: U.S. Department of Commerce, 1991); and Ramon G. McLeod and Tim Schreiner, "Racial Economic Gap Remained Wide in '80s: Census Reveals Two-tiered Society in State," *San Francisco Chronicle* (May 11, 1992).

14. Dinesh D'Souza, *Illiberal Education: The Politics of Race and Sex on Campus* (New York: Free Press, 1991).

15. Ling-chi Wang, "The Vision of the Civil Rights Movement since the 1960s: A Reappraisal from an Asian American Perspective," paper presented at Annual Asociation of Asian American Studies Conference, Honolulu, Hawaii, May 31, 1991.

16. Gertrude Ezorsky, *Racism and Justice: The Case for Affirmative Action* (Ithaca, New York: Cornell University Press, 1991).

17. Gary Becker, *Human Capital* (Chicago: University of Chicago Press, 1967).

18. Robert Pear, "Number of Poor in U.S. Is the Highest since 1964: Census Bureau Also Finds Drop in Buying Power," *San Francisco Chronicle* (September 4, 1992).

19. Bennett, *The Asian and Pacific Islander Population.*

20. Howard Gleckman et al., "Race in the Workplace: Is Affirmative Action Working?" *Business Week* (July 8, 1991); see also, America Assembly of Collegiate School of Business, *Minorities in Management: The Program to Increase Minoroties in Business* (St. Louis, Missouri: America Assembly of Collegiate Schools of Business, August 1988).

21. U.S. Commission on Civil Rights, *Civil Rights Issuing Facing Asian Americans in the 1990s.*

22. U.S. Bureau of the Census, *We, the Asian Pacific Islander Americans* (Washington, D.C.: U.S. Department of Commerce, 1988).

23. Since the early 1970s, the State of California has recognized Filipinos as a distinct racial group, separate from all other Asian and Pacific Islander groups.

24. Seymour M. Lipset, "Equal Chances versus Equal Results," *Annals of the American Academy of Political and Social Science* 523 (September 1992); Nathan Glazer, *Affirmative Discrimination* (New York: Basic Books, 1975).

25. Japanese Americans and Asian Indians are excluded from University of California's Boalt Hall student affirmative action program; other Asian Americans are included. All Asian Americans, including Filipinos, are excluded from the UC Berkeley's undergraduate student affirmative action admission program.

26. Keynote speech comments by Rebecca Chou in Chinese for Affirmative Action, *Report of CAA 3rd Upward Mobility Conference* (San Francisco: Chinese for Affirmative Action, 1992).

27. America Assembly of Collegiate Schools of Business, *Minorities in Management.*

28. Raj Gupta, Special Assistant/Senior Attorney to EEOC Commissioner Joy Cherian, telephone interview, November 2, 1991. In FY 1991, approximately 1 percent of the 62,806 employment discrimination

complaints filed with the Equal Employment Opportunity Commission involved allegations of race and/or national origin discrimination against Asian Pacific Islanders.

29. The Native Alaskan and Asian American cannery worker plaintiffs in *Wards Cove Packing Co.* v. *Antonio* have charged the Wards Cove cannery with overt racial discrimination, including segregated jobs, housing, and mess halls. The plaintiffs in *Wong* v. *Hamptom* prevailed in their attempt to enjoin the former U.S. Commission on Civil Service from imposing citizenship as a requirement for federal employment.

30. For example, in 1973 a group of Filipino employees filed a Title VII class action employment discrimination lawsuit against a health insurance company, charging promotional bias. Settlement in the case included promotional goals, backpay, and supervisory training. In 1974, a group of Asian American accountants filed a class action employment discrimination complaint against one of the Big Eight CPA firms for alleged entry-level discriminatory practices and then decided to withdraw the lawsuit.

31. Asian Americans have been co-plaintiffs in class action lawsuits initiated by other racial minority groups. In *Officers for Justice* v. *S.F. Civil Service Commission,* a black police officer organization, with S.F. NOW, Chinese for Affirmative Action and LULAC as co-plaintiffs, took the lead to challenge both entry-level and promotional practices at the San Francisco Police Department. In *Davis* v. *City and County of San Francisco,* Chinese for Affirmative Action joined as an intervenor to challenge discriminatory entry-level and promotional practices in the San Francisco Fire Department.

32. Charles Hamilton, "Affirmative Action and the Clash of Experiential Realities," in *The Annals of the Academy of Political and Social Science* 523 (September 1992); and John Ogbu, *The Next Generation: An Ethnography of Education in an Urban Neighborhood* (New York: Academic Press, 1974).

33. Derrick Bell, *Faces at the Bottom of the Well: The Permanence of Racism* (New York: Basic, 1992); see also book review by Patricia Holt, *San Francisco Chronicle* (September 13, 1992).

34. Julian Ku, "Asians as Victims," *Diversity and Division* 2:1 (Fall 1992). Throughout the debate over the Civil Rights Act of 1990 and 1991, former Deputy Undersecretary of Transportation Elaine Chao touted the concept of merit, traditional family values and hard work as preferable alternatives to affirmative action remedies. See also Bill Wong, *Asian Week* (July 19, 1991 and March 27, 1992).

35. America Assembly of Collegiate Schools of Business, *Minorities in Management.*

36. Chinese for Affirmative Action, *Report of 3rd CAA Upward Mobility Conference.*

37. Stanley Karnow and Nancy Yoshihara, *Asian Americans in Transition* (New York: Asia Society, 1992).

Language Rights Issues to the Year 2020 and Beyond:

Language Rights Policy

Kathryn K. Imahara

DIRECTOR OF THE LANGUAGE RIGHTS PROJECT
ASIAN PACIFIC AMERICAN LEGAL CENTER
LOS ANGELES, CALIFORNIA

This article explores the many issues surrounding language rights and discusses how they will continue to affect the Asian and Pacific Islander community in the future. Issues relating to language rights are not new in this country. Because language is intertwined with national origin, identity and culture (and therefore, indistinguishable, in many instances), language rights need to be protected.

The substantive portion of the paper is a discussion of access to services—all types of services—as we currently do not provide enough bilingual and culturally sensitive services. Unless we advocate vigorously now, we will never have the services which are available to the public at large. A discussion of the relationship of education to issue of access to services is followed by an examination of workplace issues, focusing on discrimination. Workplace discrimination revolves around issues of "appropriate" behavior in the workplace and tolerance for diversity. It is the same intolerance of diversity which drives municipalities to institute discriminatory sign requirements, the next topic of inquiry. And finally, I examine the issue of race relations, which encompasses all of the preceding issues and creates a framework to combat the racism and anti-immigrant sentiment prompting all other forms of discrimination.

By broadly defining language rights, I deal with a number of critical issues for our communities. For as long as Asians and Pacific Islanders continue to be primarily foreign born with English as a second language, the issue of language rights will necessarily be a part of every facet of our lives.

Historical Context

Language rights (or the lack thereof) have been with us since this country was founded. Early drafts of the Articles of Confederation and the Constitution were written in German and other languages to ensure that all 13 colonies would help fight the English. During this same period, slave masters were using language as a tool of domination and control. Taking away an African's language meant taking away their culture and heritage and stripping them of identity.

Language again became an issue in the beginning of the 20th century when large waves of immigrants began arriving from Western Europe. Many Americans were worried that these immigrants were not becoming "Americanized" quickly enough. It was believed that in order to be a "good citizen," one needed to speak English, and native language retention was seen as anti-American. Concomitantly, onerous language requirements were used by the federal government to limit and discourage immigration.[1] States also used language restrictions to exclude foreigners from economic and political participation. In 1897, Pennsylvania imposed residency and English-language requirements on miners. In 1918, New York passed a law requiring foreign language speakers to be enrolled in English classes as a condition of continued employment. About this same time, the New York State constitution was amended to include an English literacy requirement in order to disenfranchise over one million Yiddish-speaking citizens. Many states had similar goals and objectives.[2]

The current crusade for English as the official language and the increased membership into groups like U.S. English take on broader significance when placed into the above context. U.S. English was founded in the early 1980s by John Tanton to advocate English as the official language of the United States. Tanton was also the founder of the Federation for American Immigration Reform (FAIR), a slow-growth, anti-immigration and anti-immigrant group.[3] U.S. English believes that assimilation (how "white male" can you look and act) is the only alternative for immigrant groups. They also believe that immigration leads to language segregation and will turn the U.S. into a poly-lingual Babel. These views have been widely circulated by U.S. English as part of a direct-mail fundraising campaign.

This contemporary English-Only rhetoric is not based so much on "Americanization" as it is on anti-immigrant sentiment. Given that the Asian and Pacific Islander communities have doubled in each preceding decade, coupled with the tremendous growth in the Latino/Chicano community, it is likely that some people will be anxious. However, our communities will only continue to grow,[4] and the negative impact of the English-Only movement on our community will worsen. Unless much is done to ensure a co-equal place for Asians and Pacific Islanders, language will continue to be used against us to make us different and foreign and, therefore, relegate us to second-class status.

Identity and Culture

In order to discover why language is so important to our identity and culture, a demographic look at where we will be in 30 years is important. By the year 2020, there will be a large split within our community between those who are born here and those who are foreign born. In the United States, there will be one million foreign-born versus five million U.S.-born Asians between the ages of 0-24. For the same age category in California, there will be 500,000 foreign born and two million U.S. born. Conversely, for those in the 25-44 age group, there will be one million more foreign born than U.S. born for the country and there will be twice as many foreign born as U.S. born in California.[5] For those 45 and older, there will be 5.5 million foreign born versus 900,000 U.S. born in the country, and in California there will be 2.3 million foreign born and only 300,000 U.S. born.

	United States		California	
Age	Foreign Born	U.S. Born	Foreign Born	U.S. Born
0-24	1 million	5 million	500,000	2 million
25-44	3 million	2 million	1.4 million	700,000
45+	5.5 million	900,000	2.3 million	300,000

What this data implies is that the majority of our community will speak English as a second language well into the next century.[6] This data also implies that a greater part of our culture and identity will continue to be manifested through our language and language usage—even for those who may speak English primarily and their native language secondarily. As a result, language will become an ever greater indicator of who we are and where we have come from. Therefore, the link between language and national origin will remain strong and perhaps get even stronger.

> A language is much more than a way to communicate. By one's own language . . . one masters reality, one takes to oneself the most intimate and definitive emotions. . . . We quarrel, are jealous, love and hate with certain words, with certain tones, with certain inflections of the voice learned in childhood and adapted to a given set of gestures that also cannot be transported into another language.[7]

The laws of this country protect language and national origin for several reasons. The connection between language and national origin is so close that to limit language is to limit the rights of a person. This is also why language preservation and cultural identity are going to be crucial to continued development of our community.

One of the most widely accepted linguistic paradigms is that immigrants who come to this country lose their native language by the third generation. Historically, people who arrived from Europe spoke a language other than English. Their children were bilingual and their grandchildren were English-speaking with little or no native language retention. However, this paradigm only holds true when there is a single wave of immigration which then subsides. Studies within the Spanish-speaking population indicate that when accompanied by sustaining waves of immigration, language retention survives the third generation, and in many cases, increases the probability that those born in U.S. will speak their native language primarily and speak English secondarily.[8] Whether this theory will hold true for our community is yet to be studied, and its implications can be enormous. At the minimum, it would increase the need for bilingual services and bilingual education. It could also create a language/cultural divide within our community so great that the larger Asian and Pacific Islander movement may be pushed aside to be replaced with ethnic-specific agendas.

Access to Services

The Asian and Pacific Islander community is about 65 percent foreign born, and assuming that immigration rates will continue at current levels or even increase, we will need language-specific services everywhere in ever increasing numbers. Government, private industry, private nonprofits—all will be forced to look at the allocation of money for bilingual services. Access to bilingual and culturally sensitive services must be something that is a right, and not a "good idea" which should be funded but is not. The need to advocate aggressively for adequate services is imperative.

We must also ensure that people who have not retained native language skills but who have maintained cultural sensitivity not be left out of the equation. This will continue to be a concern because the U.S.-born population will increase by 211 percent in the U.S. and by 241 percent in California. Although our language retention rate may parallel that of the Hispanic community, it is conceivable that many Asians and Pacific Islanders born in the U.S. will not be bilingual but will maintain much of the culture.

There will be much debate and resistance to providing language-specific services. English-Only groups believe that people should learn English and, therefore, there should be no bilingual services. Ultimately, it comes down to money. Although the country will not always be in a recession, unless we can alter public policy to address our needs, even when there is money available, it will not be allocated for bilingual services. Some of our biggest opponents may be members of our own community. Like the late California Senator Hayakawa, older immigrant groups forget the language acquisition struggles of their ancestors and deny services to newer communities. We cannot allow this to occur.

EMERGENCY SERVICES

911 translator services and the people who respond to the calls are of particular concern. Although there is current legislation in California which mandates that 911 translators be available to language minority groups which comprise 5 percent of the service population, little is done to ensure that those responding to the calls are bilingual or even cultur-

ally sensitive.[9] The current system, especially for Asian and Pacific Islander languages, makes use of "language banks" or other systems such as the AT&T language line. While this does provide some form of service, it is no substitute for hiring bilingual personnel. There have been at least two instances in May/June 1992 in which the Los Angeles Police Department called the Asian Pacific American Legal Center (APALC) looking for a Chinese translator to speak to a 911 caller. This is no substitute for hiring, retaining and promoting bilingual people in the department.

CRIMINAL JUSTICE SYSTEM

Police. In the aftermath of the Rodney King beating and the L.A. riots, the idea of community-based policing is even more imperative. However, in order for this to happen, especially in Los Angeles, the police must be bilingual, or at least culturally sensitive. As of June 1992, Asian and Pacific Islander officers comprise 3 percent of the Los Angeles Police Department. Although there are "recruitment goals" and good intentions to hire more Asian and Pacific Islander officers, nothing has come about. As a result, our community continues to be underserved. The L.A. County Sheriffs' Department and the Probation Department also have 3 percent representation of Asians and Pacific Islanders. Much needs to be done to ensure that our tax money gets us the same quality and quantity of services that others receive.

A related problem is the issue of how our community is treated by the police. The APALC has received many complaints from Asians and Pacific Islanders who are stopped and often ignored by police because they do not speak English very well. There are also incidents of people who are arrested because of their lack of English skills to rebut charges or to tell their side of the story. This lack of sensitivity by police and problems with communication also have hampered attempts to report hate crimes. There have been many occasions in which Asians and Pacific Islanders have been discouraged from filing police reports. Also, when reports have been filed, there is no mention of racism.

Courts. Problems within the judicial system are everywhere. Civil servants, interpreters, public defenders, district attorneys, judges, and juries have a lack of sensitivity for our community and definitely lack sufficient bilingual staff. These problems have resulted in women not being able to file appropriate papers to obtain child support; criminal defendants waiting hours, even days, for a court-certified interpreter; public defenders not being able to speak to their client (interpreters are only for the hearing itself, not for preparatory work), and oftentimes getting defendants to take a plea bargain without advising them on the immigration consequences (the public defenders often are ignorant that some misdemeanors and all felonies place a person's immigration status at risk and deportation could ensue); district attorneys not prosecuting hate crimes, or prosecuting the wrong person because of a lack of communication; judges not listening to clients because they do not speak English well enough; and juries convicting a person because the defendant did not look them in the eye, or testified through an interpreter. Much needs to be done to ensure that bilingual and culturally sensitive services are provided for our community.

BILINGUAL BALLOTS AND VOTER ASSISTANCE

The Voter Assistance provision (Section 203) of the Voting Rights Act was reauthorized in August 1992. Prior to August 1992, a jurisdiction provided language assistance if: (1) more than 5 percent of its voting-age citizens were members of a single language minority who did not understand English well enough to participate in the electoral process; and (2) if the illiteracy rate of this group was higher than the national illiteracy rate, which is defined as a failure to complete the fifth grade. According to the 1980 Census, Los Angeles County was not covered for any language—not even Spanish.

A coalition of language minority groups was successful in modifying Section 203 to include a 10,000 voters benchmark figure. Therefore, if 5 percent or 10,000 voters in a county are limited English proficient and have a higher illiteracy rate than the national average, they will be eligible for language assistance. The chart below indicates which jurisdictions will now be required to provide bilingual ballots and voting materials.

The language minority groups were interested in establishing a benchmark figure because it appeared that language groups in large counties like Los Angeles would find it difficult, if not impossible, to reach the 5 percent requirement. The 1980 Census revealed that while 174,000 Spanish speakers could have used bilingual ballots, they did not receive them because they did not comprise 5 percent of the County. At

Hawaii

Kauai	Tagalog	covered under the 5% test
Mauai	Tagalog	covered under the 5% test
Honolulu	Japanese	19,226*
	Tagalog	17,900*

California

San Francisco	Chinese	covered under the 5% test
Alameda	Chinese	11,106*
Los Angeles	Chinese	39,886*
	Korean	35,000 are LEP but possess a lower illiteracy rate than the national average
	Tagalog	19,920*
	Vietnamese	12,870*
	Japanese	11,718*
Orange County	Vietnamese	13,906*
	Korean	10,000 are LEP but possess a lower illiteracy rate than the national average

New York

Kings	Chinese	15,796*
Queens	Chinese	19,162*
	Korean	8,500*
New York	Chinese	18,173*

*Number of people in the county who are limited English proficient (LEP) and possess an illiteracy rate higher than the national average.

the same time, 100,000 Spanish speakers in Fresno County received bi-lingual ballots.

Throughout the process to include a benchmark figure, there had been discussions as to whether it should be revised upward. These discussions generally arose in response to the great number of Asian languages which would be covered in Los Angeles. However, if the benchmark were raised to 15,000, it would wipe out Japanese and Vietnamese in every jurisdiction. If the benchmark were raised to 20,000, only Chinese would survive in Los Angeles. New York City would have missed the benchmark by 1,000 people. Therefore, it is crucial that the benchmark figure remain at 10,000 when Section 203 is reauthorized in 15 years.[10]

The task before us now is to educate our community about the availability of bilingual ballots and to encourage their use. Political empowerment is an important tool for our community, and we must utilize our voting rights to the fullest.

Education

K-12

In 1972, Congress found that language minority citizens had been subjected to pervasive discrimination and unequal educational opportunities which often resulted in high illiteracy rates. This high illiteracy rate was the cause of, among other things, systematic denial of the right to vote and low voter participation. These disturbing findings, still relevant even 20 years later, make advocacy for adequate K-12 education vital.

Bilingual Education. As the Anglo population ages and their birth rate declines, there will be a tendency to eliminate funding for K-12 education in general and for bilingual education in particular. By using the numbers from Assumption #1 of Dr. Paul Ong's Projection Model, the percentage of Asian and Pacific Islanders foreign-born children (age 15 or younger) will decrease in the next 30 years. However, there will still be 265,533 children born outside of the United States, with more than half of them living in California. If the numbers from Assumption #2 are used instead, however, the number of foreign-born children will increase by 10 percent in the country and by 24 percent in California. If Assumption #2 becomes reality, then the need for bilingual education/services will be even more critical. Given that current bilingual funding is minuscule, a 10 percent increase will mean that many Asian and Pacific Islander children will not receive an education. Even if there is a decrease in foreign-born children, if the native language retention rate is as high as predicted, then there will still be a high need for bilingual education.

There has been and will continue to be debate over the efficacy of bilingual education, and what follows are some of the pros and cons. English-Only groups argue that bilingual classes become a "crutch" so that children do not acquire the English language. They also argue that by allowing bilingual education at every grade level, the children go from grade to grade without ever acquiring the English language. They believe that the "sink or swim" approach is the best way to ensure that everyone learns English as quickly as possible.

Studies have shown that far from being a "crutch," bilingual education classes ensure that children acquire substantive knowledge while at the same time they learn English. The "sink or swim" method only ensures that the time spent in class trying to learn English means that no substantive learning is taking place. The bilingual classes are available at every grade level because children enter the school system at various ages and with various levels of prior instruction. Bilingual education is important to the transition process. Symbolically, the availability of bilingual education tells the children and their parents that although they are living in America, they are not required to leave their identity, culture or heritage at the border.

Nevertheless, no bilingual education system works without monetary and bureaucratic support. Many criticize current bilingual education programs because they do not work. But the programs are plagued by problems of lack of commitment from government and school administrations. We need to ensure that there are enough bilingual teachers, aides, and counselors available to serve our community. We cannot allow an aging Anglo population with declining numbers of school-aged children and English-Only groups to convince government officials that bilingual education is not necessary.

Parent Involvement. Regardless of whether the number of foreign-born Asian and Pacific Islander children will decrease or increase over the next 30 years, the number of foreign-born adults will significantly increase.[11] Using Assumption #1, the 25-44 year olds who are foreign born will grow by 49 percent by the year 2020 in the United States. In California, this increase is 67 percent. Assumption #2 shows that this same age group will increase by 83 percent in the country and by 104 percent in California. This means that the parents of the children in our schools will more than likely be limited English proficient. To ensure that our children stay in school and succeed, a cohesive parent-teacher-administration relationship must be established which provides bilingual communication, both oral and written. Also, cultural sensitivity cannot be ignored in the process. Just recently in Los Angeles, an elementary school's PTA began providing bilingual interpreters at the meetings. Heralding this as a model for other schools, the PTA decided to videotape the meeting to show how easily the translation could be integrated into the agenda with little or no disruption. Unfortunately, the immigrant parents saw the video cameras and thought that it was the INS looking for undocumented aliens. They left without ever participating.

Non-Citizen Voting in School Board Elections. Another means to increase the participation of parents of school-aged children is to promote the right of non-citizens to vote in school board elections. One of the legal justifications used by jurisdictions like New York City, which has allowed non-citizen voting in school board elections since the late 1970s, is that all people are guaranteed representation—citizens or not. For the affected parents, there is a vested interest in their children's education and around issues such as bilingual education. If parents were to wait the requisite three-to-five years to become citizens so they could vote, their children would be out of the school system. If non-citizen voting is to become a reality, however, bilingual ballots *must* be available.

POST-SECONDARY

Many community colleges and California State Universities are beginning to require English literacy exams as a graduation prerequisite. As a result, many students who speak English as a second language are finding it difficult, if not impossible, to graduate. From my understanding, this examination is much harder than the TOEFL (Test of English as a Foreign Language) which is *already* required for those seeking admission to these campuses. The impact of this disturbing trend is unclear. Although those within the 15-24 year old category (those most likely to be attending college) who are foreign born will decrease by 1 percent over the next 30 years, there will still be 351,795 of them in California. However, much more research needs to be done in this area to assess fully the implications of the situation.

Another issue facing many college students is the "foreign language" requirement for graduation. Traditionally, European languages have been required (German, French, Spanish). However, when Asian and Pacific Islander students request that Asian languages be allowed to count for "foreign language" credit, they are rebuffed. Opponents have argued that Asian languages should not be counted because this would give credits to a student for being Asian and Pacific Islander.[12] But as the world becomes smaller and the Pacific Rim becomes an ever increasing part of our economy, we will need to change how our education system values different languages and cultures.

Workplace

No matter what the problem in the workplace—English-Only rules, accent discrimination, or bilingual skills compensation—we must ensure competent, adequate, and continuous cultural sensitivity training for everyone (Asians and Pacific Islanders included). There must be a full commitment from white corporate America to implement diversity training. Combatting language discrimination must be included in any diversity training package. If this does not happen, then issues like language rights will always be a red herring to the real problem of intergroup conflict.

Another solution is to continue litigating language discrimination cases. However, because there has been a plethora of appointments of conservative judges since 1980, issues of concern to our community will not likely prevail. This is not to say that we should abandon litigation, but that we will need to be more selective about the cases we bring and that careful analyses should be made of potential U.S. Supreme Court claims.

ENGLISH-ONLY RULES IN THE WORKPLACE

What prompts English-Only rules in the workplace is a growing intolerance of immigrants and the languages they speak. Monolingual English-speaking workers often assume that when they hear others speaking another language, it means that they are the subject of the conversation because they equate the act with whispering or conspiracy or being un-American. Moreover, there is a misperception that people choose to speak other languages. There is a lack of understanding of the "code switching" which naturally and automatically occurs. "Code switching" is a linguistic term to describe what happens when bilingual people speak to each other. Because each knows that the other speaks both English and Spanish (or any other non-English language), their conversation is peppered with words and phrases in both languages. During the course of the conversation, no one is aware of what is being spoken in which language. All they know is that they are communicating. The naturalness or unconsciousness of this phenomenon is what makes English-Only rules so onerous. These rules force the person to adhere to what is not natural.

In order to remedy the problem of English-Only rules, we will need to continue litigating these types of cases. But until management behavior changes, these cases will continue to multiply. Both federal and state laws governing these rights are adequate, but are not publicized and made accessible to communities. Also, a substantial number of the managers who institute the English-Only rules never even bother checking with upper management, human resources departments, or a lawyer. They just assume that because speaking a language other than English in front of someone who does not understand is "rude," that regulating this behavior is within their discretion.

Accent

> Every person. . .has an accent. Your accent carries the story of who you are—who first held you and talked to you when you were a child, where you have lived, your age, the schools you attended, the languages you know, your ethnicity, whom you admire, your loyalties, your profession, your class position: traces of your life and identity are woven into your pronunciation, your phrasing, your choice of words. Your self is inseparable from your accent. Someone who tells you they don't like the way you speak is quite likely telling you that they don't like you.[13]

Hiring. The U.S. General Accounting Office (GAO) issued a report in March 1990 in which they found that of the 400,000 employers surveyed throughout the country that one-third "would refuse to hire" or "refused to hire" people who sounded foreign or had an accent. A similar survey was conducted in the same month by the Coalition for Humane Immigrant Rights of Los Angeles (CHIRLA) in which the findings were very similar, if not slightly higher. The bothersome aspect of the results is that a third of the employers surveyed openly admitted to discriminating on the basis of national origin. Most employers are not so ignorant and would have modified their answers to those questions. Therefore, there is more discrimination occurring than is documented by these reports.

Generally, the reason discriminatory hiring occurs is because the employers are afraid of the consequences if they hire an undocumented alien with forged papers. Therefore, when they come across a person who "sounds" like she does not have work authorization, they will run the risk of not hiring (after all, how often does an unemployed alien file a discrimination lawsuit?).

Glass Ceiling. According to reports from our own community, as validated by the U.S. Commission on Civil Rights Report issued February 1992 entitled *Civil Rights Issues Facing Asian Americans in the 1990s,* we face a glass ceiling in the workplace. It is already difficult for Asians and Pacific Islanders to obtain mid- or upper-level management positions. Recently, businesses have been using accent or communication skills as a "neutral" job requirement which has disproportionately affected our community. Complaints have been filed by immigrants (engineers, technicians, accountants, etc.) who apply for management positions. Many of these people have been unofficially functioning as managers for many years, but there has been no promotion or pay raise commensurate with the responsibilities. When the official position opens up, these applicants are not given the promotion because of a lack of communication skills. For many, English is a second language, but communication has never been a problem (they have, in fact, already been doing the job for which they are now deemed not qualified). There may in fact be some communication problems, but when this is the main justification for blocking promotions, there is the possibility of illegal discrimination.

BILINGUAL SKILLS COMPENSATION

Bilingual skills compensation has been a primary concern for the Latino/Chicano community in the past few years. As Asians and Pacific Islanders advocate for increased bilingual services, we will need to ensure that the people who serve our community are also properly compensated. *Cota* v. *Tucson Police Department, City of Tucson, et al.* was recently litigated by the Language Rights Project at MALDEF (Mexican American Legal Defense and Education Fund). Although the plaintiffs did not prevail, the issues raised will affect every context in which bilingual services are being provided.

One issue was a question of bilingualism. Studies within the Latino/Chicano population have shown that their Spanish-speaking abilities range anywhere from "enough to speak to my grandmother" to "can write and speak fluently in either language." Because of their higher-than-average native language retention rate, many speak Spanish conversationally, but not well enough to perform important or technical translation services. This was especially true in the Tucson police department, when often the only link to the victim and the police was the clerk/typist who happened to be working that day. This lack of training, coupled with the person's desire to help their community, added to the stress on the job.

Rarely, however, is a person's level of bilingualism taken into account when the need arises. In hospitals throughout Los Angeles, custodians and high school interns routinely are pulled into emergency rooms to translate complicated medical terminology, deal with distressed relatives, and give proper medicine dosage information. It does not matter that the person doing the translation knows no medical terminology or has no medical training.

Despite the need for interpreters (regardless of the availability of "qualified" translators), many employers refuse to compensate their employers for their translation services. As the city of Tucson told the plaintiff in *Cota*, "why should we pay you for being Mexican!?" The city's reasoning was that the employee learned how to speak Spanish at home, that this was not really a skill but part of being Mexican; therefore, there should be no extra compensation. The city does not pay Blacks for being Blacks or Whites for being Whites.

There are two points which are not being addressed. One is the problem of bilingualism. If speaking Spanish is not a skill, but a part of being Mexican, then there should be no differential in Spanish language ability between people. The second and more important problem is that the employer does not view bilingual services as an asset. As long as the employer believes that serving the non-English speaking public is neither a priority nor a significant percentage of their business, bilingual pay will not be a reality.

The last problem in this area relates to assigned job duties. While the filing clerk or the custodian spends four hours in the emergency room translating for the doctor (who just pulls in the worker and never clears it with the supervisor), the files are not being filed and floors are not being cleaned. As a result, many employees are either docked wages for non-performance of their job, or suspended for spending too much time on unrelated duties.

These predicaments confront the Latino/Chicano communities. Asians and Pacific Islanders must work very diligently to ensure that we are not similarly victimized. However, we are fortunate that the groundwork has been laid by the struggle of others. We just need to clearly articulate our priorities and advocate for fair and equal treatment.

Signage

As a means of keeping their city from becoming another "Monterey Park" (in other words, how to keep the Chinese out), many cities throughout Southern California have passed unconstitutional sign ordinances. Typically, these ordinances require half of the business sign to be in English. In 1988, there were approximately seven cities which had these sign ordinances. Monterey Park started the debate in 1986 when longstanding Anglo residents complained to their city council that Monterey Park did not look like their town anymore; that when they walked down their street, they could not read any of the signs; and that there suddenly were all these Chinese people.[14]

The issue was finally decided in *Asian American Business Group* v. *City of Pomona*, in which Judge Takasugi found that these types of sign ordinances were unconstitutional because they violated free speech and were aimed at language minority groups. Since this decision, the cities of Temple City, Rosemead and Garden Grove have rescinded, repealed or modified their sign ordinances. To date, the cities of San Gabriel, Arcadia and San Marino continue to have unconstitutional ordinances.

Since the opinion was rendered in *Asian American Business Group*, however, there have been no new instances of cities passing these types of sign ordinances. While the problem has yet to go away (there are still cities which need to be sued to remove their ordinances), it does not appear to be getting worse. This does not mean that our vigilance can waiver, however, because the anti-immigrant sentiment is still prevalent and could be resurrected.

Race Relations

Language discrimination has been a vehicle for anti-immigrant sentiment and intolerance, such as denial of access to services, adequate education, and equal opportunity in the workplace. Race relations have been affected by language discimination. On Los Angeles high school campuses, race wars are based on what language students speak. Language-specific cliques are being formed and turf wars ensue. This is not to say that differing languages cause division (this is U.S. English's line), but that it is an integral part of the problem. Deep-seated racism may be the cause of the conflict, but the rhetoric is couched in English-Only terms. The questions that must be asked are, why is language being used to divide and what can we do to stop it?

On another level, the many coalitions forming between African Americans, Latino/Chicanos, and Asians and Pacific Islanders may be strengthened or destroyed depending on how the "language" issue is handled. Language rights is but one of several issues which naturally link the Latino/Chicano and Asian and Pacific Islander communities. But the issue could distance the African American community. However, language rights do hold a special place in the African American community. African Americans were one of first groups to have their culture destroyed because of the elimination of native languages. Thus, their place within the coalition must be preserved. These linkages *must* be recognized if we are to work together. Reinforcing these linkages will become increasingly important as the Latino/Chicano and Asian and Pacific Islander communities grow and the African American community shrinks. The few gains made by the African Americans must be preserved, but the other groups must have their share as well. How we shape and settle these issues during the next 30 years will depend on how well we remember how much we have in common.

Notes

1. Edward G. Hartmann, *The Movement to Americanize the Immigrant* (New York: Columbia University Press, 1948).

2. Arnold H. Leibowitz, "English Literacy: Legal Sanction for Discrimination," *Notre Dame Lawyer* 45 (Fall 1969), 42; John Higham, "Crusade for Americanization," in *Strangers in the Land: Patterns of American Nativism, 1860–1925,* edited by John Higham (New Brunswick, New Jersey: Rutgers University Press, 1955), 72; Susan S. Forbes and Peter Lemos, "History of

American Language Policy," in *U.S. Immigration and the National Interest*, Staff Report (Washington, D.C.: Select Commission on Immigrant and Refugee Policy, April 30, 1981), Appendix A, 53.

3. Currently, FAIR has aligned itself with groups such as the Sierra Club. It appears that the slow growth and anti-immigrant movement have found sympathizers with those trying to preserve the environment.

4. All references to Asian and Pacific Islander populations and projected growth are based upon the "Ong Projection Model" as written by Dr. Paul Ong with the help from Dr. Jane Takahashi, which was developed for this project. Assumption 1 was used primarily in this paper because it was the most conservative projection. If the other projection assumptions are used, they shall be indicated in this paper.

5. While those within the 25–44 age range are predominately foreign born, it should be noted that the percentage increase for U.S. born is 320 percent for the country and 315 percent for California.

6. The assumption is that those who are foreign born will be more likely to speak English as a second language and, in most instances, be limited English proficient. For those born in the U.S., however, the assumption is that they will not speak English as a second language, nor will they be limited English proficient. As a result, language assistance will be needed for those who are foreign born. Caveat: see the discussion below about Spanish language retention and this theory's applicability to the Asian and Pacific Islander community.

7. Carlos Alberto Montaner, "Talk English—You Are in the United States," in *Language Loyalties: A Source Book on the Official English Controversy*, edited by James Crawford (Chicago: University of Chicago Press, 1992), 163.

8. Yolanda Sole, "Bilingualism: Stable or Transitional? The Case of Spanish in the United States," *International Journal of Social Languages* 84 (1990), 36.

9. The availability of bilingual translators in other jurisdictions is unknown because the research has not been conducted.

10. Note that in Los Angeles and Orange counties, Koreans will not be covered under any benchmark scenario because of their high literacy rate. Note also, however, that in Queens, New York, Koreans have a higher illiteracy rate but there are only 8,500 who are limited English proficient.

11. The assumption being made is that those between the ages of 25–44 will more likely have children in the under–15 age range. Whether they bring their children with them when they immigrate, or whether they have their children here, this age group will speak English as a second language and will probably be limited English proficient.

12. Similarly, some employers refuse to provide additional pay to bilingual employees for utilizing their bilingual skills on the job. It is generally postured as "Why should I pay for you for being Mexican?" See a parallel argument in the section in this paper, "Bilingual Skills Compensation."

13. Mari Matsuda, "Voices of America: Accent, Antidiscrimination Law, and a Jurisprudence for the Last Reconstruction," *Yale Law Journal* (1991), 1329.

14. For a fuller discussion on the politics and dynamics of this torrid time in Monterey Park's history, see John Horton and Jose Calderon, "Language Struggles in a Changing California Community," in *Language Loyalties*, 186.

Meditations on the Year 2020:

Policy for Women

Elaine H. Kim

PROFESSOR, ASIAN AMERICAN STUDIES
UNIVERSITY OF CALIFORNIA, BERKELEY

Census projections suggest that in 25 years our communities will be larger, more diverse, more dispersed, with gender configurations quite different from what they were in the days of the Chinese, Filipino, and Korean American "bachelor societies." If immigration continues at present rates and numbers, the Asian American population will be several times larger than it is now. Also, if present trends continue, we will probably not see again the geographical concentrations or the gender imbalances of the era before the passage of the Immigration Act of 1965. Projected population data give us reason to believe that by the next generation, Asian American women will no longer belong only to a small number of mostly East Asian nationality groups, but will hail from all over South and Southeast Asia as well. Ultimately, because of cultural, generational, and socioeconomic diversities, soon we may no longer be able to talk about Asian American women as a group; thus, we will need to focus in depth and in detail on the specific needs of particular communities of women.

It is impossible to predict how shifting global power relations will help shape Asian American communities in the future. The pending end of British control of Hong Kong has already profoundly affected the Chinese diaspora, and we can only imagine the effects on Asian emigration of normalization of relations between the U.S. and Vietnam or reunification of the Korean peninsula.

We do know that between 1970 and 1990, rapid industrial growth in "little Tiger" Asian societies—Hong Kong, Singapore, South Korea, and Taiwan—resulted in changes in the characteristics of emigrants rather than an actual decrease in emigration. For example, by the 1990s, South Korean immigrants to the U.S. no longer hailed from either the highest castes of the educated and urban elite or the lowest rungs of the socio-economic ladder as they did in the decades between the Korean War and the closing of the Immigration and Naturalization Service's professional and technical preference categories in the mid-1970s. As the gap between South Korean and U.S. living conditions narrowed through the 1980s, emigrants were increasingly from the lower middle and working classes and sponsored by relatives already in the U.S.

Although economic conditions in Taiwan, South Korea, Singapore, and Hong Kong are certainly pegged to those in the U.S., the gap between living standards in the U.S. and those societies can only be expected to decrease. Therefore, we can expect to see more lower middle-class and working-class immigrants from these areas in future years.[1] At the same time, U.S.-based corporations' ever-deeper reach into lower-wage labor markets in South and Southeast Asia can be expected to stimulate increasingly extensive immigration from those countries.

The notion of the "immigrants' ladder," supposedly climbed in succession by Northern, Eastern, and Southern Europeans, followed by racial minority immigrants from Asia and Latin America, appears to have always been a cruel hoax. Otherwise, how can we explain the fact that through the decades, despite the much-touted "bootstrap-model minority success story" mythology, a large proportion of Asian American women continue to be trapped in low-wage jobs, such as garment work, which still pay only a dollar an hour? Low-wage employment enclaves, such as garment factories and electronics assembly plants, which require fast turn-around and local research and testing, are likely to persist within U.S. borders. By the year 2020, we can expect to find more and more Bangladeshi, Burmese, Cambodian, Pakistani, Sri Lankan, Thai, and Indonesian as well as Vietnamese, Indian, and mainland Chinese women working in these enclaves. What may change by the year 2020, then, is the ethnicity and socioeconomic backgrounds of Asian immigrant women, rather than the numbers of immigrants or the framework for their labor in the U.S.

Empowering Asian Immigrant Women Workers

To address the needs of Asian immigrant working women, language programs must be developed to facilitate their empowerment and aid in their struggle against a host of difficulties. In the probable absence of far-reaching systemic reform, we can expect that Asian immigrant women workers will be forced to continue battling against low wages, poor benefits and working conditions, and lack of affordable health care, childcare and housing. Moreover, many predict an increase in anti-Asian violence in the next 25 years. Asian immigrant women workers, as a group with the least access to power, can also be expected to face increased sexual harassment and violence both in the workplace and in society at large. Organizing among limited-English-speaking women workers is extremely difficult, for obvious reasons. Yet the women may continue to be blamed for not standing up for their rights, voting, being counted in the census, and filing claims and lawsuits. None of the existing programs that could facilitate services to Asian immigrant women workers has sufficient language capability even to meet the needs of Chinese, Korean, and Vietnamese-speaking women at the present time; if current conditions remain unchanged, what will Bangladeshi and Indonesian women face in the year 2020?

Needless to say, empowerment cannot be accomplished by simply providing language services within existing institutions. There must be simultaneous efforts to strengthen the connections between them and other immigrant working women. Such connections can take the form of wide-ranging grassroots education and exchange programs that challenge the roots of ethnocentrism and racial biases of all kinds.

While there are many shared concerns among all Asian American women, priorities may differ according to socioeconomic status. It is important to realize that because English-speaking professional women are the ones most likely to be seen and heard from, theirs are the issues that are the most discussed. For example, tax credits for childcare may be an important issue for Asian American mothers working in the law profession, but safe, high-quality, affordable childcare itself is a far more pressing need among Asian immigrant women workers. Thus, while sexual orientation, sexual harassment, redistribution of household labor, and reproductive choice are important issues to all Asian American women, limited-English-speaking immigrant women in low-wage, unskilled and semi-skilled employment as hotel room cleaners, electronics assemblers, home health and food service workers, and garment factory operatives are typically more concerned about wages, benefits, and working conditions than about the issues highest on the agenda for middle-class Asian and other women.

Middle-Class Women:
Opposing Relegation to a "Buffer Zone"

Although we can expect the persistent clustering of far less visible Asian immigrant women in marginal self-employment and in low-wage factory and service-sector jobs, it is certainly probable that by the year 2020 there will be many more U.S.-educated Asian women working in the professions and in public and private sector middle management employment than in the past, when *de jure* and *de facto* segregation barred Asian Americans from such occupations.[2] Like other American women of their class, Asian American women in the professions will no doubt need to mobilize to protect themselves from both discrimination in salary and promotion and sexual harassment in the workplace. And like other middle-class American women, they will probably have to continue struggling against being forced to choose between professional and personal fulfillment and between social approval and freedom to express intellectual talent, different sexual orientations, and non-traditional values with regard to marriage and motherhood.

Unique to Asian American middle-class women may be relegation to a "buffer zone" similar to the "middleman" position Asian Americans are characteristically described as occupying between Anglo Americans and other communities of color. Asian American women must consciously challenge the racial sexualization of their social roles as decorative and serviceable gatekeepers. Asian American women in management and the professions in particular will have to guard against being positioned in a "no-woman's-land" as token women of color. As a wedge between white women and women from African American and Latino communities, Asian American women can be forced into mediating between those who have the power to make the rules and those who are oppressed by them. Whether as newscasters, attorneys, or middle managers, Asian American women could be positioned to serve as apologists for and explicators, upholders, and functionaries of the status quo.

Similarly, Asian American women will have to be wary of benefits that accrue to them from the oppression of other groups. Some women may gain individual social mobility by taking advantage of the popular view of Asian American women as more compliant than other women and more competent than men of color. But if the relations of power are not transformed, Asian American women will remain dependent and vulnerable to resentment from all sides unless they refuse to be used against white women in a battle against feminism, and unless they refuse to be pitted against men of color to mask the perpetuation of racism.

One of the ways in which the middle-class Asian American woman can resist the "gatekeeper function" would be her strong commitment to place first priority, in whatever work arena she occupies, on the needs of the most disenfranchised people of her community. For Asian American women who think of community in terms of gender and ethnicity, at the present these would be limited-English-speaking poor women, especially women in Southeast Asian refugee communities.

Given that the category "Asian American" is a political construct rooted in the coherence of effects of race-based treatment of Asians in the U.S. rather than in actual cultural or psychic affinities, it may take a great deal of effort for members of some groups to place high priority on the needs of people of other linguistic and ethnic backgrounds. Indeed, cultural nationalism may continue to flourish among individual national groups, as it has until now among immigrants of color in the U.S., because it has historically given meaning to lives of toil, making it possible to endure the indifference and antipathy of the dominant. My hope is that feminist ideas will take ever stronger hold among Asian Americans.[3] Besides transforming what can be spoken within families and communities, feminist ideas can help demystify the reductiveness of nationalisms (just as thinking on nationalisms has helped reveal the limitations of feminisms).[4]

Community Leadership and Advocacy

Despite persistent and intransigent obstacles, Asian American women from diverse socioeconomic strata have historically refused to allow themselves to be passive objects of history. Instead, they have insisted on complicating the scenarios of existing relations of power. This is particularly apparent in ethnic community leadership and advocacy. Except in recent immigrant and refugee communities, where men can become "leaders" because they are men rather than because of their talent or virtues, women—many of them educated, middle-class women—occupy a high proportion of directorships in grassroots community-based agencies organized to protect the welfare of members of the community in the arenas of civil rights, equal employment, labor rights, health and mental health, childcare, and care of the elderly. Asian American women have also been active in the crucially important but frequently underrecognized arena of cultural production, as writers, visual artists, and performers whose work invigorates the struggle for self-definition. Rooted in direct opposition to the indifference, hostility, and manipulation emanating from mainstream institutions, this work has helped protect many Asian Americans from both material and psychic violence, creating the basis for ongoing resistance to the forces that threaten to dehumanize and divide the members of the community.

Clearly the work of Asian American women in positions of community leadership and in artistic production needs support and encouragement, particularly in light of government abandonment of public services since the early 1980s, since which time more and more responsibility and fewer and fewer resources for social services have been passed on to community-based organizations. Government neglect of community services has meant more women assuming community leadership positions, since the rewards and power traditionally associated with these positions have greatly diminished.

Thus Asian American women community leaders have had to face the economic recession with ever-diminishing public sector support for education, affordable housing, employment services, health and mental health services, protection for victims of domestic violence, legal assistance for the poor, and childcare facilities, not to mention the critically needed language resources for limited-English-speaking members of the Asian communities. Obviously, we need to voice our collective insistence on the use of public resources for the public good.

Support for Asian American women's leadership requires recognition of the full worth of these women as individuals. Some Asian

American women who have assumed positions of leadership within the ethnic community have commented that they are tolerated because community advocacy is viewed by many Asian American men as an extension of family service. Lingering contradictions rooted in deeply embedded sexist tendencies in our communities need to be addressed. For example, we need to unmask and dismantle the ways in which sentimental glorification of women's sacrifice for family limits the development of their full potential as human beings. While it is understood that for people of color in the U.S., the family has often been the only real refuge from racism, we need to be vigilant against the danger that it will also function as one of the *loci* of oppression for women. Asian American women cannot be empowered as long as only *their* worth—as opposed to Asian American men's worth—is measured *primarily* in terms of service to and sacrifice for others.

Bringing Women's Concerns to the Center of Public Policy

Most policy studies have focused on women in the interest of "the nation" and as a side aspect of the family. Policy-makers have devoted much study to women in terms of their service to the state: thus, the emphasis on reproduction, fertility, and labor.[5] Few policy-makers have ever paid attention to what women would like, from youth to old age, to help them realize their full potential as human beings and not just as childbearers, caretakers, and workers in the service of the state. Only a few middle-class, mostly Anglo women have been able to focus from time to time on what they would like for themselves.

Women have traditionally been regarded as repositories of inherited notions of value. As such, they have been blamed in both Eastern and Western patriarchies for everything from their own disenfranchisement to their role in creating self-centered sons,[6] to national "crises" such as the so-called disintegration of "family values," to global issues such as sexually transmitted diseases and overpopulation. All women, and most certainly the women with the least access to social power, must become full political beings and not be allowed to suffer blame for social problems they had little part in creating. It makes no sense for Asian American men to blame Asian American women for racism and the problems created for them by racism. Instead of attacking and criticizing Asian American women writers and newscasters for impeding them, Asian American men should join forces with the women in an effort to dismantle the hierarchy of values and the structure that perpetuates racial exclusivity and inequality.

While diverse populations will probably continue to employ the category of "Asian American" as a political strategy to defend against racial inequities and injustices, class- and ethnic-specific issues will need to be addressed more substantively. Certainly nominal aggregation has resulted in neglect of the neediest and most disenfranchised Asian American women. But at the same time, Asian Americans, and Asian American women in particular, must be freed to think ever more globally during the next 25 years. No one can afford not to think about the epidemic spread of sexually transmitted disease, the global environment, or the links between ourselves and human suffering, wherever it occurs in the world.

Asian American women will need to continue to deconstruct, demystify, and debunk the deeply embedded racist and sexist discourses that sidestep and scapegoat us as raced and gendered beings. We must continue our efforts to generate new discourses, with the goal of nothing less than recreating ourselves and building a new world in which violence and exploitation will remain only as words describing a distant past.

Notes

I am grateful for suggestions from Norma Alarcon, Elsa Eder, Bong Hwan Kim, Susan K. Lee, Young Shin, and Ling-chi Wang. The lapses, of course, are all mine.

1. At the same time, we may see middle- and upper middle-class immigrants in search of alternative life styles. In the future, we can expect that the search for increased personal options will figure increasingly into the Asian woman's decision to immigrate to the U.S. Now that people in Asian "NICs" generally feel that they can feed their families, those who decide to leave for the U.S. and elsewhere tend to be people in search of business opportunities and life style alternatives. In previous decades, women who immigrated to the U.S. from affluent Japan were quite often single women who had passed the standard age of marriage in Japan. We might see a significant increase in educated, middle-class single women immigrants from Taiwan, Singapore, and South Korea in future years. At the same time, working and settling down in the U.S. remains an attractive option for elite women from India, the Philippines, and other South and Southeast Asian countries.

2. Of course Asian immigrant women have never been entirely relegated to low-wage employment. While some highly educated women from Asia have become visible in professional and managerial employment sectors, if race discrimination and lack of directly transferable skills continue to prevent Asian immigrants from large-scale employment in U.S. jobs commensurate to their education and job experience levels, they will probably continue to seek out ethnic-specific economic niches, such as self-employment in small businesses.

3. Strengthened by their location on the interstices of race and gender discourses and by their exposure to discussions of gender and power that will surely be taking place in the U.S. as well as in Asian societies, undoubtedly Asian American women will increasingly question and challenge at least traditional Asian patriarchal attitudes and practices.

4. One vivid example of how class and feminist analyses together might help us transcend the limits of nationalist thinking comes to mind when we compare the South Korean nationalist outrage at the use of Korean women as prostitutes ("comfort women") by the Japanese military government during World War II with the current role of South Koreans in Nike-licensed factories around Jakarta. Three-fourths of these plants are managed by South Korean concerns, which provide most of the machinery and raw materials as well as all of the managers. The layer of male South Korean management supervises female Indonesian assembly line workers, who labor in 100 degree heat, breathing air reeking of paints and glues, for 20 cents a day. Awareness of the complexities and contradictions suggested by this picture makes it difficult for Korean feminists to look long to Korean nationalism for self-definition.

5. Policy-makers have sometimes studied women of color in terms of their "service" to prevailing racial ideologies, suggesting interventions in what they define as "cultural practices." Thus, in keeping with the self-congratulatory Western view that Asian American families and communities are more patriarchal than the dominant culture, some have asserted without any concrete basis that domestic violence is more pervasive in Asian American than other American families.

6. Here of course I am referring the habit of attributing the perpetuation of patriarchy primarily to mothers who spoil their sons, tyrannize their daughters-in-law, and unquestioningly accept patriarchal attitudes and practices.

Will the Real
Asian Pacific American
Please Stand Up?

Media Policy

Diane Yen-Mei Wong

Writer & Editor
Former Executive Director
Asian American Journalists Association
San Francisco, California

Images of angry looters of all colors and all ages laden with consumer goods, running through streets lined by burning buildings juxtaposed against images of defiant Korean Americans hoisting rifles to protect their businesses.

In the heat of the rioting, journalists risked their lives trying to cover the story. It's a breaking story and everyone is frantically trying to find the right contacts to interview. Mistakes made about who participated in the disturbance and the underlying frustrations were to be expected, right?

❖ ❖ ❖

Images of an elementary school playground filled with wounded—some fatally—Southeast Asian children and their shocked and distraught parents juxtaposed against the image of a lone, crazed veteran.

Can, and should, the news media characterize the acts of this man as "racially motivated"—as the Asian Pacific American community argued—or did the police and mainstream media correctly characterize the man as someone who had just gone berserk and aimed his assault rifle at the first innocent targets he could find?

Images of a bereaved limited-English-speaking mother crying over the grave of her son, brutally killed by two white autoworkers who blamed him for their unemployed status juxtaposed against images of the two men smiling and triumphant at having beaten the charges filed against them.

The mainstream news media barely covered the killing. Only after the ethnic community media began looking into the killing and subsequent release of the two alleged killers with only a fine did other news media companies treat it as a legitimate news item. If the media didn't cover it, maybe the killing was not that important. Did community press blow this incident way out of proportion?

Images of young men clad all in black, with greased-back hair and shades, karate-kicking and gung-fu-chopping their way down a lonely dark street juxtaposed against images of short gray-haired women carrying plastic pink shopping bags of vegetables and noodles through the crowded streets of Chinatown, U.S.A.

Which is the "real" Chinatown? Or Little Saigon? Or Little Tokyo? Or International District? Or Koreatown? When the news media cover the community, how can they determine how prevalent one image is over the other? Do they care and does it matter anyway?

❖ ❖ ❖

Most of us have seen these images on television or in newspapers and magazines. We have heard and read not only about these stories but also countless others which follow a similar pattern. They constitute but just a fraction of the news stories to which we find ourselves exposed. And, they are just a few of the stories which journalists prepare and produce for their respective audiences.

They reflect only a very small slice of the lives of Asian Pacific Americans. Yet, for the majority of people in this country, those few images form the basis of their understanding of our entire diverse community.

As the population of the United States becomes more colorful, the news media and the various communities that comprise Asian Pacific

America will have to redefine and refine several ways in which they interact. This learning and growing process will, of necessity, be fraught with fitful starts and stops, radical changes in course and pace, and even, perhaps, an occasional moment of true understanding.

For the purposes of this paper, I will examine several issues facing news media companies, journalists and the Asian Pacific American community. They certainly are not the sole issues, but they are among the ones with which we must grapple if we mean to grow together as a society.

Issues for the News Media

The individual companies which comprise that social institution, the news media, vary throughout the country. Though it is tempting to treat them broadly as a uniform commodity, in truth, some companies are better than others, some chains or networks and affiliates are better than others, some regions are better than others. Whenever possible, I will try to delineate between what is the more common reality and what may be an exception.

Regardless of the differences among the companies, there is one indisputable common point: newsroom inhabitants do not often reflect the general population.

For people of color, for women, the initial impression of the news industry as a whole is fairly clear: it is a world dominated by white males. And it is this dominance that provides the perspective through which most of us receive news about the world around us. Further, it is this dominance that creates the context in which we must consider all our assumptions about, and hopes for, the news media.

At recent national gatherings of the American Society of Newspaper Editors (which represents the top level news executives at American daily newspapers), the American Newspaper Publisher Association (which includes publishers and other top representatives from primarily the business side of the American newspaper industry) and the Radio Television News Directors Association (which represents top level news executives in the broadcast industry), white males outnumber people of color and women by far. No doubt about it. Not even close.

What does this profile mean for the Asian Pacific American community?

In some parts of California, such as Los Angeles and San Francisco, you can see Asian Pacific American faces on the news programs of each major television station; you can read stories with Asian Pacific American bylines in each of the major local newspapers. In those areas, you can also pick up a newspaper or tune into a broadcast program in Korean, Chinese, Japanese, Tagalog, Vietnamese, or any of the other various languages used by longtime immigrants or recent arrivals.

California, a longtime favorite stopping place for immigrants and refugees from the Pacific Rim, is unusual, however. What I as a San Francisco Bay Area transplanted resident see, hear and read represents a skewed news world. For most people, the norm is a news team—both print and broadcast—that possesses a certain lack of skin pigment. Even in Hawaii, which boasts a large concentration of Asian Pacific Americans, most of the television newscasters are Caucasian.

News media organizations around the country, especially those outside of the West Coast, have a very hard time understanding the concept of "minority." For most of news managers and staff members, "minority" and "Black" (or African American) are completely interchangeable. Those who may be a bit more progressive, or who reside and work in areas with many Latinos, may understand that "minority" means brown or black. That the term actually includes other colors— such as yellow and red—is beyond many of them. They don't "get it" and don't even realize it.[1]

STATISTICAL OVERVIEW

U.S. Census data from 1990 peg the Asian Pacific American population at approximately 2.9 percent of the total population. Projections out of the University of California, Los Angeles, peg the year 2000 figure at 4 percent. In California, Hawaii and the Mid-Atlantic region of New York-New Jersey-Pennsylvania, the Asian Pacific American percentage of the general population is much greater.

According to 1991 figures collected by the American Society of Newspaper Editors, Asian Pacific Americans comprise only 1.5 percent (about 836) of the total workforce (55,700) in daily newspaper newsrooms. When one breaks down the overall figure of 1.5 percent, the picture becomes clearer about the limitations faced by Asian Pacific

Americans in this industry. The largest percentage of Asian Pacific Americans is copy editors (173 out of a total of 8,784, or 2 percent) and photographers (154 out of 5,761, or 2.7 percent). They comprise, however, only 0.9 percent of newsroom supervisors (122 out of 13, 315) and 1.3 percent of reporters (366 out of 27,656). Most daily newspapers in this country do not have any people of color working in the newsrooms.

In the broadcast industry, the figures paint an even bleaker picture. The National Association of Broadcasters in 1991 found that in 1990, Asian Pacific Americans comprised only 1.3 percent (2,010 out of a total of 158,779) of employees in commercial and non-commercial broadcasting. While the percentage has remained constant since 1988, the actual *number* of Asian Pacific Americans working in the industry has consistently decreased from a high of 2,247 in 1988.

The question about diversity in the newsroom requires a more in-depth observation. According to a 1990 Asian American Journalists Association study, conducted by Alexis Tan of Washington State University's communications school, the glass ceiling that prevents qualified journalists from moving up in their careers is the primary reason that many *former* Asian Pacific American journalists left the profession and one of the key reasons that *current* journalists plan to leave.[2] Without advancement possibilities, then, the few Asian Pacific American journalists there may even become rarer. And as entry-level journalists replace more experienced ones, the group becomes younger and less seasoned: contacts have to be made all over again and the pipeline to decision-making positions is disrupted.

The largest percentage of Asian Pacific Americans in the newspaper industry are photographers; in broadcast, they are found behind cameras or in other production and technical capacities. The few who work at jobs which involve high-level decision-making about news and hiring are just that—few. As of June 1992, in mainstream news media, there was but one Asian Pacific American publisher of a major metropolitan daily (Arlene Lum, *Honolulu Star-Bulletin*), one editor (William Woo, *St. Louis Post-Dispatch*), one television news director—who, incidentally, also reports—(Nimi McConigley, KGWC-TV, Casper, Wyoming).

Even with a strong economy and growing job opportunities, the challenge to have the numbers in the newsroom reflect more accurately the proportion in the general populace is great. With a struggling economy and the down-sizing and closure of news media organizations, prospects for more Asian Pacific Americans to be hired are bleak. Just in terms of sheer numbers, the road ahead remains long and tortuous.

But numbers are just the beginning.

The Asian American Journalists Association (AAJA), a national group of print and broadcast journalists, focuses much of its resources on efforts to increase the number of Asian Pacific Americans in the field. That, however, is not the end in and of itself. Rather, the increased employment is but a means to something that has much more far-reaching impact on the community: how the community is covered.[3]

COVERING A CHANGING COMMUNITY

For individuals who aspire to journalism, looking at the numbers in the industry may be of prime interest. For the Asian Pacific American community as a whole, however, the hope is that increased numbers will translate into better and more coverage of issues and the varied aspects of the community, that coverage will be more accurate, more sensitive and fairer.

A good newspaper, news magazine, and television or radio station can somehow manage to find the big or "sexy" story in a community. The smart organizations that have been able to afford to hire will have Asian Pacific Americans on staff; the not-so-smart or not-so-flush ones will be able to find translators and other contacts in the community. Somehow, they will muster resources necessary to cover the big shooting, the New Year's celebration or that unusual and exotic event or person.

These types of stories, though, result in a very skewed view of what makes up the community. Most of the stories that make up our community do not lend themselves to 30-second sound bites or ten- or 20-inch column spaces. These are the stories that pose many more problems to news media companies and to journalists: they require time and long-term contacts with the community.

To present a more complete view of a community, news media organizations will have to do a better job of including Asian Pacific Americans as regular people in non-ethnic-specific stories. For instance, in a story about lawyers who do *pro bono*, or free, legal work, one Bay Area station talked at length with a Sansei attorney who had recently been honored by his peers for his legal work. The fact that he was Asian Pacific American was irrelevant to the main thrust of the story.

However, the fact that he was Asian Pacific American did a lot in terms of providing the community—both ethnic and mainstream—with a good story and good role model.[4]

DIFFERENTIATING AMONG GROUPS

Many news media organizations have had a hard enough time trying to cover the older, more established ethnic groups which comprise the Asian Pacific American community. Now, with the increased presence of newer immigrant and refugee groups, that once-difficult job has become even more demanding.

Though it has always been important, determining when to differentiate among the many ethnic groups that comprise the Asian Pacific American community has become more critical. Most of the older immigrants and the American born within the community know and understand that Asian Pacific Americans form a politically-generated entity, not one based on a culture and value system that crosses all ethnic groups. For most newer arrivals this concept is indeed foreign; they identify themselves by their own ethnic and homeland affiliations.

There are times when that political commonality provides a more accurate perspective; and there are times when it is important to recognize the differences within the community. Culturally oriented stories should probably indicate on *which* particular ethnic group's culture the story focuses. For instance, a New Year's story should indicate whether the subject is a Japanese American *oshogatsu* festival or a Vietnamese Tet celebration. Each ethnic group has its ways of marking a special occasion. To treat them as a blanket Asian Pacific American is effectively to negate the very uniqueness that can enrich our *American* society.

On the other hand, sometimes ethnic distinctions are not warranted and are, in fact, inaccurate. In the case of crimes motivated by racial hatred, perpetrators do not care about a person's specific ethnicity; the mere fact that they *look* like the "enemy" is quite sufficient. Vincent Chin's killers did not bother to determine if the Asian Pacific American whom they were beating with a baseball bat was Japanese or Chinese American, or if that person slipping into unconsciousness was truly responsible for their unemployment as Detroit autoworkers. Vincent Chin's Chinese ethnic background could not protect him against those who looked at him and decided he was a Japanese person that symbolized Japanese auto manufacturers.[5]

Issues for Asian Pacific American Journalists

Asian Pacific American journalists face their own set of concerns when trying to do their job. The 1990 AAJA study cited above also indicates that both current and former journalists selected the field because they like the excitement of the job and the opportunity to help the community. The journalism occupation carries with it many responsibilities that go beyond merely going out and recording events and disseminating information.

BEING LEADERS

Many minority professionals not only have to do the job for which they are hired; many also feel obligated to make themselves available as resources to the community. Coupled with their visibility, this often means the community calls upon them to emcee fundraisers, participate in panels and as speakers. And more often than they may want, journalists find themselves held up as role models. While most people don't seek out the responsibility that this entails, and some may not even admit that they are role models, young people do look up to them.

Young people watching the small screen at home may not see too many Asian Pacific Americans in situation comedies, hour-long mysteries or made-for-television movies; the big screen fares no better in presenting realistic images. The one time they may see an Asian Pacific American—at least on the West Coast and in some of the larger urban areas—is on the news. Similarly, when perusing the school reading list or combing through the stacks at the local library, not too many Asian Pacific American names appear—unless, again, the readers reside on the West Coast or in those larger metropolitan areas. It might be possible, though, to see an Asian Pacific American name as a byline in the newspaper or a national magazine, or as a photo credit.

Almost all current (78 percent) and former (77 percent) journalists nationally are Chinese and Japanese Americans.[6] Much smaller numbers come from Filipino, Korean, Vietnamese and other Asian Pacific American ethnic backgrounds. Given the changing face of the community, the near-absence of South Asian, Southeast Asian, Korean, Filipino, and Pacific Islander journalists to act as community resources and role models may prove to be another obstacle along the path of adjusting to American life in these newer and smaller communities.

Pan-Asian Perspective

Unless and until more representatives from these other communities find themselves in America's newsrooms, current Asian Pacific American journalists must fill that void, serving not only their own ethnic communities but also these others. This is a heavy load for people who already have to work long, irregular shifts at demanding, pressured more-than-full-time jobs. Along with developing contacts in their own ethnic community, Asian Pacific American journalists must expend resources on identifying and nurturing contacts in other communities. At its best, this means spending time with people, learning about customs and beliefs, maybe learning a new language, gaining their trust and trusting others. At its worst, this means superficial treatment and coverage of these newer and smaller groups in ways no different than mainstream journalists.

Ironically, in many ways, this pan-Asian approach corresponds to the tendency for news media companies to want their few Asian Pacific American journalists—usually Chinese or Japanese, and maybe Filipino or Korean—to communicate and cover equally all the other ethnic groups. For some employers, this may reflect limited hiring resources; for others, this may be the objective manifestation of an inability to understand that each ethnic group that makes up this Asian Pacific American community is unique.

Better still it is for Asian Pacific American journalists to encourage the training and hiring of more and different journalists from the Asian Pacific American communities.

Being Liaisons and Educators

The need for more journalists from other, non-Chinese, non-Japanese ethnic groups becomes even more critical in light of the major role that journalists play as liaisons between the ethnic communities and mainstream community. It is journalists who must take complex and sensitive issues from within the community and somehow communicate them to others.

Coverage of the 1992 riots in Los Angeles after the acquittal of the police officers whose videotaped beating of black motorist Rodney King provides a very recent and troubling example of an event that may have been covered quite differently had more Asian Pacific American journalists been assigned to cover it and had more non-Asian Pacific American journalists had a more in-depth understanding of the racial tensions growing among the many different communities in the Los Angeles area.

Despite the popular news media picture painted in the early days of the rioting, battles did not involve just Blacks and Whites. Hispanics and all Asian Pacific Americans—not just Koreans—were involved. And, despite news media depictions to the contrary, the armed reaction to looting of Koreatown stores is not reinforcement of the image of Asians as valuing life less or of Koreans as more prone to violence.

Los Angeles Times reporter John H. Lee, a Korean American, eloquently describes the problems of presenting these inflammatory images without history and context. He describes how one merchant resorted to arms only after drive-by shooters had made his store into a target five times and after his 911 calls and pleas to the police for help resulted in total inaction. Viewers saw rifles and handguns but not the frantic fear that the police had all but abandoned the community.[7]

In 1990, in the very multiethnic, multicultural city of San Francisco, with a news staff more diverse than most, the *San Francisco Examiner* came out with a story which, according to AAJA's *Project Zinger* media analysis report, quickly became the "center of controversy and heated debate." The article, "Asian Women, Caucasian Men: The New Demographics of Love," focused on what writer Joan Walsh described as the "hot trend" of interracial dating. Critics say that Walsh relied on anecdotal evidence to support racial stereotypes about the exotic and passive natures of Asian women and the unattractive and sexless natures of Asian men and that she accepted these images without analysis or critique.[8]

That the topic was interesting and worthy of discussion was not at issue; that Walsh had the right to write about the topic was not an issue. What caused problems among readers was what many believed to be the insensitive, sensationalized and superficial treatment of a very complex and sensitive topic. Perhaps Walsh, in her story, demonstrated the understanding of a white woman, but, critics argue, this understanding is not enough. *Zinger* coordinator Jon Funabiki, himself a journalist with many years' experience, and his staff suggest that news companies should consider "community sensitivities" about the presentation of such pieces and that they "may wish to ask ethnic minority journalists for additional sources, background and advice on community sensitivity."[9]

This is not to suggest or advocate that only Asians can, or should, cover Asian communities. Asian Pacific American journalists can, however, bring in different perspectives, develop different sources, understand subtleties of ethnic culture, and can bring up story ideas and issues that normally might not make it to the table. At the same time, though, while Chinese and Japanese Americans may be able to cover refugee and immigrant communities and demonstrate an understanding of racism and discrimination, the challenge is to have more members of the newer communities to go into journalism.

RELATIONSHIPS WITH OTHER MINORITIES

The educational role Asian Pacific American journalists must play includes sharing information about the ethnic groups with other journalists of color and with white journalists. Having access to information and contacts means that when major stories affecting the community are happening or about to happen, Asian Pacific American journalists have a responsibility to make waves about how the stories are written, produced or aired and if they are at all.[10]

And, as if this were not enough, Asian Pacific Americans must be sensitive to the needs and concerns of communities beyond their own. As society becomes more racially diverse, there will be many occasions for Asian Pacific American journalists to speak up about coverage of other communities of color. To do this with conviction and strength means that journalists of various colors must communicate with each other to educate each other. Journalists of color are natural allies. However, as the Asian Pacific American community changes, and, hopefully results in concomitant changes in the newsrooms, other minorities must learn about the newer groups.

The four national minority journalism organizations joined together in 1988 to form a separate group, Unity '94, whose goals include a unified response to issues affecting all or any of the group's members. The commonalities among the groups' struggle to have an impact on the news media industry form the foundation of the new entity. Actions have included, among other things, black and Hispanic journalists taking a very verbal and visible position when a white male columnist attacked a Korean American colleague with graphic sexual and racial epithets. It has also meant Asian, Black and Hispanic journalists joining with Native Americans in commending a newspaper's decision not to refer to sports teams by names offensive to Native American nations.[11]

The process of working with each other requires a great deal of time and trust. For journalists from the newer immigrant and refugee communities, the mere idea of working closely with other minorities can cause anxiety and friction. On the other hand, for American-born Asian Pacific Americans and others who have been in this country long enough to be exposed to the common history of racial discrimination shared by people of color, working with Blacks, Hispanics and Native Americans may be a challenge but not necessarily a source of fear. It is up to the American born and/or raised journalists to help set a cooperative tone.

Once identified, these issues may then give direction to leaders about political and social policies.

Resorting to Stereotypes

Journalists need to learn how to cover a community that no longer corresponds to the already inaccurate "model minority" stereotype that many journalists held. The "community" always was actually more a collection of many different communities, but now, these common stereotypes will become even less applicable as the smaller ethnic groups that more recently arrived here in the United States grow larger.

Journalists, by definition, operate under deadlines. They need to find information fast and get it out even faster. If they don't already have the facts on hand or in their news files, they have to do some research. Or, they may rely on what they believe to be true. Unfortunately, in many instance, this has meant resorting to stereotypes.

Any journalist can be guilty of doing this—color and ethnicity are no guarantees against use of stereotypes. Journalists from the more established Asian Pacific American communities must work hard to avoid including stereotypes about the newer immigrant and refugee groups, and vice versa. And, beyond this one community, Asian Pacific American journalists are in the position to be more sensitive about inaccurate stereotypes applied to different groups.

To ensure that journalists have the latest, most accurate information, the community must take some responsibility for educating them.

Issues for the Community

The third important component in this discussion of the relationship of the changing Asian Pacific American community and the news media is the community itself. While journalists are still an integral part of the community, there are some specific issues with which the latter must grapple.

JOURNALISTS OR COMMUNITY ACTIVISTS?

Some of the most difficult questions facing Asian Pacific American journalists are: am I a journalist first or an Asian Pacific American first? How does that affect work as a journalist? Do I advocate or do I remain totally neutral?

In reality, there is no such thing as total objectivity. The only achievable goal is to be fair. Journalists must acknowledge that they can influence how readers and viewers and listeners feel about an issue when they decide what story to pursue, which contacts to interview, even which adjectives and adverbs to use. A community, especially one that is new to the idea of Western journalism with its tenets of freedom of the press and the "right to know," may want journalists to be advocates and, indeed, may even expect its "own" journalists to be out there right in front of the battle.

To place this type of demand on Asian Pacific American journalists unfortunately often puts them in an untenable situation: they may want to cover a community, but once they are perceived as being outright advocates, editors or directors may feel it is time to pull them off and assign them to beats or stories in which they have no personal agendas. No, this is not necessarily fair to individual reporters, but it is an option still exercised by many managers and it is an issue still unresolved in the news media industry as a whole.

For the community, the challenge is to develop and maintain contacts with Asian Pacific American or other sensitive journalists and to keep them informed about what is happening in the community.

AFFECTING WHAT STORIES ARE COVERED

These contacts can be critical in reporting stories and perspectives that reflect sensibilities that differ from the majority of news industry decision-makers, who are, not surprisingly, white and male. Decisions about which stories make it to the news—and which don't—often result in defining which issues are considered newsworthy and deserving of attention from the general public and political leaders. The community must fight to have a say in those decisions. There is very limited space and time for stories. After all, how many sound bites can fit within a 30-minute broadcast, and how many articles in a daily newspaper? If the Asian Pacific American community as a whole has not been well covered thus far, how much more will it be neglected or misrepresented now that there are more ethnic groups and our numbers are growing?

The importance of these decisions should not be underestimated. This relationship between the news media and the community can be critical in identifying and defining what an important issue is. This concept has been used by older, more established Asian Pacific American communities that have learned news media savvy.

In one instance, a group of primarily Japanese American attorneys learned how to work effectively with the news media to call attention to an obscure legal procedure, writ of *coram nobis*, that was to be the vehicle through which these attorneys hoped to right the legal wrong visited upon the Japanese American community during World War II.

When attorneys and community activists decided to take on the *coram nobis* case of Fred Korematsu, they wanted the support of the general public. To achieve this, they would need to educate people about the importance of the case and the injustice not only of Korematsu's original criminal conviction for disobeying the World War II orders to relocate but the injustice of the entire internment.

They knew that many people did not even know about the internment. Further, many who *did* might believe that the camps had been necessary to protect either the Japanese Americans against society or society against the Japanese Americans. Thus, to build support for Korematsu (and the two companion cases involving Minoru Yasui and Gordon Hirabayashi, both of whom also refused to obey wartime orders aimed at controlling the movement and choices of Japanese Americans), they joined the campaign of the Japanese American Citizens League to convince the mainstream media about the newsworthiness of the topic. Together, they worked with such news media entities as *The New York Times* and *60 Minutes* to educate them about the nuances of the case and the potential significance not only for Asian Pacific Americans but for all people concerned with protecting the Constitution.

The *coram nobis* action presented the court with newly discovered evidence showing that the federal government had suppressed, altered and even destroyed evidence which would have exonerated Japanese Americans from any charges of sabotage and espionage. This new evidence demonstrated that the federal government had perpetrated fraud against the court. Such a charge was so grievous that the court chose to reopen the *Korematsu* case even though four decades had passed.

With all the media attention on the unusual case, more people learned about the internment camps and the unjust imprisonment of 120,000 Americans of Japanese descent. The news media, by choosing to cover the issue, helped to depict and define it as an important issue for all Americans. The media attention also coincided with, and reinforced, efforts by Congress to develop the redress and reparations plan for those held in the camps. The case resulted not only in a legal victory but an educational one as well.

An Honorable Profession

Some media critics may argue about the respectability of being a journalist. Generally, however, Asian Pacific Americans born and/or raised in this country have grown up with principles such as the First Amendment and the public's "right to know." They understand that being a journalist does not automatically mean that one's life is meaningless, useless and distasteful; most may even believe that there are some journalists who are worthy of respect, honor and well wishes.

For many Asian Pacific American immigrants and refugees, however, journalism is synonymous with working as the voice of government and not exercising any independent thought, with fearing that criticism of the government means sure loss of job and possible loss of life. For young people from these communities, there is little encouragement from parents to enter journalism; instead, they encounter persuasion to become doctors, dentists, business leaders, bankers and engineers. With so much loss in their recent past—loss of jobs, homes and lives—it is understandable why so many refugee and immigrant parents worry about their children being able to make a living at a good job that will bring not only money but honor and that will not risk their survival. Several student members of AAJA have mentioned time and again how hard it has been to convince their immigrant parents that journalism is all right as a profession, that they will manage to survive. Most of these students report pressure to go into other, more financially rewarding and more prestigious fields.

And, yet, for many of those communities, it is precisely more journalists that they need—journalists who have a clearer insight into issues and concerns and who have gained the ability to communicate those issues and concerns. Community leaders and parents need to work at supporting those who choose journalism as careers.

ONE COMMUNITY'S STRATEGY

Recently in one local community, some leaders took matters in their own hands in the fight to improve the media's coverage of its issues and concerns.[12] Though some of the news media in the city had done an adequate job of covering major issues in the Asian Pacific American community, many had not. Only one paper and one television station had a reporter assigned to cover the community on a semi-regular basis. Many issues that were less conducive to one-time only pieces went by unheeded by most of the media. Plus, many in the community felt that the media companies were not too responsive.

A small group of community activists met and brought in representatives from other ethnic groups, especially some of the newer or smaller communities. During the course of their meetings, they outlined some goals and strategies, including a list of which news companies to approach first.

They identified sympathetic Asian Pacific American journalists who worked at the targeted companies. The journalists and community leaders met with each other to determine where their respective objectives overlapped and how they could help each other. With one company, for instance, journalists wanted to be able to do more stories on the community; the community wanted more coverage. The strategy became clear: the community representatives would meet with the company's top-level managers and say that though the company was doing fair so far, they wanted more coverage and they would encourage their friends and other community members to support that paper.

At another company, community leaders again met with sympathetic Asian Pacific American journalists employed there. They learned that one of the reporters wanted to cover the community as a beat, but that paper had not identified that community as newsworthy enough to have a reporter specially assigned to cover it. At their subsequent manager's meeting, the community group made it quite clear that it was not happy with that company's spotty coverage. As a matter of fact, members said, they all preferred to follow the company's rival since it had assigned someone familiar with the community and its players to cover the community on a regular basis. Disturbed by what it was hearing, the second news company suddenly found a way to assign one of its reporters (who just happened to want the beat) to report on the Asian Pacific American community.

From the beginning, the group knew that the journalists alone would have a tough time putting pressure on their employers about beats and coverage. With the community making similar demands, however, editors and news directors would feel more compelled to act. And that has proved true.

The meetings constituted only the first step. The group has now pledged to try to follow up to make sure that promises are kept. Follow-up includes monitoring the media to see if coverage has increased and improved. They also plan to continue meeting with other local news companies.

Challenge for the Future

Both the news media and the changing Asian Pacific American community will face challenges. Those who can adjust will be better able to survive and thrive in the coming decade; those who cannot will be left behind wondering what the fuss was all about and thinking there is nothing that can be done anyway.

As a fast-growing community of color, we cannot accept a defeatist attitude about the news media. What we read, hear or watch must be just the beginning of what we and they learn.

It's not that journalists have the *only* perspective or the *correct* perspective. It's not that they have some inherent knowledge about issues or events that endows their opinions with more weight. No. What journalists as a group have that the ordinary Asian Pacific American does not is easier access to the channels through which information can be disseminated, through which opinions are formed. It is critically important for the community and journalists to work closely together and for them both to fight for what they believe in an effort to make the news media industry more sensitive, accurate and fair in its coverage.

Notes

1. Many of my observations come from my four and a half years as national executive director of the Asian American Journalists Association, a non-profit organization of print and broadcast journalists and journalism students.

    When discussing Asian Pacific American issues with news media editors, publishers and news directors from all over the country, it became increasingly evident that especially on the East Coast, Midwest and South, Asians were not considered a minority, or, if they were, they were not a minority that should benefit from any affirmative action programs or the like.

2. Alexis Tan, "Why Asian American Journalists Leave Journalism and Why They Stay" (San Francisco: Asian American Journalists Association, 1990), 1, 3, 6. The survey, which was sent to 700 working journalists and 40 former journalists, generated a 38 percent response from the former group and a 70 percent response from the latter. Results also showed a dismayingly high 36 percent of current Asian Pacific American journalists said they were likely or very likely to leave the field within five years.

3. The Asian American Journalists Association's four objectives include (a) increasing the employment of Asian Pacific American journalists; (b) assisting students who are pursuing journalism as a career objective; (c) ensuring that coverage of the Asian Pacific American community is accurate and fair; (d) providing mutual support for Asian Pacific American journalists. These overall goals are similar to those held by the other national minority journalism organizations: National Association of Black Journalists, National Association of Hispanic Journalists and the Native American Journalists Association.

4. This story, which appeared in the mid-1980s, was so unusual in this respect that I wrote to the station commending the reporter and producer for their work.

5. Vincent Chin died on June 23, 1982, after a baseball bat beating by two white men, Ronald Ebens and Michael Nitz. For their roles in Chin's death, the two men each received five years' probation and a $3,000 fine. The incident served as a catalyst for the Asian Pacific American community to organize against anti-Asian violence.

6. According to the Tan study, among former journalists Japanese comprise the largest ethnic group (47 percent), followed by Chinese (30 percent). Among current journalists, Chinese American journalists outnumber Japanese Americans (47 percent versus 31 percent).

7. John H. Lee, "You Have to Explain How We Feel," *AAJA Newsletter* (Summer 1992). That issue of the newsletter also contains several other

articles about Asian Pacific Americans who covered, or commented on coverage of, the Los Angeles riots.

8. Center for Integration and Improvement of Journalism, *Project Zinger: The Good, the Bad and the Ugly* (San Francisco: Asian American Journalists Association, 1991), 7, 8. The project was headed by long-time journalist Jon Funabiki, who heads the center. When it submitted the article to the center as an example of poor coverage, the San Francisco Bay Area Chapter of AAJA called it an "egregious example of shoddy reporting, sensationalism and woefully irresponsible editorial judgment."

9. *Ibid.*, 8.

10. In "The L.A. Riots and Media Preparedness" *AAJA Newsletter* (Summer 1992), *Los Angeles Times* business writer and AAJA-LA Chapter president Dean Takahashi took on his own paper and observed that many of its minority reporters had been assigned to work out of suburban bureaus and that only a very few worked in the more prestigious downtown Metro section. When the riots began and it "became apparent that a number of white reporters could not gain access to the story, minority reporters, some from the suburbs, were shipped into the riot zone." Takahashi made waves in his newsroom when he wrote about his observations about how the *Los Angeles Times* covered the riots. His article first appeared in the news media industry publication, *Editor & Publisher* (May 23, 1992).

11. Unity '94 includes the Asian American Journalists Association, National Association of Black Journalists, National Association of Hispanic Journalists and the Native American Press Association. It plans a joint national convention in 1994 in Atlanta.

    The first incident occurred in 1990 when *Newsday* (NY) columnist Jimmy Breslin became angry at remarks made by reporter Mary Yuh. The incident was covered widely in the news and resulted in the two-week suspension of the Pulitzer Prize-winning Breslin. The second occurred in spring 1992, when *The Oregonian* (Portland) announced its new policy that it would no longer refer to sports teams by racially-oriented names, such as the Washington Redskins.

12. Because the group is still in the process of meeting with news media groups, I have chosen not to reveal the names of the people, news media organizations or even the location. Suffice it to say that the group includes representatives from many different Asian Pacific American ethnic groups (including Chinese, Filipino, Japanese, Korean and Vietnamese) and from many different walks of life. The news media are located in a large metropolitan area where there is a concentration of Asian Pacific Americans.

South Asians in the United States with a Focus on Asian Indians:
Policy on New Communities

Sucheta Mazumdar

Assistant Professor, Department of History
State University of New York, Albany

In this article I am going to focus primarily on Asian Indians—a community which has grown considerably during the decade of the 1980s but on whom there is, as yet, very limited research. Though there are several other communities of immigrants also from South Asia, as indicated below, the absence of published literature makes it difficult to discuss them in any detail. I start each section with the available data from 1980/1990 and then develop the discussion based on the projections. I have included a brief discussion of the Immigration Act of 1990 and its anticipated impact on Asian Indian immigration.

Background Information
on South Asian Immigrants

"South Asia" is comprised of Bangladesh, Bhutan, India, Pakistan, Nepal and Sri Lanka. There are relatively few immigrants in the U.S. from either of the two Himalayan countries, Bhutan and Nepal; data are not available from the printed records of either the census or the Immigration and Naturalization Services (INS). Up to 1980, separate data were also not available for immigrants from Pakistan, Bangladesh or Sri Lanka. However, the 1980 Census did count all the major South Asian groups in separate categories. The various South Asian groups share common cultural, linguistic and religious affiliations, as well as a common colonial history. Community newspapers such as *India West* and *India Abroad* reflect these regional ties and carry some news of all the South Asian communities.

Asian Indians: Asian Indians are the largest group of immigrants from South Asia. "Asian Indian" is a "self-identified category" so that it is possible that some immigrants of Indian origin from Fiji, Guyana, Britain and Africa are not accounted for in the total count of Asian Indians in the census which poses the question of ancestry as a question of national origin. Some community newspapers and political alliances use the term "Indo American" to denote "Asian Indian."[1] For purposes of this paper I will use the term "Asian Indian" as it is the official designation for immigrants from India and is used in the census.

The Preliminary Counts of the 1990 Census (June 1991 release) recorded a total of 815,447 individuals, making the Asian Indians the fourth largest group among the Asian Americans and slightly more numerous than the Koreans. The 1980 Census had noted 387,223 Asian Indians. That was the first time Asian Indians had been counted as a separate category. Asian Indians have thus grown 125.6 percent in the 1980s, making them one of the fastest growing Asian American communities, second only to the Vietnamese in the percentage increase during the decade. Asian Indians make up about 19 percent of the total Asian American Pacific Islander population of the United States. The actual total of Asian Indians as noted by the 1990 Census actually may have been slightly higher. In the fiscal year 1990, INS data show 30,667 Indians were admitted as immigrants.[2] Some of these immigrants may not have been accounted for in the 1990 Census.

The projection is that the Asian Indian community will continue to grow rapidly in the decade of the 1990s through immigration not only in the categories of skilled workers and professionals, but also as more Asian Indians become eligible to sponsor close relatives outside the preference system. Among those naturalized in 1990 by country of foreign citizenship, Indians represented the fifth largest group (11,499) following (in numerical order) naturalizations from the Philippines, Vietnam, Mexico and mainland China.[3]

Under the Immigration Act of 1990 (IMMACT90), all family-sponsored preferences have been reorganized.[4] This second preference (spouses and minor children) category has been increased considerably over that of 1965 (from 70,200 to 114,200). This should help ease the backlog facing many Indians. Some have had to wait three to five years before their spouses could join them in America.

IMMACT90 has also radically changed the employment-related categories, with preference given to skilled workers, professionals with advanced degrees, "aliens of exceptional ability" and "outstanding professors and researchers." These provisions will be beneficial for countries with skilled professional category immigrants such as India. The slowdown, and indeed, economic crisis of the Indian economy means there will be many with professional degrees seeking to immigrate. Already by 1990, the Indian unemployment bureau listed 30 million unemployed. Of these, 2.8 million held graduate or postgraduate degrees.[5] So in the 1990s we are likely to see an increase in the number of educated and skilled immigrants from India.

The potential pool of Asian Indian immigrants has also been increased by the larger number entering the country as students. In 1990-91 there was a 10 percent increase over 1989-90 in the number of students from India for a total of 28,900 students.[6] Studies done on Indian migration show that, on an average, one-third of those coming in as students from India adjusted their status to that of immigrant in the 1980s.[7]

In 1990, besides the students, over 120,000 individuals entered the country from India as temporary visitors for either business or pleasure, and over four thousand entered as "temporary workers and trainees."[8] On an average during the 1980s, around six thousand of those coming in as visitors converted their status to immigrants each year as did around two thousand of those in the "trainee" category. These trends will probably also continue, adding to the size of the community as a whole.

Pakistani: The 1980 Census had accounted for only 15,792 Pakistanis. This was probably an undercount, for the 1990 Census notes 81,371 Pakistanis. This figure too may be an undercount. The 1990 Census data on "Foreign-born population by Place of Birth" gives the total of 83,663 for Pakistan.[9] Even if one accepts that there may be over two thousand individuals born of American parents in Pakistan who were excluded from the census count, the addition of American-born children to the Pakistani immigrants should lead to a higher total than that given in the

1990 Census. Overall, the size of the Pakistani population is likely to show a sharp upward increase because as many as 49,986 Pakistanis entered the country in 1990 as "non-immigrants" in 1990, of whom over 33,000 were visitors and almost five thousand students.[10] A portion of these "non-immigrants," given the current political situation in Pakistan, is likely to seek change of status as immigrants.[11] Perhaps presaging this trend, overall annual Pakistani immigration increased from 8,000 in 1989 to 9,729 in 1990.[12] Thirty-four percent (27,876) of all Pakistani immigrants live in the northeastern states.

Bangladeshi: The total number of Bangladeshi noted in the 1990 Census was 11,838. Almost 60 percent of the Bangladeshis are also concentrated in the northeastern states of the U.S. Like the Pakistani community, the Bangladeshi community shows an increase in recent immigration. In 1989 Bangladesh had only 2,180 immigrants but the number more than doubled to 4,252 in 1990.[13] So it is likely that both the Pakistani and the Bangladeshi communities will grow rapidly in the decade of the 1990s.

Sri Lankan: The 1990 Census indicates there are 10,970 Sri Lankans in the United States. In contrast to all the other South Asians who are located primarily in the northeast, 38.3 percent of Sri Lankans live in West Coast states. Around one thousand Sri Lankans immigrated in 1990.

Other South Asians: There are also over seven thousand Fijians of Indian origin, most of whom live in California. There are around fifty thousand Guyanese Indians who live primarily in New York (Queens and Manhattan) and California (Long Beach).[14] Both the Fijians and the Guyanese Indians are linked to the Asian Indian community through linguistic, cultural and religious ties. There are also a small number of Caribbean (mostly Trinidadian) Indians, located in New York.

Impact of Asian Indian and South Asian Immigration

The high level of immigration from South Asia in the 1980s has made South Asians a far more important component (almost 19 percent) of the Asian American population than previously anticipated. By the year 2000, Asian Indians, now the fourth largest group, will probably emerge as the third largest group, especially as part of a South Asian contingent.

While some links between Asian American political organizations and South Asian ones have been established, especially in California, far more needs to be done. Otherwise, the political potential of Asian Americans, representing approximately 14 percent of the American population by 2010, as projected by Paul Ong, will not be realized.

Overall, in terms of data on all Asian Americans, not just Asian Indians, there are some basic problems with the types of data available. Many studies on Asian Americans rely on the Current Population Survey (CPS). However, the sample size of the data for Asian Americans used for this survey is very small and the data set do not allow many types of analysis. This observation is made by William P. O'Hare in his study on Asian Americans.[15] He points out that a few years ago when Hispanics faced the same problem, the Census Bureau began to increase their sample size in the CPS. A similar policy decision should be made for the Asian American data.

Regional Distribution of Asian Indians

Like the four other major Asian American groups (Chinese, Filipino, Japanese and Korean), Asian Indians live predominantly in metropolitan areas. The only major rural agricultural Asian Indian community is the Punjabi Sikh community in Central California. Seventy percent of the Asian Indians live in eight major industrial-urban states—New York, California, New Jersey, Texas, Pennsylvania, Michigan, Illinois and Ohio. Of the 815,447 Asian Indians counted in the 1990 Census, California had the largest number of Asian Indians (159,973), followed by New York with 140,985. However, unlike the other Asian American groups, Asian Indians continue to be concentrated in the Northeastern states. Thirty-five percent of Asian Indians in the United States live in the northeast. The distribution of states with the largest number of Asian Indians, besides California and New York are: New Jersey: 79,440; Illinois: 64,200 and Texas: 55,795. Overall in eight states—Alabama, Connecticut, Michigan, New Jersey, North Carolina, Ohio, Tennessee and West Virginia—Asian Indians are the largest subgroup of the Asian Americans.

Though the Metropolitan Statistical Area data for 1990 are not available yet, the major settlements are likely to be the same as they were in 1980. The 1980 Census data (which showed a total count of 387,223

Asian Indians) indicated the five largest Standard Metropolitan Statistical Areas (SMSA) with Asian Indians were: New York—56,815; Chicago—33,541; Los Angeles—18,770; Washington, D.C.—15,698; and San Francisco—12,782.

Because most other Asian Americans are concentrated in the West, Asian Indians formed a relatively smaller proportion of the total Asian American population in the metropolitan areas of the Pacific coast states in 1980. On the other hand, already in 1980, Asian Indians represented 29.6 percent of the Asian American population in New York, 23.7 percent of the Asian American population in Chicago, and 23 percent of the Asian American population in Houston.[17] It is possible that with the increase in total numbers in 1990, Asian Indians represent an even higher percentage of Asian Americans in these areas and will continue to do so well into the next century.

This spatial diversity raises some problems in terms of coalition building. Asian Indians, and most South Asians, are concentrated in the Northeast, versus other Asian Americans who are concentrated in California and Hawaii. Educational strategies have to be developed to link the two shores; otherwise, a significant Asian American population group remains underrepresented in the formulation of public policy and discussions of the Asian American experience.

Economic Profile and Changing Pattern of Asian Indian Immigration

Though India, with 1,016 individuals entering the country in the third preference category of immigration (professional and highly skilled workers), was second only to Taiwan in the worldwide count in the number of immigrants entering in this category in 1990, the vast majority of the Indian immigrants came under other preference categories. In 1990, of the 19,157 Asian Indians immigrants permitted entry under the worldwide numerical limitation system, the number of individuals coming in on the second preference (spouses and unmarried sons and daughters of permanent resident aliens) and the fifth preference (adult brothers and sisters of U.S. citizens and their spouses and children) were 6,396 and 8,842 respectively. On the other hand, the number of immigrants coming in on the third preference (and their spouses and children) totalled only 2,038.[18] This may suggest that the pattern of immigration from India has been changing from the exclusively highly trained professionals in the earlier decades to those who may not have the same level of professional training as the initial sponsor.

In the 1980 Census, 35.5 percent of Asian Indian women and almost 70 percent of men were college graduates.[19] Among the ranks of the professionals, engineers were the most numerous, followed by physicians. Overall, 47 percent of Asian Indians were in the high-status categories of managers, professionals and executives.[20] Associations of engineers of Indian origin in the U.S. are organized along lines of technical specialization, and many of the engineers are linked by alumni association membership. Because there is no single national organization, though the engineers are a significant and relatively wealthy segment of the community, their impact on the American economy remains difficult to ascertain. The physicians, on the other hand, are organized in a national organization, the Association of American Physicians from India (AAPI), with local chapters in all the metropolitan areas. The AAPI suggests that there are approximately 26,000 physicians of Indian origin in the United States at present, the second largest number of foreign-born medical personnel after the Filipinos.[21] As discussed below, the economic power of this group, along with their active national organization, has given them a political presence both in the community and in terms of national politics. Overall, physicians have not been as adversely affected by the recession as some other segments of the Asian Indian professionals. The sluggish economy of the northeastern states throughout the 1980s and the layoffs in the aerospace industry in California in particular have forced many with professional engineering degrees to turn to alternative avenues of employment. For those with some capital, or access to financing, starting small businesses has been one common strategy.

Throughout the 1980s there has been a rapid increase in the number of Asian Indians going into small businesses. The Chinese, with 89,717 firms, have the largest number of businesses among the Asian Americans; followed by Koreans (69,304); Japanese (53,3720); and Asian Indians (52,266).[22] Asian Indian-owned businesses increased 119.9 percent between 1982 and 1987. The growth in receipts for these Asian Indian firms was even more marked, with an increase from $1.66 billion in 1982 to $6.715 billion in 1987, an increase of 304.6 percent. The vast majority of these firms are individual proprietorships.[23] Average receipts per Asian Indian firm were $128,477. This indicates the highest level of earnings among all Asian American firms, though as is well known, average figures of income such as these blur distinctions between the two poles.

The three metropolitan areas with the largest number of Asian Indian firms are New York (5,744), Los Angeles-Long Beach (4,037), and Chicago (3,049). In twelve states—Alabama, Connecticut, Delaware, Florida, Indiana, Kansas, Michigan, New Jersey, Ohio, South Carolina, Tennessee and West Virginia—Asian Indians are the dominant non-black, non-Hispanic business group.[24] Broken down by industry sector, the primary areas of Asian Indian investment are the following: services, 29,787; retail trade, 9,314; finance, insurance and real estate, 3,537; transportation and public utilities, 2,812; wholesale trade, 1,634; construction, 1,199; manufacturing, 878; agriculture and forestry, 358; and mining, 112.[25]

Economic Sectors with Significant Asian Indian Involvement

The prominence of Asian Indians in the service sector in the *Economic Census* above reflects their involvement in the lodging industry. Unfortunately, the data for minority-owned hotels and lodging places is not broken down by different Asian American groups.[26] But survey data from elsewhere as well as media reports establish the high degree of Asian Indians' involvement in the lodging industry. By 1987, for example, 28 percent of all motels in this country were owned by Asian Indians.[27] Most of the hotel and motel owners are from the western Indian state of Gujarat (hence the common last name of Patel for many of the owners), though there are some owners from other Indian states. The motels and hotels owned range from decrepit downtown residential hotels to motel chains such as Days Inn and Best Western to isolated properties on interstate routes. Approximately five thousand of the hotel-motel owners are originally from East Africa, and immigrated either to the U.S. or to Britain when Indians were expelled from Uganda. As British passport holders, some of them immigrated first to Britain, where they established small businesses such as grocery stores, and then to the United States, bringing their investment capital with them. Others, direct immigrants from India to the United States, have entered the lodging business after investing savings from white-collar professional jobs, such as in pharmacy or engineering, where they did not perceive opportunities for economic mobility for themselves. Some, especially on the West Coast, who had degrees in construction engineering, have started construction companies along with the hotel-motel business. The operation of the smaller hotels and motels, as well as common areas of ethnic enterprise such as restaurants and grocery stores, rely extensively on unpaid family labor. Women, often the wives and sisters of the motel owners, do all the work of cleaning the rooms and laundering the sheets and towels in addition to tending the hotel desk.[28]

Investing in such economic niches as the hotel-motel industry seems to have been more the result of networks within the community and the particular juncture of when and where these immigrants were entering the U.S. economy than any experience prior to immigration which would have predisposed the immigrants to a particular line of business. The absence of other choices for those with small amounts of capital seems to have been a determining factor. However, the motel and hotel industry has reached a plateau, and in some areas with the decline in tourism and travel due to the recession, motel owners are facing an economic crisis. Increased investment in this sector is unlikely to continue at the pace of the 1970s and 1980s.

Other small business preferences for Asian Indians and Pakistanis in New York and California include the operation of 7-11 stores. In New York, South Asians seem to have a virtual monopoly of subway newsstands.[29] Like the small hotel-motel business, these enterprises also operate through combinations of kin and ethnic networks and low capital requirements. However, women do not seem to be directly involved in operating businesses such as newsstands.

On the other hand, there are sectors where the recent rapid increase in Asian Indian presence is a result of prior experience. Gujarati Jains have controlled the South Asian diamond trade for centuries in India. In the U.S. they form the second largest ethnic group, after the Hasidic Jews, in the New York Diamond District.

A more visible and numerically more significant area of business for Asian Indians, also based on prior experience, has been the entry of Punjabi Sikhs into the transportation industry. In India, this community dominates the transportation sector with more than 80 percent of the bus and trucking services being run by them. Some trucking stops, including the nation's fifth largest stop (located in Maryland), are owned by Asian Indians.[30] In New York City 43 percent of the applications for cab drivers and, in the boroughs, 15 percent of the applicants are of subcontinental origin.[31] This reflects a threefold rise over the last eight years. The vast majority of the cab drivers are Punjabi Sikh.

Gas stations have been another major area of investment and employment for many Punjabis. In New York City, the Department of Consumer Affairs estimates that 40 percent of the city's gas stations are owned and operated by South Asians.[32] Though there are some white-collar professionals who own these gas stations, many of the Sikh Punjabi gas station owners and operators are either from farming backgrounds or from working-class backgrounds in India. This type of class and educational background reflects, to some extent, the changes in the pattern of immigration from South Asia.

These two niches, gas stations and taxicabs, have provided points of entry into the economy for a group of immigrants coming to the U.S. in the midst of a long recession. In the Northeast, particularly New York, the economic downturn has existed for much longer than in the western states. Both gas stations and taxicabs are labor intensive and require 12-hour days but seem to provide high returns for those who are owner operators.[33] However, they are also high-risk enterprises. Crimes against cabdrivers are among the most common of all crimes in the city; in the boroughs like Queens, Bronx and Brooklyn the rate of crime involving cabdrivers is even higher. Gas stations are also frequently held up. One station owner interviewed by the *New York Times* indicated the station, in Harlem, was held up an average of two times a month and that two Indian employees have been shot and killed during holdups.[34]

With the increase in the size of the community, we see Asian Indians are no longer only professionals and executives. Yet there are very few community organizations among South Asians which are even interested in building alliances across class lines. On the other hand, as victims of racism, such alliances are increasingly necessary.

The increase in the South Asian component of Asian Americans is also leading to competition between them and other Asian Americans. As the economic pie has shrunk, such competition has intensified. For example, the recently well-publicized case recommending that Asian Indians be excluded from contracts given through the minority business ordinance in San Francisco was initiated by Harold Yee of Asian Inc.[35] Educational programs are needed to prevent such internal divisions.

Women's Issues

Perhaps the most important and most problematic area of immigration legislation affecting women is the 1986 U.S. Immigration Marriage Fraud Amendments Act. Passed in an environment of political hysteria about "sham" marriages and immigration, the legislation provides for conditional residency status to spouses of green card holders for the first two years after entering the U.S. To convert the conditional visa to a permanent resident status, a joint petition has to be filed by the couple three months before the end of the conditional residency period. A divorce, prior to the expiration of the two-year period, unless contested and special petitions submitted to the INS, makes the spouse on the conditional visa deportable. This two-step process and long, drawn-out process of application are to be continued under the Immigration Act of 1990.

Among South Asians, unlike the immigration pattern from the Philippines and even China, the typical pattern of immigration has been predominantly male.[36] After acquiring the green card, individuals return and get married and sponsor the wife. In a troubled marriage, the conditional residency status of the wife gives the husband additional power. Frequently, as reported by crisis-intervention centers and battered women's centers nationwide, husbands hold the threat of deportation over the wife, refuse to file the joint petition, or serve divorce papers just prior to the two-year expiration date.[37] In several cases, women continued to live in abusive marriages because of the fear of divorce and deportation. National data on this subject are lacking. But in one example, which may be typical of many, a Cook County Commissioner noted that of the 2,500 impoverished Indian women in Illinois in 1985, most had been abandoned by their husbands.[38]

Female-headed households are relatively less numerous among Asian Americans than among other ethnic groups. Asians also have the lowest level of family dissolution through divorce and widowhood among the foreign-born immigrant groups.[39] The percentage of divorced and widowed females in the Asian-born category is, however, almost three times as high as the number of divorced and widowed Asian-born males, suggesting that males remarry far more quickly than the female cohort.[40] The national aggregate data also disguise local realities. A Chicago-based social worker suggested that in 1990 there were over 25,000 divorced South Asian women in the Chicago metropolitan area alone.[41] While this figure is certainly an overestimate, it is indicative of a growing trend both in South Asia and in the immigrant community. Support networks for women need to be developed and all Asian American community groups, and South Asians in particular need to undertake research projects and active data-collection projects on the women in the community. The level of information available is distressingly little.

Some comparative work is needed to ascertain how other Asian immigrant groups have been affected by the 1986 U.S. Immigration Marriage Fraud Amendments Act. The legislation, at least as suggested by the South Asian experience, needs to be rethought and perhaps revoked. While technically the routes to petition and appeal to the INS are supposed to prevent the type of abuse outlined above, the "conditional residency" status leaves women in an unfairly vulnerable position.

Poverty among Asian Indians

Data are not yet available to indicate how the Asian Indian fared overall in the labor market in the 1980s. The 1979 data showed that 14.4 percent of the Asian Indian males who were in the labor force had some period of unemployment. The average period of unemployment was 11.5 weeks.[42] The relatively higher percentage of unemployment among U.S.-born Asian Indians (7.6 percent), when compared to other U.S.-born Chinese and Japanese Americans (1.5 percent), suggested to the U.S. Civil Rights Commission that Asian Indians faced labor-market discrimination.[43]

It is possible that this trend of labor-market discrimination may actually have been accentuated in the second half of the decade due to the passage of the Immigration Reform and Control Act of 1986 (IRCA). While data are not available on the direct impact of IRCA on Asian Indians and their employment, there is evidence that labor market discrimination increased as a result. Directed primarily at Hispanics, and therefore receiving all too little opposition from the Asian Americans who assumed they would not be affected, a recent report from the U.S. General Accounting Office (GAO) found that employers were practicing discrimination in two forms: first, not hiring applicants whom they suspected of being unauthorized aliens because of their accents or appearance; and second, applying IRCA's verification system only to those who had a foreign accent or appearance.[44] Some employers used both practices. The same study found that levels of discrimination were higher in areas with high Hispanic and Asian populations. It is thought that there are around ten thousand illegal immigrants from South Asia.[45] With the ongoing civil war in Punjab and in Sri Lanka, it is possible that the numbers have increased slightly. There is a small increase also in the numbers applying for refugee status from both these regions, though many more have been accepted into Canada. How these individuals may have fared on the job market and indeed how Asian Indians have been affected by this legislation remains to be ascertained.

A closer examination of the 1980 data also shows that not all Asian Indians enjoyed the same degree of upward economic mobility. On the one hand, the 1980 data showed that the Asian Indian income levels were, like that of Japanese Americans, above the median level of full-time white workers. However, among those who had immigrated between 1975-1980, 10.7 percent lived below the poverty level.[46] This was a higher level of poverty than among Japanese Americans and Filipino Americans. Approximately 17 percent (16.9 percent) of Asian Indians received Social Security payments in 1979.[47] Many were the elderly, some of them survivors of the first groups of immigrants from earlier in the century. With inflation and increased health costs, some of the elderly may also be among the impoverished. A study of the Civil Rights Commission, *The Economic Status of Americans of Asian Descent*, also based on the 1980 data, found that poverty level among American-born Asian Indians was 20.2 percent, or five times that of other Asian American groups.[48] Many of the American-born Asian Indians are in the Central California Valley and are farmworkers. With the increase in the number of female-headed households and changes in the immigration pattern, it is possible that with the recession, and indeed depression in the northeastern states where many of the Asian Indians reside, poverty levels have probably risen in the intervening decade among Asian Indians in some other regions as well.

Political Participation and Anti-Asian Indian Violence

Not since 1956, when Dalip Singh Saund became the first Asian American to be elected to the U.S. Congress, have South Asians succeeded in being elected to either the Congress or the State Assembly. The year 1992, however, marks a turning point of sorts. South Asians entered electoral politics in larger numbers than ever before. Most of the candidates running for office were in California where four South Asians ran for Congress, two as Democrats and two as Republicans. Two also ran for the State Assembly, one as a Democrat the other as a Republican. A couple of people ran for County Supervisor.[49] None were elected in the June primaries and most cited their meager resources as the main obstacle and noted they were outspent by their rivals by more than three to one.[50] This financial crunch seems all the more noteworthy because the South Asian community has been very active in raising funds for both Bush and Clinton, as well as for several non-South Asian candidates in California, sometimes raising as much as $100,000 at a single event. Though the majority of South Asians profess support for candidates running from the Democratic party, like wealthy Cubans in Florida, many have now become ardent supporters of the Republican Party as well. Already by June 1992, Asian Indians had contributed close to a million dollars to Bush's war chest.[51] To some extent this may be a belief in backing a winning ticket and the politics of opportunism. But it is also a reflection of class politics. Wealthy South Asians, often earning well over a hundred thousand dollars and living in exclusive suburban areas, have little sympathy for the problems of inner cities and those who do not seem to be able to make it up the economic ladder.[52] However, the politics of race and the increasing number of racially motivated attacks against South Asians make the issue of political alliances somewhat more complicated.

The 1986 U.S. Commission on Civil Rights Report, *Violence Against Asians*, did not contain coverage of Asian Indians or South Asians. Nor did the Asian American Legal Defense Fund keep data on Asian Indians. However, even by the mid-1980s, when the South Asian immigrant population was about half the size of the present one, there had been extensive levels of violence against South Asians, a trend which has continued.

Like the Koreans, Asian Indians have faced violence for owning businesses formerly owned by other ethnic groups. Over a three-month period in Chicago, in 1986, Indian grocery stores, electronics stores and restaurants were vandalized and attacked 47 times.[53] The police believed the vandals were white competitors, some of whom had owned these stores.

There have been numerous beatings and attacks on Asian Indians with serious injuries and one death in various cases on Staten Island, in the Bronx, and Jersey City Heights, Middlesex County (New Jersey). Forty anti-Asian bias-related incidents were reported in Hudson County (New Jersey) in 1991 alone, and statewide 58 such incidents against Asian Indians were reported the same year.[54] Specifically anti-Indian gangs have developed in New Jersey; in addition to the infamous "Dotbusters" in Jersey City Heights, a gang known as "The Lost Boys" has been recently very active in the Edison-Iselin area.[55]

Similarly, across the country on the West Coast, Indian homes and businesses have been vandalized, property destroyed and racial epithets spray-painted in Fremont, Union City, Artesia (California), Springfield (Washington), and Portland (Oregon). All these incidents were reported in 1991.

In addition to racial prejudice, Hindu and Muslim South Asians also face discrimination due to perceptions of their religions. In Chino, California, for example, Christian fundamentalist groups put out anti-Hindu pamphlets in 1991. One pamphlet, entitled "The Traitor," proclaimed Hinduism a bloodthirsty religion which calls for human sacrifice, and asserted that "Satan created all the gods of India" and that they are demons who will "rob your soul and take you into hell."[56] In 1988, in Aurora, Illinois, when the City Council met to consider the Indian community's request for permission to build a temple, it was turned down because many at the hearing believed that the temple "would possibly cause rat-infested streets, human sacrifices, and become a haven for terrorists."[57] Rev. Zarris, a Baptist minister said at the hearing, "The Hindus are always associated with the drug culture. . . . Theologically we are opposed to the Hindus because they are practicing a false religion."[58] Similarly, Dr. Nazeer Ahmed and Nisar (Nick) Hai, Muslims who ran for office from southern California in the 1992 primaries, found that prevalent notions about Islamic fundamentalists and terrorists were fully exploited by opponents during the campaigns.[59] Many Muslim South Asians, as well as those whose names sounded as if they could be

Muslim, got harassed and received death threats throughout the country during the Gulf War.

These experiences have forced many South Asians to become far more actively involved with the political process. Indian Chambers of Commerce have been founded in most areas with Indian businesses; various types of lobbying groups have been set up in other places. Some groups started to make efforts to link up with local branches of the Asian American Legal Defense and Education Fund and the NAACP. There are also four national associations which have sought to organize Asian Indians politically and provide lobbying services in Washington and some of the state capitals. These are the Association of Indians in America (AIA), the Federation of Indian Associations (FIA), the Indian American Forum for Political Education (IAFPE) and the National Association of Americans of Asian Indian Descent (NAAAID). The Indo-American Political Association (IAPA), a group dedicated to enhancing political participation in mainstream politics, has succeeded in getting some delegates elected to the County Central Committees of the Democratic Party. All five organizations have been active in debates on the 1990 Immigration bill, on issues affecting medical personnel (Foreign Medical Graduates, or FMG), voter-registration drives, as well as in fundraisers for various political candidates. Given the increased level of political involvement noted in the most recent primaries, some Asian Indian representatives will probably be elected to some political offices in another three or four years.

However, as the numbers of Asian Americans increase, along with the number of Asian Indians and other immigrants from South Asia, the thorny question of racism against visible minorities remains a difficult problem.

In conclusion, I would like to raise the question of coalition building. There is all too little discussion of how Hispanic American and Asian American coalitions are to be built, particularly in states like California where both groups are increasing rapidly. Similarly, on the East Coast, with many new African American immigrants, particularly from Haiti, Guyana and the Caribbean countries, there is very little discussion of developing new coalitions with African Americans. Asian Americans will become numerically far more significant by 2010 and 2020 than they are now, but so will the other minorities. An increase in total numbers does not obviate the need for political coalitions among minorities.

Notes

1. Robert Gardener et al., *Asian Americans: Growth, Change and Diversity* (Washington, D.C.: Population Reference Bureau, 1985), 6; see figure 2.

2. U.S. Immigration and Naturalization Service, *Statistical Yearbook of Immigration and Naturalization Service* (NTIS) (Washington, D.C.: Government Printing Office, 1991), 52; henceforth noted as *Statistical Yearbook INS.*

3. *Ibid.*

4. For a fuller discussion of IMMACT90 on Indian immigration, see the four-part series by Indra M. Gandhi, "Immigration Act of 1990," *India West* (September 20–October 25, 1991). Gandhi is an attorney who writes the regular immigration column.

5. *India Today* (September 15, 1990), 37.

6. Institute of International Education, New York; report released October 16, 1991.

7. Binod Khadria, "Migration of Human Capital to the United States," *Economic and Political Weekly* (August 11, 1991), 1790.

8. *Statistical Yearbook INS,* 124, table 40.

9. Foreign-Born 1990 CPH-L-90. This data includes persons born abroad of American parents. Data for foreign-born persons by place of birth, citizenship and year of entry will not be available until 1993.

10. *Statistical Yearbook INS,* 124, table 40.

11. Briefly, the availability of arms and military weaponry has increased enormously in Pakistan as a result of its position as a U.S. supplier during the war in Afghanistan. Pakistan is one of the largest producers of heroin for the world market. The links between the drug and arms traders, combined with the rise of Muslim fundamentalist politics and the consequent unstable political situation, has meant that many from the middle classes are seeking to emigrate.

12. *Statistical Yearbook INS,* 51, 64, table 8, and 86, table 20.

13. *Ibid.,* 64, table 8, and 86, table 20.

14. These counts are based on community estimates, such as those of *India West.*

15. William P. O'Hare and Judy Felt, *Asian Americans: America's Fastest Growing Minority Group* (Washington, D.C.: Population Reference Bureau, 1991), 13.

16. *1980 U.S. Census of Population; Supplementary Report PC80-S1-5, 1981 Standard Metropolitan Statistical Areas and Standard Consolidated Statistical Area,* tables 1 and 4.

17. Surinder M. Bhardwaj and N. Madhusudhana Rao, "Asian Indians in the United States: A Geographic Appraisal," in *South Asians Overseas,* edited by Colin Clarke, Ceri Peach et al. (Cambridge, United Kingdom: Cambridge University Press, 1990), 205–207.

18. *Statistical Yearbook INS*, 58.

19. Gardner et al. *Asian Americans*, 24.

20. *Ibid.*, 30.

21. Figure provided by Dr. Shanti Lunia, former president, Albany, New York, Capital District chapter AAPI.

22. U.S. Department of Commerce, *Economic Censuses: Survey of Minority Owned Business Enterprises*, Washington, D.C., August 1987, 4.

23. *Ibid.*, table 10.

24. *Ibid.*, table 5.

25. *Ibid.*, table 2.

26. *Ibid.*

27. *Wall Street Journal* (January 27, 1987).

28. Suvarna Thaker and Sucheta Mazumdar, "The Quality of Life of Asian Indian Women in the Motel Industry," *South Asia Bulletin* 2:1 (1982), 68–73.

29. Johanna Lessinger, "The Indian Immigrant Experience," paper presented at Asia Society conference, April 20, 1986.

30. "Ethnic Niches Creating Jobs that Fuel Immigrant Growth," *New York Times* (January 12, 1992), 20.

31. "Long Road from Home," *India Today* (June 15, 1992), 48g.

32. "Ethnic Niches," *New York Times*, 1.

33. Those who lease cabs indicated that they can earn around $200 per day; a well-located gas station can earn a net profit of $4,000. See "Ethnic Niches," *New York Times*, 20; "Long Road," *India Today*.

34. "Ethnic Niches," *New York Times*, 20.

35. *India West* has had a lengthy coverage of this issue starting from May 24, 1991.

36. U.S. Department of Commerce, *Studies in Fertility*, CPR Series P-23, issued October 1991, 40.

37. Viji Sundaram, "Divorce to Deportation," *India West* (June 22, 1990), 41.

38. *Ibid.*

39. Data on family dissolution from U.S. Department of Commerce, *Studies in Fertility*, 23.

40. *Ibid.*, 45, table 7.

41. Sundaram, 41.

42. Gardner et al., *Asian Americans*, 30.

43. "Economic Status of Indo-Americans," *India West* (October 14, 1988), 32; based on U.S. Commission on Civil Rights report, *The Economic Status of Americans of Asian Descent*, 1988.

44. O'Hare and Felt, *Asian Americans*, 113.

45. Indian Consulate, 1986; cited by Amrita Basu, "Political Activity of Indian Immigrants: 'Model Minority' Dissidence," unpublished paper, prepared for Asia Society conference, New York, April 1986, 26.

46. Gardner et al., *Asian Americans*, 34.

47. *Ibid.*, 35.

48. *India West* (October 14, 1988), 32.

49. *India West* (May 29, 1992), 28.

50. *India West* (June 12, 1992), 1.

51. *India Today* (June 30, 1992), 48b.

52. Lavina Melwani, "Republican vs. Democrat: Wither Go Indo-Americans?" *India West* (July 26, 1991), 1, 36–37.

53. Basu, "Political Activity of Indian Immigrants."

54. *India West* (April 24, 1992), 27.

55. *India West* (July 12, 1991), 35.

56. Francis Assisi, "Two Booklets Propagate Anti-Hindu Material," *India West* (July 26, 1991), 52.

57. "Letters to the Editor," *India West* (September 22, 1989), 5.

58. *Ibid.*

59. *India West* (June 12, 1992), 31–33.

Appendix

Specific Policy Recommendations

An Overview of Asian Pacific American Futures:
Shifting Paradigms

Shirley Hune

*Acting Associate Dean, UCLA Graduate Programs, Graduate Division
Visiting Professor, UCLA Urban Planning Program*

1. That Asian Pacific Americans be included in policy-making and that their expertise, concerns, and perspectives be incorporated into policies, especially in matters directly impacting their welfare.

2. That Asian Pacific Americans be included on task forces, commissions, and in other relevant advisory capacities.

Education K-12 Policy

Peter N. Kiang

Assistant Professor, Graduate College of Education and American Studies Program, University of Massachusetts/Boston

Vivian Wai-Fun Lee

Director, National Center for Immigrant Students of the National Coalition of Advocates for Students, Boston

1. That teachers, schools, and school districts—supported by appropriate teacher training and instructional resources—provide students with systematic, in-depth opportunities throughout the K-12 curriculum to learn about the historical and contemporary experiences of Asian Pacific Americans.

2. That educational policy-makers and practitioners develop timely, appropriate measures to respond to incidents of anti-Asian bias in schools, and that they establish school environments that are safe, supportive, and respectful of the cultural and linguistic strengths and needs of Asian Pacific American students and their families.

Higher Education Policy

L. Ling-chi Wang
Chair, Ethnic Studies, University of California, Berkeley

1. That Asian Americans actively monitor and participate in the ongoing debate over criteria for admissions and be prepared to take action against any unfair targeting of Asian Americans for exclusion.

2. That Asian Americans—as a racial minority who have benefitted and will continue to benefit from affirmative action programs—continue to support legitimate affirmative action programs and forcefully oppose efforts by Whites and some Asian Americans to challenge and dismantle such programs.

Health Policy

Tessie Guillermo
Executive Director, Asian American Health Forum, San Francisco

1. That policy-makers prioritize the institution of culturally competent health care service delivery in all proposals for health care reform.

2. That policy-makers modify current national and state data collection methods and reporting systems to codify Asian and Pacific Islander populations by ethnicity and, where appropriate, break down morbidity, mortality, health care use and expenditures by specific ethnic group.

Mental Health Policy

Stanley Sue

Professor of Psychology and Director, National Research Center on Asian American Mental Health, University of California, Los Angeles

1. That policy-makers place immediate attention on the initiation and funding of research dealing with Asian American mental health issues.

2. That policy-makers develop culturally relevant mental health services and interventions geared for Asian Americans.

Arts Policy

Gerald D. Yoshitomi

Executive Director, Japanese American Cultural and Community Center, Los Angeles

1. That policy-makers support culturally specific institutions, particularly for emerging Asian American organizations that did not benefit from the arts and cultural expansion programs of the 1970s and 1980s; and that this support have priority over efforts to "democratize" large arts institutions; no culture can survive if its interpretation and transmission are controlled by outsiders.

2. That policy-makers encourage the development of audiences for the arts which more closely reflects the demographics of each locality, and that programs in the arts encourage audiences to explore the diversity and richness of all cultures.

Cultural Preservation Policy

Franklin S. Odo

Director, Ethnic Studies Program, University of Hawai'i, Manoa

1. That policy-makers allocate resources and energies to institutions dedicated to preserving and interpreting the history of Asian Americans, including recent immigrant and refugee communities.

2. That bilingual and ESL programs include agendas that promote immigrant Asian cultures and languages, and that specific programs incorporate into the learning process respect for ethnic histories and cultures.

Immigration Policy

Bill Ong Hing

Associate Professor of Law, Stanford Law School

1. That family reunification remain the primary goal of this nation's immigration laws, because this policy has strengthened this country and has provided a means for professionals as well as working-class immigrants to enter the U.S. Due to historical discrimination against Asians in U.S. immigration laws and a legalization program that places undocumented migrants ahead of immigrants, severe backlogs have occurred for the categories of siblings and relatives of lawful permanent residents from many Asian Pacific countries. Additional visa numbers must be provided in order to clear these backlogs.

2. That naturalization procedures be streamlined in order to meet the aspirations for citizenship by Asian Pacific immigrants. This streamlining should include the recognition of the newly offered written examination by all INS offices; the reevaluation of the English literacy requirement, given the ever-growing presence of immigrant language media that keep non-English speakers informed; and the reduction of the residency requirement to three years.

Labor Policy

Paul Ong

Associate Professor, UCLA Graduate School of Architecture and Urban Planning

Suzanne J. Hee

UCLA Asian American Studies Center

1. That policy-makers support the creation of more English language instructional and job-related programs that will help immigrants

currently trapped in low-wage jobs. Creation of these programs will help to fight poverty in the Asian Pacific American community, which is considerably higher than the rate of poverty in the non-Hispanic white population.

2.   That legislation be enacted to protect Asian Pacific American workers from employment discrimination, including protection against practices that create a "glass ceiling" limiting upward mobility to top management positions, and from unfair labor practices based on language and cultural biases.

Civil Rights Policy

William R. Tamayo

Managing Attorney, Asian Law Caucus, San Francisco

1.   That Congress repeal immediately the Employer Sanctions provision of the Immigration Reform and Control Act of 1986. According to a U.S. General Accounting Office's Report (March 1990), these sanctions have caused widespread discrimination against Latinos and Asians and subjected workers to employer abuse.

2.   That policy-makers promote massive public educational efforts to inform the U.S. population about the strengths and benefits of a diverse and multicultural society, so that government, labor and business leaders cease viewing immigrants as a harm to the economy.

The Case of the Southeast Asian Refugees:
Policy for a Community "At-Risk"

Ngoan Le

Deputy Administrator, Division of Planning and Community Services, Illinois State Department of Public Aid

1.   That Congress and the Administration provide adequate funding to assist refugees admitted to the U.S. Loss of funding, substantial decrease, would result in undue pressure at the state and local levels where resources are already extremely limited. In addition, the funding mechanism at the federal level needs to promote the coordination and partnership between the public and private sectors,

which are critical to the success of resettlement efforts at the local community level. Current initiatives to minimize the role of states and refugee self-help organizations in providing initial resettlement assistance for newly arrived refugees from Southeast Asia and other parts of the world will have major impact on their comprehensive care.

2. That policy-makers restore programs and funding to support refugee children at K-12 public schools. The majority of public schools need assistance to work effectively with these children who face multiple problems ranging from language barriers to social and cultural adjustment. Early intervention could prevent drop-out and gang-related behaviors, which would demand more costly solutions at a later time.

Political Policy

Stewart Kwoh
President and Executive Director, Asian Pacific American Legal Center, Los Angeles

Mindy Hui
Asian Pacific American Legal Center, Los Angeles

1. That legislators extend voting rights protection to Asian Pacific Americans in districts where they comprise a significant minority of the population. Such legal protection would help redress the problem of fragmentation of Asian Pacific American population centers in the redistricting process.

2. That Asian Pacific American community and political leaders take the responsibility to develop a process for a comprehensive agenda for political empowerment, given the situation where few others are willing to take the lead.

Race Relations Policy

Michael Omi

Assistant Professor, Asian American Studies, University of California, Berkeley

1. That policy-makers move beyond an exclusive "black/white" focus on race relations and frame and assess their policies with respect to their impact on increasingly large ethnic/racial minority groups in this nation. Issues such as immigration, welfare, bilingual education, and community economic development have a differential impact on different groups, and policies on these issues also shape the relations between groups.

2. That political leaders vigorously repudiate and challenge the increasing "racialization" of politics. Playing the "race card" should be explicitly disavowed as an election strategy, since it serves to polarize the electorate, detract attention from broader political and economic ills, and exacerbate the already existing tensions between racial groups.

Affirmative Action Policy

Henry Der

Executive Director, Chinese for Affirmative Action, San Francisco

1. That Asian Pacific Islanders develop strong employee organizations to guide and monitor on a regular basis the implementation of affirmative action goals and timetables and to negotiate and secure a reasonably retaliatory-free framework for providing direct feedback and advice to employers regarding goals. The presence of strong Asian Pacific Islander employee organizations reinforces the need for employers to embrace and implement institution-wide practices and policies that eradicate the "glass ceiling."

2. That Asian Pacific Islander employees seek out opportunities to inform and educate appropriate federal and state anti-discrimination officials about the different forms of promotion bias. Enforcement

officials need to be sensitized about the employment needs of established and emerging Asian Pacific Islander groups.

Language Rights Policy

Kathryn K. Imahara

Director, Language Rights Project, Asian Pacific American Legal Center, Los Angeles

1. That policy-makers make yearly language needs assessments for various jurisdictions (e.g., school districts, prison populations, qualified individuals for welfare programs, etc.) and provide bilingual language assistance based on the 5 percent population benchmark.

2. That legislators repeal all English-Only laws across the U.S. and oppose new initiatives.

Policy for Women

Elaine H. Kim

Professor, Asian American Studies, University of California, Berkeley

1. That policy-makers support linguistically appropriate services and information/education for Asian immigrant women for such issues as employment rights, reproductive choice, spousal abuse and domestic violence, parenting in a multiracial community, sexual harassment, and sexual violence.

2. That policy-makers support affordable, quality and culturally appropriate child care.

Media Policy

Diane Yen-Mei Wong

Writer & Editor; Former Executive Director, Asian American Journalists Association, San Francisco

1. That the news media industry diversify its staff and actively seek assistance from this diverse staff in identifying and accurately covering issues affecting the Asian Pacific American community.

The community should play a critical role in this process: it should target media groups lacking diversify, present concerns to these groups, and monitor the groups' progress on an ongoing basis.

2. That existing Asian Pacific American journalists—in this period of inadequate diversity of newsrooms—recognize their unique position as liaisons between the Asian Pacific American community and other communities, and develop a pan-Asian perspective so they can better cover issues affecting different ethnic groups within the larger Asian Pacific community.

South Asians in the United States with a Focus on Asian Indians:
Policy on New Communities

Sucheta Mazumdar
Assistant Professor, Department of History, State University of New York, Albany

1. That policy-makers support creation of outreach programs for working-class and elderly South Asians to inform them of social services provided by the state. South Asians are one of the most class-divided new immigrant groups, with large numbers of highly educated professionals and large numbers of working-class newcomers. The problems of the latter group have received scant attention.

2. That Asian Americans (particularly Koreans and South Asians) join in dialogue with African Americans and Latinos in all major urban centers. These efforts need to be supported through public and private initiatives. Churches and temples from all communities also need to be involved in these educational programs.

Chapter Authors

Asian Pacific American
Policy Experts

Henry Der is the executive director of Chinese for Affirmative Action, a San Francisco-based civil rights organization. A 1968 graduate of Stanford University, he has been appointed to many federal and state commissions and advisory panels in recognition of his contributions to the civil rights arena. He is currently the vice-chair of the California Postsecondary Education Commission and is recognized as one of the most effective civil rights advocates in the San Francisco Bay Area.

Tessie Guillermo is the executive director of the Asian American Health Forum, a national health policy and advocacy organization. She received her education in Economics from the University of California at Berkeley and California State University, Hayward. She currently serves on several community boards and policy committees, representing Asian and Pacific Islander interests nationwide.

Suzanne J. Hee is a graduate student in Asian American Studies and a research assistant for Professor Paul Ong at the UCLA Graduate School of Architecture and Urban Planning.

Bill Ong Hing is an associate professor at the Stanford Law School where he has served on the faculty since 1985. He received his BA in Psychology from the University of California at Berkeley and his law degree from the University of San Francisco. Specializing in immigration law, he has served in numerous advisory capacities for various agencies and organizations and has authored books, manuals, and articles on immigration law.

J. D. Hokoyama is the president and executive director of Leadership Education for Asian Pacifics (LEAP). A graduate of Loyola University of Los Angeles with a BA in English Literature and MEd in Educational Administration, he is a former Peace Corps Volunteer who served in Ethiopia. He advances understanding of Asian Pacific American issues and concerns by conducting cultural awareness, cultural diversity and leadership development workshops, as well as who served on various community boards and committees.

Mindy Hui received her BA from UCLA. She serves as the coordinator of the Coalition of Asian Pacific Americans for Fair Reapportionment and currently works at the Asian Pacific American Legal Center of Southern California.

Shirley Hune is an acting associate dean for Graduate Programs in the Graduate Division at UCLA. Born in Toronto, Canada, as a third generation Chinese Canadian, she received her BA in History from the University of Toronto and her PhD in American Civilization from George Washington University in Washington, D.C. As a widely published scholar, she has had her works translated for publication in Asia, Africa, Latin America, and Europe.

Kathryn K. Imahara received her BA in Political Science from the University of Southern California and her law degree from the University of Southern California Law School. As the director of the Language Rights Project of the Asian Pacific American Legal Center of Southern California, she is the principal litigator for the Legal Center's civil rights cases focusing on language rights.

Peter N. Kiang is an assistant professor in the Graduate College of Education at the University of Massachusetts in Boston and also holds a position in the American Studies program where he teaches undergraduate courses in Asian American Studies. He received his BA in Visual and Environmental Studies and Geological Sciences as well as his EdD from Harvard University. He has published a wide range of articles on Asian Americans, many of which focus on Asian American educational issues.

Elaine H. Kim is a professor of Asian American Studies and faculty assistant for the Status of Women at the University of California at Berkeley. She received her BA in English and American Literature from the University of Pennsylvania, an MA from Columbia University, and a PhD in Education from UC Berkeley. She has authored books and numerous articles and essays on Asian Americans and Asian American women's issues. She was a recipient of a Fulbright Fellowship in 1987.

Stewart Kwoh, a graduate of UCLA and the UCLA Law School, serves as the executive director and president of the Asian Pacific American Legal Center of Southern California. A past president of the Los Angeles City Human Relations Commission, he is currently a board member of Rebuild LA, the organization primarily responsible for rebuilding riot-torn areas of South Central Los Angeles. He is a founder and current board member of the National Asian Pacific American Legal Consortium.

Ngoan Le, currently the deputy administrator of the Illinois Department of Public Aid's Division of Planning and Community Services, came to the United States as a refugee from Vietnam in 1975. A graduate of Illinois State University, she served as the executive director of the Vietnamese Association of Illinois and as special assistant for Asian American Affairs to former Governor James Thompson. She is a highly regarded national expert on refugee resettlement issues and has often been called upon in advisory capacities to assist federal agencies concerned with refugee matters.

Vivian W. Lee is the director of the National Center for Immigrant Students, a program of the National Coalition of Advocates for Students in Boston. She received her BA in Economics from Harvard University and an MA at the Institute for Learning and Teaching at the University of Massachusetts, where she is currently an MEd candidate in Bilingual and ESL Studies. Prior to assuming her current position, she was an education specialist in the K-12 Boston school system.

Sucheta Mazumdar is an assistant professor in the History Department at the State University of New York at Albany, and an associate director for the Institute for Research on Women at the same institution. She received her BA from UCLA in East Asian Languages and Literature, and an MA and PhD in History at UCLA. Her writings include articles on Chinese history and comparative Asian history, as well as articles on Asian American and women's issues.

Don T. Nakanishi, director of the UCLA Asian American Studies Center and associate professor at the UCLA Graduate School of Education, earned his PhD in Political Science from Harvard University after receiving his BA from Yale University. Active as a board member, speaker, consultant and advisor to various agencies, institutions and organizations nationwide, he has also written over 50 articles and books on the subject of Asian Pacific Americans. He serves as the co-chair of the LEAP Asian Pacific American Public Policy Institute.

Franklin S. Odo, director and professor of the Ethnic Studies Program at the University of Hawai'i at Manoa, earned his BA from Princeton University, his MA in East Asian Studies from Harvard University, and his PhD in Japanese History from Princeton. He serves as an advisor and consultant on Asian American culture and history to various institutions and agencies. His many articles have focused on Japanese American social and cultural history.

Michael Omi is an assistant professor of Asian American Studies and Ethnic Studies at the University of California at Berkeley. He received his BA in Sociology from UC Berkeley and his MA and PhD from the University of California at Santa Cruz. An expert on ethnic community race relations, he has written and spoken extensively on the subject as well as authored numerous articles on modern American popular culture.

Paul M. Ong is an associate professor at the UCLA Graduate School of Architecture and Urban Planning, and past associate director of the UCLA Asian American Studies Center. He received his BS in Applied Behavioral Science from the University of California at Davis, his MA in

Urban Planning from the University of Washington and his PhD from UC Berkeley. He has authored and co-authored numerous articles on Asian Americans and issues of racial inequalities. His demographic analyses have played a major part in reapportionment efforts in Los Angeles.

Stanley Sue is a professor of Psychology and director of the National Research Ceanter on Asian American Mental Health at UCLA. He received his BS from the University of Oregon, and his MA and PhD from UCLA. Considered one of the nation's foremost experts on the subject of Asin American mental health issues, he has been called upon in consulting and advisory capacities by numerous agencies and institutions throughout the country. He is among the most widely published scholars on Asian American mental health concerns.

William R. Tamayo received his BA from San Francisco State University and his JD from the University of California at Davis. He is currently the managing attorney fror the Asian Law Caucus in San Franciso and serves as the chair of the National Network for Immigrant and Refugee Rights. He also serves on the board of directors of the Northern California chapter of the ACLU and the Coalition for Immigrant and Refugee Rights and Serrvices, of which he is a co-founder.

John Tateishi, an independent public affairs consultant, earned a BA and MA in English Literature from UC Berkeley and UC Davis, respectively, and taught in the baccalaureate program at the University of London during his three years in England. Leaving a teaching career at the City College of San Francisco, he directed the congressional campaign to seek redress for the World War II internment of Japanese Americans. He is the author of *And Justice for All*, an oral history of the internment experience.

L. Ling-chi Wang is the chair for the Department of Ethnic Studies and coordinator of Asian American Studies at the University of California at Berkeley. He received his BA in Music from Hope College in Michigan, a Bachelor of Divinity in Old Testament Studies from Princeton Seminary and an MA in Semitic Studies from UC Berkeley, where he has been teaching Asian American Studies since 1972. Author and lecturer on Asian American history, civil rights and educational issues affecting Asian Americans, he has been a strong civil rights advocate in the San Francisco Bay Area.

Diane Yen-Mei Wong received her BA in Social Welfare and MA in Higher Education Administration from the University of Washington and a law degree from the Boston University School of Law. Currently a freelance writer and editor, she served as the past executive director of the Asian American Journalists Association in San Francisco and was the former director of the Washington State Commission on Asian American Affairs. She has written widely on Asian American issues and on media images of Asian Americans.

Gerald D. Yoshitomi is the executive director of the Japanese American Cultural and Community Center (JACCC) in Los Angeles, one of the largest ethnic cultural centers in the United States. He received his BA in Economics from Stanford University and MA in Public Administration from Arizona State University. Prior to joining the JACCC, he served as deputy director, Arizona Commission on the Arts and Huamnities, and vice president and director of operations of the Western States Arts Foundation in New Mexico. He has served on numerous national arts policy advisory panels and committees.

Leadership Education for Asian Pacifics (LEAP), Inc.

Leadership Education for Asian Pacifics (LEAP) is a nonprofit, community organization founded in 1982 to develop, strengthen, and expand the leadership roles played by Asian Pacific Americans. LEAP provides leadership development training through its Leadership Management Institute, its Community Development Institute, and its cultural awareness and diversity workshops which it has conducted for public, private, nonprofit and community sector organizations nationwide. LEAP established the Asian Pacific American Public Policy Institute in 1992. The Public Policy Institute, the first in the nation dedicated to researching Asian Pacific policy issues, is headquartered at the LEAP offices in Los Angeles with a Research Center and Information Clearinghouse on the UCLA campus.

Leadership Education for Asian Pacifics (LEAP), Inc.
327 East Second Street, Suite 226
Los Angeles, CA 90012–4210
TEL. (213) 485–1422
FAX (213) 485–0050

UCLA Asian American Studies Center

The UCLA Asian American Studies Center, founded in 1969, is one of four ethnic studies centers at UCLA. The Center does research in the social sciences and the humanities, public policy and urban planning, immigrant and labor history, public health and social welfare, literature and film studies; administers undergraduate curriculum and graduate programs; develops and disseminates publications; works with student and community groups; and maintains one of the world's largest research archives in Asian American Studies.

UCLA Asian American Studies Center
3230 Campbell Hall, 405 Hilgard Ave.
Los Angeles, CA 90024–1546
TEL. (310) 825–2974

Don T. Nakanishi, *Director*

Center Staff

Cathy Castor, *Administrative Assistant of Center Management*
Enrique de la Cruz, *Assistant Director*
Yuji Ichioka, *Research & Adjunct Professor in History*
Mary Kao, *Graphics and Production Assistant*
Marjorie Lee, *Librarian & Library Coordinator*
Russell C. Leong, *Editor, Amerasia Journal*
Brian Niiya, *Associate Librarian*
Julie Noh, *Assistant Coordinator, Student/Community Projects*
Glenn Omatsu, *Associate Editor, Amerasia Journal*
Sandra Shin, *Administrative Assistant, Center Management*
Jean Pang Yip, *Publications Business Manager*
Meg Thornton, *Coordinator, Student/Community Projects*
Christine Wang, *Coordinator, Center Management*

Faculty Advisory Committee

James Lubben (Chair), *Social Welfare*

Emil Berkanovic, *Public Health*
Lucie Cheng, *Sociology*
Clara Chu, *Library & Info. Science*
King-Kok Cheung, *English*
John Horton, *Sociology*
Yuji Ichioka, *History*
Snehendu Kar, *Public Health*
Harry Kitano, *Social Welfare*
Jinqi Ling, *English*
Takashi Makinodan, *Medicine-GRECC*
Mari Matsuda, *Law*
Valerie Matsumoto, *History*
Ailee Moon, *Social Welfare*

Robert Nakamura, *Theater, Film & TV*
Kazuo Nihira, *Psych. & Biobehavioral Sci.*
Paul Ong, *Urban Planning*
William Ouchi, *Management*
Geraldine Padilla, *Nursing*
Kyeyoung Park, *Anthropology*
Julie Roque, *Urban Planning*
George Sanchez, *History*
Gregory Sarris, *English*
Shu-mei Shih, *Comp. Literature*
Stanley Sue, *Psychology*
James Tong, *Political Science*
Cindy Yee-Bradbury, *Psychology*